Introduction to
Modern Behaviorism

Introduction to
Modern Behaviorism
Second Edition

Howard Rachlin
State University of New York
at Stony Brook

W. H. FREEMAN AND COMPANY
San Francisco

Library of Congress Cataloging in Publication Data

Rachlin, Howard, 1935–
    Introduction to modern behaviorism.

    Includes bibliographies and index.
    1. Conditioned response. 2. Behaviorism
(Psychology) I. Title. II. Title: Modern
behaviorism. [DNLM: 1. Behavior. 2. Conditioning
(Psychology). BF319 R119i]
BF319.R33   1976   150'.19'43   76–1151
ISBN 0–7167–0493–5
ISBN 0–7167–0492–7 pbk.

Printed in the United States of America

9 8 7 6 5 4 3 2 1

Contents

Preface to the Second Edition

There are two major additions to this edition. First, in response to just criticisms of the first edition, I added a chapter on the biological limitations on learning. Second, I modified several sections in the chapter on new directions. The self-control experiment described there was changed from one by Ainslie to one by Leonard Green and myself. I believe the new presentation is easier to understand and fits better with the quantitative material that precedes it. I have also added a new section on language and the talking chimpanzees; certainly, this is an interesting new direction for modern behaviorists.

I should mention that I have borrowed freely back and forth between this book and a longer book I have just written on the same subject entitled *Behavior and Learning*. This book is intended for only part of a semester course, whereas *Behavior and Learning* is intended to occupy a whole semester. Where it was convenient to repeat long sections of one book in the other, I felt free to do so.

HOWARD RACHLIN
January 1976

Preface to the First Edition

This introduction to modern behaviorism is designed to supplement standard textbooks in introductory psychology and animal learning. Such texts are notoriously weak in their discussions of the topics covered in this volume. Indeed, because of the deficiencies of standard texts and because of the importance of the historical and philosophical background of behaviorism to the study of animal behavior and learning, this book may also prove useful at the beginning of some intermediate courses.

At the outset, it should be pointed out that many of the historical statements made here as though they were incontrovertable facts and many of the experiments cited here as though they were the last word on the subject are actually matters of some dispute. From time to time in the text it is indicated that there has been little agreement on certain important issues among psychologists and philosophers; in a few cases both sides of an argument are presented. However, an introductory book is no place for tracing out the details of esoteric debates. The main purpose of this volume is simply to give the reader an idea of what sort of things psychologists who call themselves behaviorists do and why they do them.

If there are any ideas in this book that are new and worthwhile, they arose from conversations with Richard Herrnstein and with graduate students in the animal behavior laboratory at Harvard University. I would also like to thank the following people who read and criticized parts of the manuscript: William Baum, Robert Boakes, David Cross, Marvin Frankel, Charles Gross, Peter Killeen, John Schneider, and Richard Solomon.

HOWARD RACHLIN
October 1970

Introduction to
Modern Behaviorism

1
Background

Organisms try to influence the behavior of other organisms by a variety of means and for a variety of purposes. Indeed, much of the interaction among humans and other living creatures consists in efforts to influence behavior. Consider a cow nudging its newborn calf, or for contrast, a victorious alley cat driving an intruder from its territory.

Of course, not all interactions are so one-sided. Organisms often simultaneously modify each other's behavior. Even when one organism is clearly dominant over another, as in the relations between ant and aphid or doctor and patient, there may still be an element of mutual influence. If we examine the teacher–student relationship, which, in formal terms at least, seems rather one-sided, we may find that a given student is trying to get a good grade as actively as his teacher is trying to impart information and stimulate thinking. Thus what the teacher sees as learning on the part of the student may be, from the student's point of view, simply a means of influencing the teacher and obtaining a good grade.

Given a situation in which one organism is trying to influence the behavior of another organism, the purpose of the effort may not be readily apparent. A parent may spank a child to keep him from playing in the street. This punishment is intended "for the child's own good." On the other hand, if a parent spanks a child for not making his bed or cleaning his room, it may be the parent himself who hopes to benefit from the change in the child's behavior. Thus the motives behind the modification of behavior and the benefit to be derived from the modified behavior may critically determine the nature of a given interaction.

Let us consider one final example along these lines. A radio announcer may urge us to "Eat apples for health!" because he is paid to advertise apples. If the speaker were an apple grower, instead of a radio announcer, the same statement might be a form of benign propaganda. But if a nutritionist or doctor gives us this advice, the statement may express more concern for our health than for the selling of apples. The very same statement could be used in all three attempts to modify our behavior.

The type of relationship between organisms that will be discussed in this book is that of experimenter and subject. On the surface this relationship appears one-sided, with the experimenter observing, manipulating, and modifying the behavior of the subject. But in a deeper sense a truly reciprocal interaction occurs, for the subject helps determine the experimenter's behavior and causes him to modify old theories, to formulate new theories, and to design new experiments.

A look at the titles of articles by experimental psychologists in the field of learning yields clues to the objectives of learning studies. Here, for example, is a hypothetical set of titles corresponding to the experimental observations shown in Figure 1.1:

a. Variables influencing the rate of motor learning
b. The sense of time
c. A study of appetite
d. Anxiety as a determiner of performance

Although authors almost always qualify such broad titles in subtitles or introductions, the titles do reveal the questions that the experimental reports are meant to elucidate.

Psychologists seem to expect to be able to understand and explain all kinds of behavior. But looking at Figure 1.1, we see that they study narrowly defined bits of behavior in their laboratories. How, then, do they justify these grand expectations?

This chapter will be devoted to the theoretical and historical

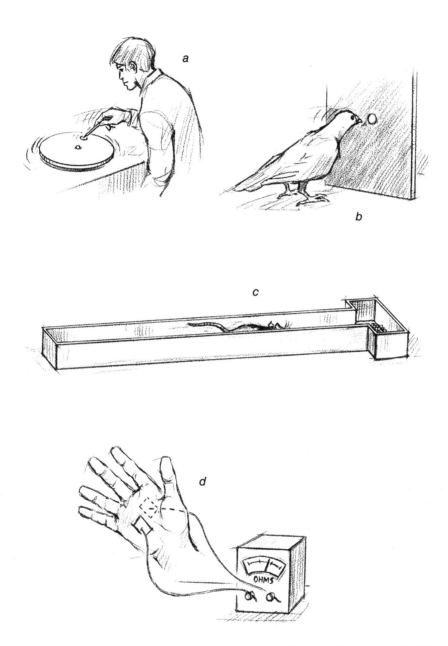

Figure 1.1 Four forms of behavior observed in the laboratory: (a) a man following a moving spot with a stylus; (b) a pigeon pecking at an illuminated disk on the wall; (c) a rat running down a straight alley with food at the end; (d) a change in electrical resistance due to sweat secreted on the palm of a hand.

Cartesian Dualism

influences that have guided research in learning. Because the history of psychology is lengthy and complex, we shall concentrate primarily on one central problem: What kinds of events should a psychologist study? Through an understanding of some of the intellectual roots of modern psychology, we may come to understand the behaviorist's purpose when he observes a human following a moving spot with a stylus, when he observes a pigeon pecking at an illuminated disk on the wall, when he observes a rat running down a straight alley to reach some food, or when he observes a man's sweating palm.

CARTESIAN DUALISM

In the Middle Ages, the theology of Western Christendom viewed reason as a handmaiden to faith. Faith had resolved the essential nature of man; reason's job was to support faith. Clearly, the intellectual climate was not hospitable to the scientific study of human behavior.

At the dawning of the modern age, science began to question many traditional beliefs. For example, in 1616, Galileo Galilei (1564–1642) earned harsh censure from established authority for denying the theological truth that the earth was fixed at the center of the universe. René Descartes (1596–1650) was about twenty years old when the Church first censured Galileo. When Descartes later undertook to study the nature of man, he found a way to compromise with tradition rather than clashing with it head on.

Descartes was already a great mathematician and philosopher when he published his first essays concerning human and animal behavior. In these essays, he felt obliged to reconcile his findings with the fundamental precepts of theology. Descartes thus took the position—a position adopted by most subsequent philosophers *—that there are two broad classes of human behavior: voluntary and involuntary. Descartes said that voluntary behavior is governed by the mind (a nonphysical entity) and that involuntary behavior has nothing to do with the mind, but instead is purely mechanical—as mechanical as the behavior of animals. According to theology, animals had no souls; Descartes therefore considered them to be essentially like clockwork mechanisms. For this reason, their behavior could be studied directly.

Descartes may have gotten the idea that many human behaviors could also be mechanical from watching the movements of the mechanical statues constructed by ingenious seventeenth-century ar-

---

*The term "scientist" was not coined until 1840.

Figure 1.2 *This illustration from Descartes' De Homine was designed to show the response of an organism to a stimulus. [From F. Fearing, 1930.]*

chitects and hydraulic engineers. Many of these grotesque mechanical figures were activated, like the chimes of clocks, by internal forces, but some had a unique feature—they were triggered unknowingly by the observer of the mechanism. For instance, as the observer walked down a path he stepped on a hidden treadle that activated a hydraulic mechanism that, in turn, caused a grinning Saracen automaton to emerge from the bushes brandishing a sword. (Similar mechanisms are still to be found at amusement parks like Disneyland.) To Descartes, this feature of the mechanisms, their response to a signal from the environment, was critically important. He reasoned that if human behavior could be simulated so well by these mechanical figures, then perhaps some of the principles on which the mechanisms operated also applied to the humans they were designed to imitate.

Figure 1.2 is a diagram by which Descartes showed the operation of an involuntary, purely mechanical, act. The overall effect is that the fire (A), touching the foot (B) of the boy, causes him to withdraw his foot. The mechanism acts through the nerve. The lower end of the nerve is set in motion by the fire, and this motion is transmitted

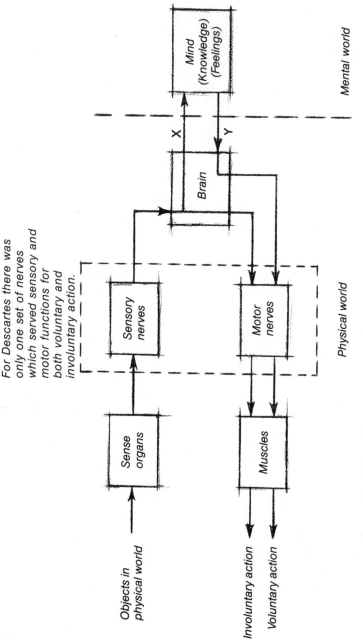

For Descartes there was only one set of nerves which served sensory and motor functions for both voluntary and involuntary action.

Objects in physical world

Sense organs

Sensory nerves

Brain

X

Y

Mind (Knowledge) (Feelings)

Motor nerves

Muscles

Involuntary action

Voluntary action

Physical world

Mental world

Figure 1.3 A diagram of the dualistic system of Descartes. Objects in the physical world, acting through sense organs and nerves, send signals to the brain. Involuntary actions are caused by the direct transmission through the brain of signals to the motor nerves and muscles. The mind can sense input through arrow X. Voluntary actions are caused by the mind, which sends out signals at Y.

upwards to the brain (de) ". . . just as, by pulling one of the ends of a cord, you cause a bell attached to the other end to ring at the same time." At the brain, a substance (which Descartes called "animal spirits") is released from the cavity (F). The animal spirits travel back down the nerve, swell the muscle in the calf, and cause the foot to be pulled back. At the same time, animal spirits go to the eyes, head, and hand to direct them toward the fire. Although this primitive explanation is crude by today's standards, it was a great departure from earlier conceptions of the workings of the body in that it tried to explain the boy's action in physical terms—without recourse to his will, his mind, or his emotions.

The dualism of Descartes' psychology is the feature that is essential to our understanding of the history of psychology. As we have noted, both mind and body were considered necessary to explain the totality of human behavior. Figure 1.3 is a schematic diagram of human behavior as it was conceived by Descartes. In his view, objects in the physical world affect the sense organs, which send messages through the nerves to the brain. At the brain, two things happen. First, in a purely mechanical way, the brain causes action by sending animal spirits through the nerves to the muscles. (This mechanical chain of effects from the sense organs to the brain and back to the muscles, by means of the nerves, eventually became known as a *reflex arc.*) At the same time, the body interacts with the mind at the pineal gland, near the center of the brain. This interaction allows the mind to be aware of both kinds of the body's actions—reflex, involuntary actions, over which it has no control, as well as voluntary actions, over which it exercises complete control. All actions involve the same nerves and muscles, but voluntary actions originate in the mind, a nonphysical realm, and involuntary actions originate in objects in the physical world. Only humans possess the extra pathway that leads to voluntary action (Figure 1.3). According to Descartes, since much behavior (including all animal behavior) is as mindless as the behavior of a stone, it can be considered subject to the same physical laws that govern a stone's behavior. On the other hand, the actions of the mind are not subject to physical laws but are determined by other laws, unknown, and perhaps unknowable.

The effect of Descartes' dualism was to divide up the study of behavior: involuntary behavior came to be studied by physiologists specializing in the study of the body; voluntary behavior remained in the realm of philosophers. These two branches of study had, at first, virtually nothing in common. They are of interest here because they gave rise to two distinct methods of collecting psychological data. We shall discuss first the mental branch of study and then the physical branch of study that grew out of Descartes' dualism.

THE MIND

Psyche is a Greek word meaning breath, spirit, or soul. Originally, psychology was that branch of knowledge that dealt with the human soul or mind. (Although "soul" and "mind" are not synonyms, the concepts are inextricably linked and the terms are often used interchangeably.) According to the dualism of Descartes, the mental world (which was identified with the soul) was the true realm of psychology, and the physical world—including the human body—was outside that realm.*

Introspection

In the age of Descartes, the concept of mind provided the very basis of philosophical speculation concerning human nature. How could the mind be studied? As we have noted, the study of mind through behavior was held to be impossible because (1) involuntary behavior was not determined by the mind; (2) voluntary behavior, which was governed by the mind, was considered to be unpredictable, determined by man's free will. Since the only observation a philosopher could make of others was their behavior (speech being included as a form of behavior), the minds of others were closed to him.

The most that one can do, these philosophers contended, is to study one's own mind by looking inward. Such a study was thought to be reliable because the information carried from the body to the mind (arrow X, Figure 1.3) was considered to be orderly and to affect the mind in orderly ways.

To this day introspection remains a common technique for studying mental activity.

Innate Ideas

If we accept, for the time being, the notion that the mind can be examined by introspection, and that the object of the examination is to determine the nature and origin of its contents, we can focus on one of

---

*The modern psychologist turns these priorities around: for him, the object of psychology is to study behavior. He feels required to look for the explanation of all human and animal behavior wherever his quest takes him. His ultimate objective is to explain behavior. If the concept of mind is useful in that respect, it must be part of his explanation. If it proves not to be useful, he is free to ignore it.

the key questions that troubled Descartes and the philosophers who came after him. That is, to what extent does the information entering the mind from the senses (arrow X in Figure 1.3) determine the contents of the mind? In other words, what is the effect of experience on ideas and emotions?

All philosophers agree that experience plays an important part in forming ideas. As we learn more about the world around us, our ideas change radically. A baby, for instance, sees a coin as a toy or as something to put in his mouth; an adult sees it quite differently. The question under debate was not whether experience modifies our ideas, but *to what extent* it modifies our ideas. Descartes himself, while believing that experience played a role in forming some of our concepts of the world, held that our most basic ideas are innate. That is, they are common to all human beings simply because they are qualities of the soul and because all human beings possess a soul. The idea of God, the idea of the self, the geometrical axioms (for example, that a straight line is the shortest distance between two points), the ideas of space, time, and motion are thus all said to be innate; experience is thus believed to fill in the details. (For example, experience can tell you what sort of objects move fast and what sort of objects move slowly or stay still, but the basic idea of motion in the world is present before experience.)

Those who hold that there are innate ideas, or that innate ideas are more basic and important than what is learned from experience are called "nativists." Those who deny the existence of innate ideas or hold that the idea of innate ideas is relatively unimportant are called "empiricists." The controversy between nativists and empiricists is a theme that runs through philosophy and psychology to the present day. However, contemporary psychologists (who de-emphasize *mind* as an explanatory concept) argue not about innate ideas but about innate *patterns of behavior.* Note that the nativism-versus-empiricism dispute can apply to both halves of Descartes' bifurcated model of man. Although we have been discussing innate ideas, that is, inborn mental qualities, there are also innate physical qualities. Just as one can argue about the extent to which the idea of space is modified by experience, one can also argue about the extent to which the structure of the nervous system is modified by the environment. By and large, the beliefs of most contemporary psychologists fall somewhere between extreme nativism and extreme empiricism. Descartes, who is usually considered a nativist, played a role in the development of empiricism. For example, although he held that the idea of space was innate, he showed how experience might give rise to the ideas of size and distance.

The more extreme view, that all or almost all ideas are due to experience, was not formulated until after Descartes' death. The development of this more extreme form of empiricism took place in England, and its adherents came to be known as the "British associationists." This school of philosophy was a direct predecessor of experimental psychology, and we shall turn to it next (after a cautionary note).

Principles of Association

The British empiricists accepted Descartes' dualistic theory of human nature (Figure 1.3). They also accepted Descartes' belief that the seat of knowledge is in the mind; they generally agreed with him that the proper subject for psychological study is the mind of man; they accepted his idea that the mind could be known by "reflection upon itself," in other words, by introspection. However, they did not accept Descartes' notion that man is born with a set of ideas. Their basic axiom was that all knowledge must come from the senses. Man may be born with the capacity to acquire knowledge, but everything we know, they held, comes from our experience. If we lived different lives, if our experiences were different, if we had been transported to a foreign land in infancy, then our knowledge would be different, and we would be, essentially, different people. This assumption is stated clearly by John

Locke, one of the earlier associationists, in 1690 in *An Essay Concerning Human Understanding*:

> Let us then suppose the Mind to be, as we say, white Paper, void of all Characters, without any *Ideas;* How comes it to be furnished? Whence comes it by that vast store, which the busie and boundless Fancy of Man has painted on it, with an almost endless variety? Whence has it all the materials of Reason and Knowledge? To this I answer, in one word, From *Experience:* In that, all our Knowledge is founded; and from that it ultimately derives it self. Our observation employ'd either about *external, sensible Objects; or about the internal Operations of our Minds, perceived and reflected on by our selves, is that, which supplies our Understandings with all the materials of thinking.* These two are the Fountains of Knowledge, from whence all the *Ideas* we have, or can naturally have, do spring.

The empiricists held that all knowledge comes from the senses. But the senses, by themselves (unaided by innate ideas), could provide only sensations: eyes alone could detect a spot of color but could hardly provide the knowledge that the spot of color is a round red ball.

The empiricists faced a dilemma. If we have no innate idea of a book, how do we know that a patch of light that is before us is an object that can be opened and read? that when we open it we can expect to find print on the pages? that the pages will be numbered consecutively? How do we know, in fact, that this object will not disappear after we have touched it? that it is capable of being lifted up without falling apart? or, for that matter, that it won't bite us or explode and destroy us? In other words, how is the mere sight of the object associated with sensations we do not feel but can *expect* to feel once we have lifted the object, opened it, and started to read it?

What the empiricists needed to find was some sort of "mental glue" to hold together all of the sensations capable of being experienced from a given object. "Association"—hardly a new idea—served this purpose. Aristotle (384–322 B.C.) formulated one of the first sets of associationist principles. He said that we remember things together (1) when they are similar, (2) when they contrast, and (3) when they are contiguous. This last principle, that of "contiguity" is by far the most important, since all subsequent formulations of the principles of association contain it. It is perhaps worth stating formally:

> If two (or more) sensations are felt at the same time often enough, then one alone felt later can invoke the memory of the other (or others).

To summarize, then, the empiricists took as their basic axiom: All knowledge comes from the senses. Realizing that isolated sensations cannot convey the meanings or the connotations of objects, these philosophers adopted a further principle to explain how sensations are connected. This principle was the principle of association by contiguity: If sensations occur together often enough, one alone can cause the memory of the rest.

The task of the empiricists then became to explain how the principle of contiguity acts in particular instances to produce complex experiences from simple sensations.

Visual Distance

One kind of complex experience that concerned the associationists was the experience of distance. The world appears to us in three dimensions, yet the retina of the eye is a thin, fairly flat surface. How does the three-dimensionality of experience come from impressions on the retina? According to the associationist George Berkeley (1685–1753), one possibility was that our idea of visual distance comes from the sensation of moving the pupils of the eyes together. Here is Berkeley's argument. For closer objects we have to move our eyes closer together to focus the objects; for farther objects we must move them apart. The sensations in the muscles of the eyes correspond to the distance of the objects. Other, nonvisual sensations corresponding to distance are those involved in reaching for or walking to the object. These sensations of walking, reaching, and so forth, become attached to the sensations in the muscles of the eyes by association by contiguity. In other words, whenever we have to reach only a short distance to touch an object, our pupils have to move close together to focus on the object. Whenever we have to reach far to touch an object, our pupils must move farther apart. Thus, the movement of our pupils and the movement of our hands become associated, and when we look at an object without touching it and only our pupils move, we remember the other sensation—that of our hands moving. This memory of our hands' greater or lesser movement is, according to Berkeley, what we mean when we say an object is far away from us or near.*

Meaning

Another problem faced by the associationists was that of meaning. How do we learn, for instance, the meaning of the word "chair"? The solution of this problem by the associationist James Mill (1773–1836)

---

*Berkeley seems to have favored different explanations at different times. This account of his argument is based on proposition 45 in "An essay towards a new theory of vision," Dublin, 1709. Reprinted in Berkeley, *Works on Vision* (Indianapolis: Bobbs-Merrill, 1963, p. 39).

was essentially an extension of Berkeley's solution of the problem of perceived distance. Here, in brief, is James Mill's reasoning. As we experience chairs in our lifetime, we see them, touch them, sit on them, and so forth. All these activities in relation to chairs produce their own sensations as well as containing many sensations in common. The "sittableness" of a chair is an association of the visual experience of chairs with the kinesthetic sensation of sitting. Also, the simultaneous seeing and hearing of the word "chair" produces sensations that become associated with each other and with the sensations resulting from the sight and touch of chairs. These all mix together in a huge bundle so that when we hear the word "chair" the memories or ideas of all the other sensations come to our minds. These memories and ideas were conceived by Mill to be less vivid than the actual sensations, but otherwise identical to them. The meaning of a word would thus be nothing but the bundle or total sum of associated ideas called to mind when the word is spoken or read. (Figure 1.4 illustrates the process by which meaning is established.)

Mental Chemistry

A more sophisticated concept of meaning was advanced by James Mill's son, John Stuart Mill (1806–1873), whose thinking was clearly influenced by the advancing science of chemistry. The younger Mill suggested that simple ideas might interact in a way analogous to a chemical process rather than by simply mixing together like salt and pepper. John Stuart Mill argued that just as the properties of water differ from those of its elements, hydrogen and oxygen, the properties of the meaning or connotation of a word could differ from the properties of the sensations that went into forming it. As he wrote:

> When many impressions or ideas are operating in the mind together, there sometimes takes place a process, of a similar kind to chemical combination. When impressions have been so often experienced in conjunction, that each of them calls up readily and instantaneously the ideas of the whole group, those ideas sometimes melt and coalesce into one another, and appear not several ideas but one . . . [Mill, 1843]

The idea that the operations of the mind could be studied in an experiment was a direct outgrowth of such speculations by the British associationists. The groundwork for experimental psychology was laid when the apparent chaos of our thoughts, the infinitude of images and ideas that seem to float so haphazardly in our minds, was seen to be a function of a restricted set of elements ("sensations") and of principles

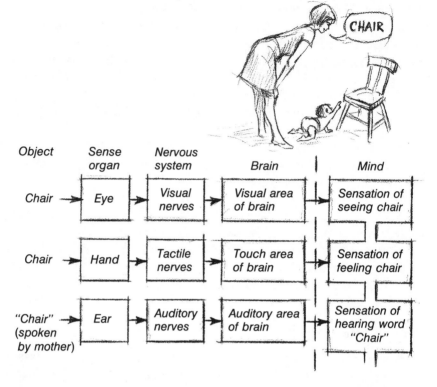

Figure 1.4a *A common view of the way meaning becomes established through association. The sketch shows a child touching a chair and hearing his mother say the word "chair." The diagram shows the inputs to the various sensory systems of the child. The three sensations occur together and are associated with one another by the child.*

of association. The early experiments in mental experimental psychology took two forms: studies of sensations themselves and studies of their combination.

Studies of Sensation

The idea that a sensation, as it occurs in the mind, is not identical to a sensory process in the body had been present since ancient times, but the idea that sensation as a mental phenomenon could be studied and measured seems to have come into being in German universities in the nineteenth century. It is to that time and place that most experimental psychologists today trace the origins of their science.

The first psychological experiments sought to explain the way in which sensory impulses pass from the physical world to the mental world (arrow X in Figure 1.3). Two lines of investigation started

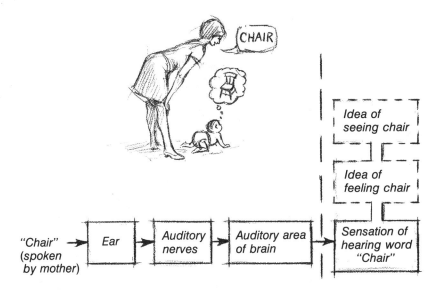

Figure 1.4b *This sketch shows the child at a later time, hearing the word "chair" when there is no chair present. The diagram shows that the word "chair" is now associated with past visual and tactile sensations.*

separately and eventually fused. One line studied the intensity of sensations and the other studied the quality of sensations. Let us discuss each of them in turn.

Intensity of Sensations

To some early investigators, the mental world, in contrast to the physical world, seemed discontinuous. Consider the following hypothetical experiment. Imagine a light controlled by a dial capable of producing a continuous range of intensity from complete blackness to blindingly intense light (Figure 1.5). An experimenter, starting at zero, turns the dial up very slowly until a subject reports that he can see some light. The amount that the intensity must increase from zero before light is reported is called the *absolute threshold* (or "absolute limen"). Then the dial is turned farther, until the subject reports that the light is noticeably brighter than it was before. Then it is turned farther still, until the subject again reports an increase in brightness. Each interval of brightness between reports is called a *just noticeable difference* (jnd). As the light is continuously increased in physical intensity, the intensity of the sensation (brightness) seems to go up in discrete jumps each jump corresponding to a jnd. It was noticed by Ernst Heinrich Weber (1795–1878) that for many different stimuli

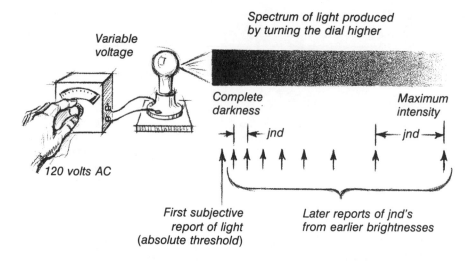

Figure 1.5 *A light used to measure* just noticeable differences *(jnd's) of* *brightness. The arrows across the bottom of the brightness spectrum indicate* *points at which a subject reported a difference in brightness as the brightness was* *gradually increased. Note that the jnd's at the dark end of the spectrum are* *smaller than those at the bright end.*

there was an orderly relation of jnd's to the magnitude of the stimulus. The bigger the stimulus, the bigger the increase required to notice that the stimulus increased. This relationship, in rough form, is quite obvious in everyday life. If a goldfish grows two inches longer over-night, its owner is likely to notice it the next morning; however, if an elephant grows two inches longer, no one is likely to notice it—even if it takes place in front of his eyes. Weber's significant contribution was quantifying this observation. He stated that the increase in the stimulus for one jnd was exactly proportional to the intensity (or size) of the stimulus. The importance of this correlation was seen by Gustav Theodor Fechner (1801–1887). He reasoned that since all jnd's had in common the fact that they were the smallest increment it was possible to see, then, as far as the subject who is watching for a change is concerned, any jnd is equivalent to any other (in other words, Fechner reasoned that all jnd's are subjectively equal). But, whereas the jnd's may be *subjectively* equal, they are not *physically* equal. If the jnd's vary in the physical dimension as Weber's theory states, and if all jnd's are subjectively equal, then the relation of subjective to physical size can be plotted (as in Figure 1.6). According to Fechner, in this relation-ship ". . . one has a general dependent relation between the size of the

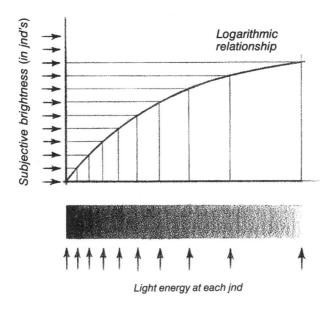

Figure 1.6 *This graph shows the relationship between jnd's in brightness and the magnitude of the stimulus (measured by the voltage regulator). All jnd's are considered to be subjectively equal.*

fundamental stimulus and the size of the corresponding sensation. . . . This permits the amount of sensation to be calculated from the relative amounts of the fundamental stimulus and thus we have a measurement of sensation [Fechner, 1860]." Fechner believed that their relation bridged the gap between the mental (psychic) and physical worlds (arrow X in Figure 1.3). Accordingly he chose the name *psychophysics* for this new science of the measurement of sensations, a name that persists today for the study of sensory magnitude.

Quality of Sensations

The theory of the associationists was that complex mental phenomena could be constructed from a limited group of elements. What, then, are the elements? How can they be distinguished from complex mental phenomena?

Johannes Müller (1801–1858), another German scientist, made the argument that the thing that distinguishes one sensation from another is not the stimulus itself, but the particular nerve stimulated. In other words, a sound seems different to us from a light, not because sound energy is essentially different from light energy, but because sound and light activate different nerves. Here are Müller's views. The mind decides whether a given stimulus was a light or a sound; if a light, what color; if a sound, what pitch. But the mind has no contact with the light or sound itself. The mind can only be sensitive to the nervous impulses leading from the receptors to the brain. The nerves alone tell the mind what sort of stimulation is impinging on the body. Any one of a certain group of nerves can signal that a sound has occurred (the particular activated nerve corresponds to the pitch of the sound). The ear is constructed so that it allows sounds of only that particular pitch to stimulate that particular nerve. But, Müller argued, under certain circumstances the mind can be fooled. If the energy that usually goes to our ears and causes us to hear a sound could be made instead to stimulate the nerve that goes from our eyes to our brain, we would experience the sound as a light. In fact any form of energy that succeeds in striking the nerve that corresponds to a given sensation would be capable of causing that sensation. He pointed out that electricity as well as sound energy could cause us to hear sounds when it was applied to the nerves of the ears. Müller's contention that the nerve rather than the stimulus determines the quality of sensation became the doctrine of *specific nerve energies.* This principle led to more questions. How many specific nerve energies are there? In vision, for instance, is there one for each color? In hearing, is there one for each tone?

A great deal of subsequent experimentation was directed towards answering such questions. In vision, for instance, all the colors were shown capable of being constructed by various combinations of three elementary colors, the primaries, red, green, and blue. These, then, could be the elementary sensations that reach the mind, and the vast array of colors that we see could be products of mental chemistry. Similar research was carried out for the other senses. Usually the method used was introspection and verbal report. Early experimental psychologists believed that a person could be trained to analyze his complex experience into its elements. For instance, an untrained observer experiences *wetness* as a unitary sensation, but observers experienced in introspection could analyze the experience of wetness into *pressure* and *cold.* As a check on this analysis it was shown that a dry, cold, uniform pressure on the finger, for instance, cannot be distinguished by a blindfolded observer from actual wetness.

Experiments in the analysis of sensations are still being carried on today, albeit in a more sophisticated way than those described here.

Secondary Laws of Association

Once it is accepted that simultaneously experienced sensations become associated in the mind, there is nothing more that the simple, unvarnished law of association has to say about them. How many times must they be experienced together before becoming associated? Which of several simultaneous sensations are more likely to become associated, or will they all become equally associated? Do sensations, once they become associated, remain so forever, or do they eventually separate again? These questions were not of great importance to the British associationists. However, the early experimental psychologists deemed them to be important because only by answering such questions would they be able to measure associations, and only by measurement would they be able to predict the occurrence of an association. It was the Scottish philosopher Thomas Brown (1778–1820) who first tried to answer these questions by formulating nine laws he called secondary laws of association (the three primary laws being those of Aristotle: contiguity, similarity, contrast). The secondary laws were held to modify the primary laws and to enable one to predict which sensations out of a group of sensations were more likely to become associated. Because of their importance for psychology it is worth listing Brown's secondary laws. They stated that association between sensations is modified by:

1. the length of time during which the original sensations endured
2. the intensity of the original sensations
3. the frequency of their pairing
4. the recency of their pairing
5. the number of other associations in which the sensations to be paired are involved
6. the abilities, capacities, and dispositions of the person experiencing the sensations
7. the emotional state of the person experiencing the sensations
8. the bodily state of the person experiencing the sensations
9. the similarity of the association itself to other, previously acquired, associations

The nine secondary laws of association set forth by Brown, as he himself recognized, contained no new facts but were merely a new way to organize facts that separately were well known. However, new facts about association did come from Hermann Ebbinghaus (1850–1909), who was the first to perform formal experiments in learning. His object was to study the quantitative relations implied by the nine secondary laws of association, particularly the third and fourth, which state that the mental association of two elements is modified by the frequency and recency of their pairing. Ebbinghaus chose nonsense syllables to be the elements he would use in his research and prepared lists of them to be memorized.

Ebbinghaus's nonsense syllables were three-letter combinations like BIV, RUX, JIC, and KEL, with the first letter a consonant, the second a vowel, and the third another consonant. It is worth knowing the claims Ebbinghaus made for nonsense syllables, because similar claims have frequently been made by psychologists about the kinds of material they use in their experiments and about the kinds of behavior they choose to study. In fact, the various, apparently trivial, observations depicted in Figure 1.1 are used in psychological experiments today for some of the same reasons that nonsense syllables were used in Ebbinghaus's classic studies. (Indeed, nonsense syllables themselves are still used in many studies of learning.) The advantages claimed for such materials are:

1. *They are relatively simple.* (It is important to understand the reason behind the search for simplicity in psychology. Many of the experiments that psychologists do will otherwise seem incomprehensible. Essentially, the reason that simplicity is sought is that psychologists hope that the underlying laws of behavior will prove to be simple and that the complexity we observe in everyday life will prove to be the result of the concatenation of simple basic processes. The reason for this hope is that in other sciences a similar hope has frequently been fulfilled. For example, it is virtually impossible for a physicist to predict the everyday behavior of physical objects except in a most general way. When a piece of paper is dropped in a room, it is impossible to predict the path it will take as it flutters to the floor. But it is relatively easy to predict the path the paper would follow if it were dropped in a vacuum, a simplified environment where several second-order phenomena—like friction and air resistance—are not present. The vacuum is artificial, so is the nonsense syllable. The intent of scientists, however, is the same in both cases: to find an area in which laws operate simply and directly and in which behavior can be easily predicted. Psychologists are continually seeking to devise a test condition that is the psychological equivalent of a physical vacuum, and many of their methods

reflect this effort. Just as the vacuum eliminates friction and air resistance, the nonsense syllable, according to Ebbinghaus, eliminates meaning. For Ebbinghaus, as for the earlier associationists, meaning was equivalent to the accumulation of sensations attached to a given word. Because the syllables he devised were not words, not associated with any objects, and therefore not associated with any particular sensations, they had no meaning.)

2. *They are relatively homogeneous.* (This means simply that no one nonsense syllable stands out from the rest.)

3. *They form an inexhaustible amount of new combinations, each of which can be compared to the other.* (In other words, a given list of ten nonsense syllables has no more meaning than any other list of ten nonsense syllables. Also, they may be compared in reverse. That is, CEV MEB has no more meaning than MEB CEV.)

4. *They are capable of quantitative variations, and may be divided at any point.* (The only difference between a list of five nonsense syllables and a list of ten nonsense syllables, no matter how they are arranged, is that the latter is twice as long. On the other hand, consider the differences between these two lists:

I	II
TOM	BUT
MEN	SIX
SIX	MEN
BUT	SAW
HIS	TOM
	GET
	HIS
	BIG
	RED
	CAR

The difference between them is not only that the second is twice as long, but that it is a meaningful sentence whereas the first is not. The second list, although twice as long as the first, is easier for most people to memorize because of its meaning.)

The object of Ebbinghaus's experiments was to use nonsense syllables in a quantitative analysis of the development of associations. He was not satisfied to know merely that greater frequency of pairing

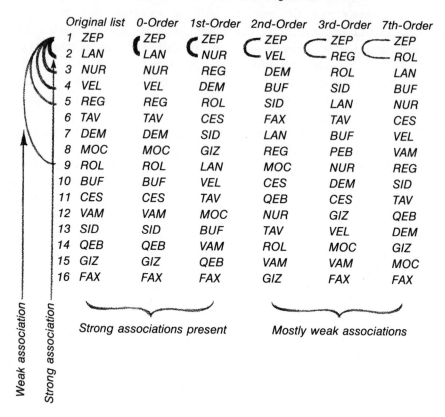

Original list	0-Order	1st-Order	2nd-Order	3rd-Order	7th-Order
1 ZEP	ZEP	ZEP	ZEP	ZEP	ZEP
2 LAN	LAN	NUR	VEL	REG	ROL
3 NUR	NUR	REG	DEM	ROL	LAN
4 VEL	VEL	DEM	BUF	SID	BUF
5 REG	REG	ROL	SID	LAN	NUR
6 TAV	TAV	CES	FAX	TAV	CES
7 DEM	DEM	SID	LAN	BUF	VEL
8 MOC	MOC	GIZ	REG	PEB	VAM
9 ROL	ROL	LAN	MOC	NUR	REG
10 BUF	BUF	VEL	CES	DEM	SID
11 CES	CES	TAV	QEB	CES	TAV
12 VAM	VAM	MOC	NUR	GIZ	QEB
13 SID	SID	BUF	TAV	VEL	DEM
14 QEB	QEB	VAM	ROL	MOC	GIZ
15 GIZ	GIZ	QEB	VAM	VAM	MOC
16 FAX	FAX	FAX	GIZ	FAX	FAX

Weak association   Strong association

Strong associations present   Mostly weak associations

Figure 1.7 *Lists of nonsense syllables prepared by Ebbinghaus.*

leads to greater association. He wanted to know exactly how much pairing was necessary before an association would be formed.

In the course of his investigations, Ebbinghaus studied many different aspects of association. To better understand his method, let us consider one of his experiments. The purpose of this particular experiment was to test the conception that an association is formed in the mind of a subject between all members of a list of nonsense syllables when he reads that list, and that the association is stronger for items on the list that are closer together and weaker for items on the list that are further apart. Consider the "original list" in Figure 1.7. According to Ebbinghaus, once the list is memorized, associations are formed between each item and all the other items. The association between neighboring items is strongest; the association between distant items is weak. This would imply, for instance, that ZEP LAN becomes strongly associated, ZEP NUR moderately associated, and ZEP ROL only weakly associated. In order to test this notion, Ebbinghaus invented what is called the *savings method.* He memorized several lists like those in the left-hand column of Figure 1.7; 24 hours later, he tried to relearn the same lists. The relearning of the lists, he found, took an average of 420 seconds less than the learning of the original list. The 420 seconds he saved he considered to be a measure of the strength of the associations 24 hours after they were formed. He reasoned that if he had forgotten the list completely he would have shown no saving (learning and relearning times would be equal), and if he had remembered the list completely he would have maximum saving (relearning time would equal zero). Thus, the amount of time saved would be an index of how well he had remembered the list.

Then he constructed, from the original list, a series of derived lists. "A derived list of zero order" is simply the original list. A derived list of the first order contains the items of the original list so arranged that all but one of the adjacent items in the derived list were separated by one item in the original list. A derived list of the second order is arranged so that most of the adjacent items in the new list were originally separated by two items. Higher order derived lists were constructed by the same principle. If, as Ebbinghaus theorized, the association on the original list was greatest for adjacent items, then a zero-order derived list, which retains the same adjacent items, should produce the most saving. A first-order derived list, which contains items from the original list spaced one item apart, should produce less saving. A second-order derived list with items spaced two apart should show still less, and so on. When the experiment was performed, this was exactly what Ebbinghaus found. A graph showing the decreasing amount of saving as the associations on the list became more remote is shown in Figure 1.8.

The experiments of Ebbinghaus were the first formal experiments in association, just as the experiments of Weber and Fechner were the first formal experiments in sensation. The goal of these experiments was to describe and measure scientifically the properties of the mind. The subjects were invariably human. The data collected was in the form of verbal reports. The preferred method of obtaining this data was by introspection on the part of the subject, although whether Ebbinghaus's experiments really relied on introspection is open to question. The introspective method in which the experimenter and subject are the same person was so influential, however, that even in his rather objective experiments, Ebbinghaus always served as his own subject.

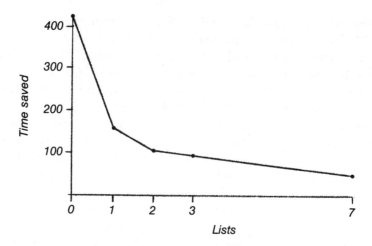

Figure 1.8 *Results of Ebbinghaus's experiment. This graph shows that the amount of time saved in relearning lists decreases as a function of their remoteness from the original list (0). The time saved is the number of seconds required to learn the original list minus the number of seconds required to learn one of the derived lists 24 hours later.*

For many years all scientists who called themselves psychologists were engaged in studying mental phenomena by methods like these. In the early part of the present century, however, such methods were seriously challenged by physiologists who claimed that phenomena such as memory, emotion, and knowledge, hitherto seen as mental, were actually capable of being explained as bodily functions. Thus, they contended, the proper people to study such phenomena were not psychologists trained in introspection, but physiologists trained in analyzing the discrete and delicate functions of the body and, in particular, the system of nerves that regulate bodily functions.

THE BODY

For a hundred years after Descartes, the methods of investigating the mind and the body could not have been more widely separated. On one hand, the British associationists and the German experimental psychologists studied the mind of man by means of introspection. On the other hand, physiologists studied the body by methods akin to those of physics. In general, the physiologists accepted Descartes' division: psychology, the study of the mind; physiology, the study of the body.

However, as their science gained precision, physiologists could account for much of the behavior previously thought to be controlled by the mind. For instance, in the seventeenth century, physiologists showed that after death (when, presumably, the soul had left the body) hearts could be kept beating. In fact, instances of hearts beating when removed entirely from the body were reported. Today we know that the heart operates like a muscle and that muscles can be activated by stimulating them appropriately even when they are detached from the body, but in the seventeenth century most people believed that the soul gave life to the heart. There are two possible resolutions to the problem that was posed by the observation that the heart, the muscles, and other organs were capable of functioning separately from the body. First of all, one could say that each of these organs had a soul—an animating force—of its own. This resolution was counter to the traditional belief that a human soul was in essence an *immortal entity:* such an entity obviously could not be divided up into several bits and pieces, some of which remained in human organs after death. The other solution to the problem was to deny that the soul had anything to do with the operation of the organs and to say that human organs worked "mechanically," like those of animals. This was the position that most physiologists took and the notion that is generally accepted today. (Not many people object to heart transplant operations on the grounds that they interfere with a patient's soul.)

With each new advance, the physiologists found mechanistic explanations for processes that were traditionally held to be controlled by the mind. Some people reasoned that physiology might continue to advance until it eventually captured the entire province of the mind. Might not all human behavior eventually be explained in mechanistic terms? By this reasoning, to say that a function was "controlled by the mind" was the same as saying that its causes were unknown, and that physiology had not yet advanced far enough to explain it. Perhaps Descartes' dualism was wrong, ran this mechanistic reasoning, and perhaps human behavior as well as animal behavior could eventually be explained without any reference to an animating force like the mind or the soul. In the words of Julian Offray De La Mettrie (1709–1751), one of the first thinkers to espouse a completely mechanical explanation of behavior:

> To be a machine, to feel, to think, to know how to distinguish good from bad, as well as blue from yellow, in a word, to be born with an intelligence and a sure moral instinct, and to be but an animal, are therefore characters which are no more contradictory, than to be an ape or a parrot and to be able to give one's self pleasure ... I believe that thought is so little

incompatible with organized matter, that it seems to be one of its properties on a par with electricity, the faculty of motion, impenetrability, extension, etc. [La Mettrie, 1748]

Most physiologists did not go so far as La Mettrie, preferring mechanical explanations for those functions of the body that they could bring under their scrutiny, and mental explanations for those functions that they had not yet investigated.

The subsequent physiological investigations that had the greatest effect on psychology were those that dealt with the reflex, that is, with the direct response of an organism to a stimulus in the environment. (We recall Descartes' example of the boy recoiling from the fire.)

As recently as the beginning of the twentieth century, there were still two principal areas of behavior that remained virtually unaffected by physiological research and almost wholly within the province of the mind:

1. Behavior seeming to arise from within the person himself, such as (a) an apparently voluntary raising of the arm for which no cause or stimulus can be found in the environment or (b) complex behavior (singing an operatic aria in the shower, for instance) for which no correspondingly complex environmental stimulus can be found.
2. Learning. Most reflexes seem to be permanently fixed in the body. How can they explain learning to sing a song, for instance, or learning a whole repertoire of songs?

However, it was in the late nineteenth century and early twentieth century that the Russian physiologists Ivan Michailovich Sechenov (1829–1905) and Ivan Petrovich Pavlov (1849–1936) asserted that even these two areas of behavior could be understood in terms of reflexes.

In the next several sections, we shall trace the history of the physiological investigation of the reflex. We shall see how the concept of the reflex has become vital in psychology, especially in the study of learning. Let us begin by returning to the world of Descartes to look for the origins of the concept of reflex action in early discussions of nervous conduction.

Nervous Conduction

In general, early theories of nervous conduction held that the mind governs behavior through the transmission of some kind of vapor or substance to the muscles. Such theories reflected both traditional doctrine and the state of knowledge in the physical sciences. For

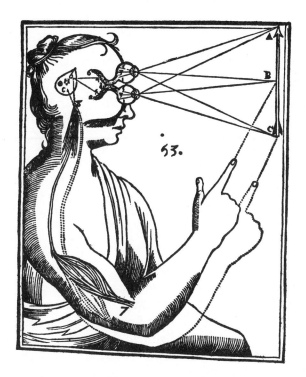

Figure 1.9 *The central role of the pineal gland in Descartes' physiology is shown in this diagram from l'Homme. Images fall on retinas (5, 3, 1) and are conveyed to the cerebral ventricles (6, 4, 2); these then form a single binocular image on the pineal gland (H), the site from which the soul controls the body. Stimulated by the image, the soul inclines the pineal gland, activating the "hydraulic system" of the nerves (8), causing a muscle to move (at 7). [Courtesy of the Curators of Bodlein Library, Oxford University.]*

Descartes, nervous conduction was based on a hydraulic model. As we recall, his opinion was that the soul interacts with the body in the pineal gland, near the middle of the brain. This gland, he thought, directs "animal spirits" through the nerves to activate the muscles mechanically. In 1662, he wrote that even though animal spirits must be "very mobile and subtle, they nevertheless have the force to swell and tighten the muscles within which they are enclosed, just as the air in a balloon hardens it and causes the skin containing it to stretch." (See Figure 1.9.)

Descartes' views were highly influential. For a hundred years, controversy raged, not about whether animal spirits existed, but rather

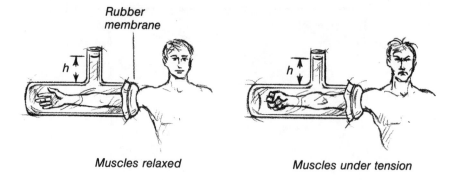

Rubber
membrane

h

Muscles relaxed

h

Muscles under tension

Figure 1.10 Glisson's attempt to show that muscles do not gain in substance when they are contracted. The height of the water, h, is identical whether the subject's arm is tensed or relaxed.

about what they consisted of. Some physiologists rejected Descartes' hydraulic model and adopted a pneumatic model; that is, they claimed that a gas, rather than a liquid, runs from the nerves to the muscles. Some (called iatro-physicists) claimed that there is a mechanical transmission of force, and others (called iatro-chemists) claimed that the phenomenon is basically a chemical process. This speculation was generally nonexperimental. A clear experimental advance, however, was made by Francis Glisson (1597–1677), who showed in 1677 that whatever nervous conduction occurs when muscles contract, it does not consist of the transfer of a substance, either liquid or gas, from the nerves to the muscles. Glisson's experiment was simple. He had a subject put his hand in a tube full of water, as shown in Figure 1.10, and then contract and relax his muscles. When the muscles were contracted Glisson found that the height of the water did not increase above the height for relaxed muscles, showing that no substance could be flowing into the muscles when they were contracted. From this evidence, it followed that muscles work by themselves once they receive proper stimulation. The question that remained was: what sort of stimulation do the nerves supply to the muscles?

Actually, a more sophisticated experiment had been done by John Swammerdam (1637–1680), prior to Glisson's work, but had not become widely known. In 1660 Swammerdam had surgically isolated a nerve and muscle of a frog and had shown that mechanical stimulation of the nerve was sufficient to contract the muscle. In other words, no infusion of animal spirits or any other substance was necessary for the contraction of the muscle; simple irritation of the nerve was sufficient. Whether such a mechanical irritation is the actual process that takes

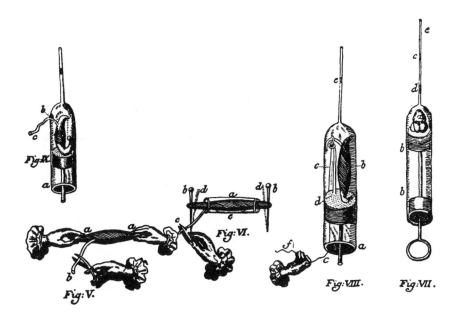

Figure 1.11 *Early illustrations of Swammerdam's experiments.* [*From Fearing, 1930.*]

place in the body when a muscle is contracted was another question. Figure 1.11 shows some of the illustrations of Swammerdam's experiments with nerves and muscles of frogs—experiments that have been repeated by countless students of elementary physiology.

In general, until late in the eighteenth century, some kind of mechanical conduction of energy was held to activate muscles, but the question of the exact nature of the energy was not resolved. For instance, according to David Hartley (1705–1766)—whose ideas we shall refer to again later—the nervous impulse consisted of minute mechanical vibrations transmitted through the nerve like a wave. By the beginning of the nineteenth century, physiologists came to agree that however nerves might work, they were not adequately explained by references to animal spirits, mind, or soul.

Around 1800 there was great interest in electricity and much fruitful study of the subject. Some scientists speculated that nervous conduction might be electrical. As research progressed in the middle of the nineteenth century, it became increasingly clear that some form of electrical impulse was present in the nerve. Today, the nerve impulse is thought to be a combination of electrical and chemical events.

So we have, in the history of speculation about nervous conduction and research into its nature, a progression of theories—hydraulic to pneumatic to vibratory to electrical and chemical. These theories became more sophisticated and complex as the physical sciences offered successively better ways to understand the way the human body functions.

The Reflex Arc

To those who have considered animal behavior (and much of human behavior) to be machinelike, the basic element of that machinelike behavior has been the *reflex arc*, the pathway leading from the sense organs through the nerves to the muscles. Descartes thought that sensory and motor signals travel through the same nerve. According to him, the sensory signal from the sense organ to the brain operated like a pull chain; the motor signal was hydraulic, consisting of the flow of animal spirits down through the nerve and into the muscle.

After Descartes' time, experimenters began to dissect animals to look for the organs necessary for various reflex functions. They found that certain parts of the nervous system (for instance, the cerebrum of the brain) could be entirely removed without destroying most reflexes; but they also found that severing some parts (notably, the spinal cord) immediately destroyed reflexes. This kind of investigation of the body may be compared to a mechanical investigation of an unknown machine. In order to discover whether a certain part of the machine is necessary for a certain function, you could remove or disconnect that part and see what functions are impaired. Does the carburetor of an automobile belong to its steering mechanism? One way to find out is to remove the carburetor and see if you can still steer the automobile. Because of experiments of this nature with animals, physiologists began to look upon the spinal cord and the base of the brain—but not the cerebrum—as necessary centers of reflex action. But what happens in the spinal cord or base of the brain between the input and output was still a matter for speculation. According to George Prochaska (1749–1820), an early reflexologist, "This part, in which, as in a centre, the sensorial nerves, as well as the motor nerves, meet and communicate, and in which the impressions made on the sensorial nerves are reflected on the motor nerves, is designated by a term, now adopted by most physiologists, the *sensorium commune* [Prochaska, 1784]." But it was not clear in Prochaska's time, nor is it fully clear today, exactly what occurs in the *sensorium commune*, now called the central nervous system.

Although information on the central nervous system was scanty in the eighteenth century, physiologists were able to make lists of types

TABLE 1.1

Special Sense	Automatic Motion
1. "Feeling"—touch, pain	Crying, distortion of face, laughter following tickling, grasping, putting muscles into contraction following painful stimulation.
2. Taste	Sucking, mastication, deglutition, distortion of mouth, peristaltic motion of stomach and bowels, vomiting, hiccough, expulsion of faeces, spasms.
3. Smell	Inspiration of air to "increase" odor, contraction of the fauces and gullet, sneezing.
4. Sight	Motions of globe of eye, motions of the eyelid, contractions of the lacrymal glands, contractions of the muscular rings of the iris, and the ciliar ligaments
5. Hearing	Contraction of small muscles of the auricle in adjusting to sound, contraction of muscles belonging to small bones of the ear.

of behavior that they thought were governed by reflexes. Table 1.1 shows one made in 1749 by Hartley, classified according to the sense organ stimulated.

In the early nineteenth century, physiologists began to develop a better picture of reflex mechanisms. In independent experiments with animals, François Magendie (1783–1855) and Charles Bell (1774–1842) discovered that when they cut the posterior branch of spinal nerves in an experimental animal, the animal could still move the innervated limb but did not react to a pinprick on the limb, whereas, when they cut the anterior branch of nerves, the animal responded to a pinprick but was not able to move the limb. This discovery established a clear distinction between nerves with a sensory function and nerves with a motor function. Meanwhile, lists of reflexes such as Hartley's were being expanded. Postural reflexes, such as those that allow a man to walk on a tilting ship or allow a cat to land on its feet when dropped upside down, and tendon reflexes, such as the knee jerk, were studied in detail. However, no matter how the list of automatic actions was extended, there still remained a host of actions, including most of the complex actions of everyday life, such as speaking, reading, and writing, that were unexplained by the physiologists and therefore classified as voluntary acts. We now turn to the attempt by the Russian physiologists Sechenov and Pavlov to explain such complex acts mechanistically.

Complex Behavior

Although the notion that all behaviors could be classified as either voluntary or involuntary (automatic) was a basic legacy of the dualism of Descartes, many observable behaviors simply could not be fit into either classification. Sneezing and laughing seem involuntary enough, yet they can be suppressed; with much practice, some people have even learned to exert some control over the size of the pupils of their eyes. And what about breathing? We normally consider it to be quite automatic. But when a doctor puts a stethoscope to our chest we breathe in and out at his command; we can also hold our breath at will for short periods of time.

A different type of hard-to-classify behavior is represented by fast and accurate typing. Most skilled typists say that fast typing is automatic, and that they do not concentrate on the pressing of each individual key. In fact, if they try to think of each key, they slow down considerably. Yet, clearly, when someone starts learning to type, he or she must concentrate on each key that is struck. This voluntary effort seems to become involuntary with practice. A similar shift from voluntary to automatic behavior can be seen in the acquisition of almost any skill. As an advertisement for a standard-shift Volkswagen puts it, "After a while, it becomes automatic."

Recognizing (1) the tendency of many voluntary acts to develop into involuntary acts and (2) the modifiability of many involuntary acts, nineteenth-century physiologists had to admit that they knew little or nothing about many forms of behavior. Nevertheless, they persisted in their hope that the idea of reflexes would eventually explain all behavior of organisms.

It was Sechenov who attempted to show how complex, apparently voluntary acts, can, in a broad frame of reference, be understood to be essentially involuntary. To demonstrate this, Sechenov had addressed himself to the problem of energy. One of the most basic laws of physics is that of the conservation of energy: any energy that crosses the boundaries into a system must either remain in the system or come out in some other form. For instance, in an automobile engine, the energy contained in the gasoline that enters the engine eventually may leave it in the form of kinetic energy—the energy involved in the motion of the automobile—or in the form of heat lost to the environ-

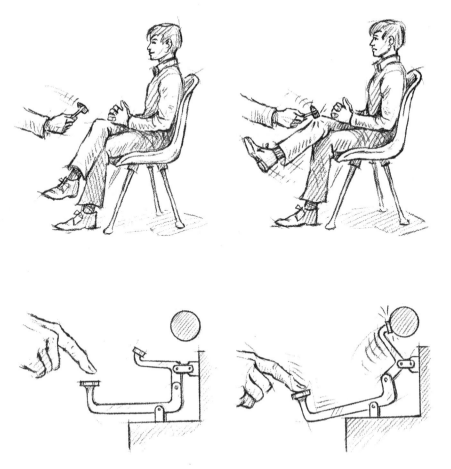

Figure 1.12 *The reflex conceived of as a simple mechanism.* Above, *a high-energy stimulus from the environment causes a high-energy response in the form of a knee jerk.* Below, *a high-energy blow on a typewriter key causes a typebar to strike the roller.*

ment, in the form of sound energy, and in the form of the chemical energy remaining in the exhaust gases. If you could keep a record of all the energy going into and coming out of the engine—or any system—you would find that the two amounts are equal.

Many movements of organisms are caused by direct stimuli in the environment. A tap on a human knee, for instance, causes a reflex jerk in the leg. The energy input here is great enough so that it does not stretch the imagination to attribute the energy output of the knee jerk to the energy input of the blow on the knee. This view of the operation of this reflex is illustrated in Figure 1.12. Even though we now know it to be a gross oversimplification, it was nevertheless possible for early

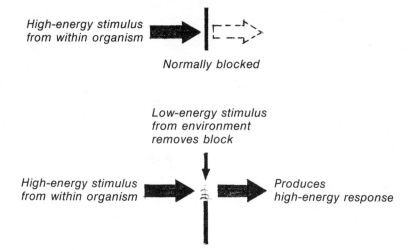

High-energy stimulus
from within organism

Normally blocked

Low-energy stimulus
from environment
removes block

High-energy stimulus
from within organism

Produces
high-energy response

Figure 1.13 *A low-energy stimulus can produce a high-energy response. This diagram suggests that the main source of energy is within the organism but that it is normally blocked. A low-energy stimulus may temporarily remove the block and thus permit a high-energy response.*

physiologists to think of the knee jerk as a mechanism that connected the stimulus to the response by various linkages within the body, with the stimulus providing the energy for the response, just as a blow on a key of a standard typewriter provides the energy for a typebar to strike the paper. But consider another reflex: a baby's sneeze. Where is the stimulus that provides the tremendous energy exhibited in a good satisfying sneeze? Could all that energy come from a mote of dust tickling the inside of the baby's nostril? It did not seem to Sechenov that it could. Instead, he proposed another kind of mechanism, one that we can compare to the electric switch that starts a fan. The energy that operates the fan is not supplied by the movement of the switch. The switch merely releases electrical energy to the fan, energy that is far greater than that required to turn the switch. While the switch is turned off, the pathway of electric current is blocked; turning on the switch removes the block. (In the nervous systems of organisms such blocking is called *inhibition*, and the stimulus that removes the inhibition is called a *releasing stimulus.*) Returning to the example of the baby's sneeze, we can think of the energy for the sneeze as stored up in the body of the baby, perhaps from milk drunk the previous day, ready to activate a sneeze at any moment—but normally inhibited from doing so. When the baby's nose is tickled, the energy is released and the baby sneezes. Figure 1.13 illustrates the mechanism. For a long time, explanations of complex behaviors had relied on the idea of inhibitory and releasing mechanisms, but Sechenov was among the first actually to locate them in the body.

In one series of experiments Sechenov measured the time taken by a frog to remove its foot reflexively when an acid stimulus was applied to its extended leg. Then he showed that this reflex could be modified by removing various portions of the frog's brain. Sechenov found, essentially, that the stimulus–response reaction time decreased when he removed certain areas of the brain—indicating that he had removed an inhibitory mechanism. When he put salt on parts of the frog's brain, the stimulus–response reaction time was increased—showing that he had excited an inhibitory mechanism. Figure 1.14 shows how Sechenov supposed this mechanism to work. In a series of experiments with humans, Sechenov showed that people's reflexes work more slowly when they are tickled than when they are not tickled; furthermore, the more tickling the slower the reflexes. In other words, tickling serves to increase the inhibition of reflexes.

Sechenov reasoned that if stimuli with little energy could trigger off and control such relatively violent reactions, then perhaps all of those complex actions that appear to be voluntary (controlled from within the organism by the mind) are actually controlled from outside the organism by stimuli that have so little energy that the organism is not aware of its responses to them. Although the reactions to low-energy stimuli may be slight, they are present, and are, according to Sechenov, purely mechanical. In other words, the small, unnoticed external stimuli have two functions. First, they cause reactions within the brain, reactions we have come to call thoughts. Secondly, they activate or release inhibitions on gross motor reactions. Sechenov says of this sequence:

> It is generally accepted that if one act follows another, the two acts stand in causal relationship (post hoc—ergo propter hoc); *this is why thought is generally believed to be the cause of behaviour;* and when the external sensory stimulus remains unnoticed—which happens quite frequently—*thought is even accepted as the initial cause of behavior.* Add to this the extremely subjective character of thought, and you will understand how firmly man must believe in the voice of self-consciousness, when it tells him such things. In reality, however, this voice tells him the greatest of falsehoods: *the initial cause of all behaviour always lies, not in thought, but in external sensory stimulation, without which no thought is possible.* [Sechenov, 1863]

By this reasoning, Sechenov attempted to draw all the complexity of behavior within the realm of reflexology. No longer was a reflex seen to be a simple chain from stimulus to response; instead, it was seen as a

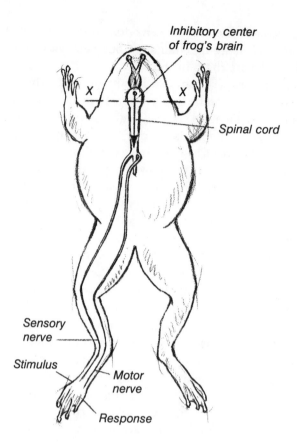

Inhibitory center
of frog's brain

Spinal cord

Sensory
nerve

Stimulus

Motor
nerve

Response

Figure 1.14 *Sechenov's experiments on inhibition. Sechenov observed that (1) salt applied to "an inhibitory center" in the frog's brain slowed down the withdrawal of its leg from an acid, and (2) severing the frog's nerves at X—X speeded up the withdrawal.*

complex machinelike process modified by unnoticed signals from the environment—much like the process by which a radio receives low-energy electromagnetic waves and uses them to modify the high energy from its battery or from an electric outlet so as to generate signals loud enough to be audible. But no matter how complex a radio may be, it is nevertheless fixed in its construction. If the signal to a radio is repeated, its response will be the same. In this respect, the behavior of an animal cannot be explained by Sechenov's theory. An animal does not always respond in the same way to a repeated stimulus. Its responses are modified, as we have seen, by experience; furthermore, the way in which responses are modified depends on the nature of the experience. It was another Russian physiologist, Pavlov, who was to show how reflexes could be modified by experience.

Pavlov realized that inborn reflex mechanisms, no matter how precise and complex, were not enough to explain the various adjustments that organisms make to their environments. In particular, such mechanisms could not explain the process that the psychologists who studied mental phenomena called *association*. For example, how could an inborn reflex explain the fact that people react strongly not only to heat on their skin, but to the sight of a fire, the smell of smoke, the word "fire" shouted in a loud voice, and the sound of fire engines in the street? Certainly it was too much to imagine that each of these stimuli is connected to an inborn reflex of its own; more likely, such groups of stimuli become associated through experience. But how? Pavlov's investigations were directed mainly towards this question.

The particular reflex that Pavlov and his students studied most closely was the salivary reflex in dogs. (We shall describe these experiments in more detail in Chapter 2.) In general, Pavlov found that dogs salivate when any stimulus is presented, such as a bell, a light, the experimenter, or a geometrical pattern, provided that the stimulus has been presented together with food a sufficient number of times. There are parallels between Pavlov's work and Ebbinghaus's. Ebbinghaus presented two nonsense syllables together and observed association. Pavlov presented a neutral arbitrary stimulus (such as a bell) together with a stimulus (food) that was closely linked to a response. Like Ebbinghaus, Pavlov found that the more the paired stimuli are presented together, the greater is the strength of the association. The strength of the association was determined by Pavlov by measuring the amount of saliva secreted when the bell was sounded. As the amount secreted at the sound of the bell approached the amount secreted when food itself was present, the strength of the association was said to be increasing.

Pavlov decided that all organisms must possess two sets of reflexes:

1. *A fixed, innate set of relatively simple reflexes.* (According to Pavlov, the path of these reflexes runs from the sensory nerves through the spinal cord to the motor nerves; these simple reflexes can be modified by innate inhibitory mechanisms, as Sechenov had shown, but essentially they are fixed.)

2. *A set of acquired reflexes.* (These reflexes, called *conditioned* reflexes by Pavlov, are formed by pairing previously neutral stimuli with a stimulus that triggers off an innate reflex; the

path of these acquired reflexes goes through the upper parts of the brain, the cerebral hemispheres; when these parts of the brain are removed, the acquired reflexes disappear, leaving only the simple innate reflexes.)

It was Pavlov's view that:

> the basic physiological function of the cerebral hemispheres throughout the ... individual's life consists in a constant addition of numberless signalling conditioned stimuli to the limited number of the initial inborn unconditioned stimuli, in other words, in constantly supplementing the unconditioned reflexes by conditioned ones. Thus, the objects of the instincts [our desires for food, and the like] exert an influence on the organism in ever-widening regions of nature and by means of more and more diverse signs or signals, both simple and complex; consequently, the instincts are more and more fully and perfectly satisfied, i.e., the organism is more reliably preserved in the surrounding nature. [Pavlov, 1955, p. 273]

Pavlov held that we (organisms) steer ourselves through our environments by means of signals conditioned through experience to remove us from trouble and to lead us to the things we need. He contended that all complex learned behavior is brought about through the combination of several simple conditioned reflexes, which are physiological—not mental—processes. He believed that through objective investigations, physiologists would eventually be able to predict all of the behaviors of animals and humans.

THE RELATION OF PHYSIOLOGICAL PSYCHOLOGY TO MENTAL PSYCHOLOGY

In regard to the associationists we pointed out that the parties to theoretical disputes are often seen from the perspective of time as essentially similar in basic outlook. To some extent, this applies to the reflexologists versus the associationists. The reflexologists, like Sechenov and Pavlov, thought that all complex behavior is mechanical; the associationists, like Ebbinghaus, thought that all complex behavior is influenced by the mind. Although these theorists differed in many obvious respects, they nevertheless retained several basic similarities.

Both the associationists and reflexologists believed that complex behavior is the result of the combination of simple elements. The associationists believed that the elements are simple sensations or ideas, that a complex idea is the combination of a group of simple ideas, and that the blending of simple ideas into complex ones takes place in the mind. The reflexologists believed that the elements are simple reflexes, that a complex action or behavior is the combination of a group of simple reflexes, and that the blending of simple reflexes into complex ones takes place in the brain.

The parallels between the basic concepts of these two outgrowths of Descartes' dualism, although often obscured, were not unnoticed at the time. Both the mentalists and Pavlov claimed that conditioned reflexes might shed light on the concept of association. Even as early as the eighteenth century, the associationist philosopher Hartley, who was also a physician and a physiologist, attempted to explain all of human behavior in terms of both association and physiology. He believed that mental and physical processes could exist side by side, that together they could account for all complex phenomena, each on its own terms, without interaction between them: in Hartley's book *Observations on Man* ... (1750) the chapters alternate, one on the physical explanation of a phenomenon and the next on the mental explanation of that phenomenon. There is one chapter on the mental association of ideas and a tandem chapter—which anticipates Pavlov—on associative interactions within the brain.

An important point about both mental association and physiology as explanations of complex behavior is their common *structural* nature. Both systems have elements; the research pertinent to both systems has to do with the rules for the combination of these elements and the nature of the compound formed from the elements. In both systems the repeated pairing or grouping of stimuli attaches elements together in some way to build compounds. The general term for such systems is *structuralism.*

The next section is concerned with an alternative to and an attack on the structural method of analyzing behavior.

Molarism

So far, what we have said about psychology can be understood in terms of Figure 1.3, Descartes' system for understanding man. We have looked at the work of both the associationist Ebbinghaus and the physiologist Pavlov. Since both of these experimentalists relied on the idea that elements become combined into complex entities, both are described as structuralists.

Structuralism is surely not the only doctrine by which man may be understood. For example, consider again how we might come to understand such a complex entity as an automobile.

The engineer who built the automobile knows the relation between the temperature in the combustion chamber and the power output, and he knows the diameter of each opening in the carburetor. The mechanic who regularly repairs the automobile knows that it needs a little extra oil in certain areas where leaks occur, that the wheels are currently out of line, and that the exhaust system has another thousand miles to go. The driver knows that the car is hard to start, that the steering is rather loose, that the back seat is cramped, and that the windshield washers and the clock do not work. If we offered $1000 to the person who knows the car best, who would be entitled to the prize?—the engineer, the mechanic, or the driver? They all "know" the car quite well, and no one area of knowledge is really more "basic" than the others. The engineer may argue that his knowledge is the most basic because without him the car wouldn't exist. But the driver might claim that since the ultimate purpose of a car is to be driven, to know how to drive an automobile well is to know an automobile in its most basic sense. There is much room for heated—and unproductive—argument here. One must finally accept the fact that the ways in which the engineer, the mechanic, and the driver know the automobile are all valid ways of knowing automobiles, and that, in fact, there are other valid ways to know automobiles. Consider the traffic policeman, the road-builder, the city planner, the traffic engineer, the automobile salesman, and the pedestrian, to name a few.

Similarly, there are many ways in which the behavior of animals and man may be studied and known. The structural approach, whether mental or physiological, corresponds to an engineer's understanding of a car—the structuralist wishes to know the components and how they are put together. *Molarism* is another approach in psychology, one that attempts to know man as a whole. To return to our analogy, we might say that a driver has a molar view of a car's steering, acceleration, and braking characteristics. When a psychologist says he is a molarist, we can understand him to mean that he studies large units of behavior rather than looking for discrete "building blocks." The molarist also differs from the structuralist in the way in which he goes about his study and especially in the kind of data he collects and the kind of observations he makes.

The molarist observes a large psychological unit (like "personality") directly, without trying to break it into its elements, and, just as there are structuralists on both the mental and physical sides of Descartes' dualism (for example, Ebbinghaus versus Pavlov), there are also molarists on both sides. A group of molarists who addressed themselves to mental phenomena were the Gestalt psychologists.

Gestalt Psychology

In Germany in the early twentieth century, the predominant approach in psychology was both mental and structural. The research was similar to that which had been done previously by Ebbinghaus, Weber, and Fechner, and mainly consisted in trying to discover laws pertaining to the association of mental elements such as sensations and ideas.

Gestalt psychology arose in reaction to the structural aspect of German psychology. The emphasis of the Gestalt psychologists was on the study of whole entities rather than parts.

Let us consider a specific example of a phenomenon to which the Gestalt psychologists felt their argument was relevant: melody. The elements of a melody are tones. But, according to the Gestaltists, the essence of a melody is its organization. After all, a melody may be played in different keys (with different sets of tones). It may be sung by various singers, played on various instruments, and rendered in various styles. Yet it remains the same melody. If we try to break a melody down into discrete tones, we lose the very quality by which we can identify it—the way in which it organizes tones. It is fruitless, according to Gestalt psychologists, to study a complex process like a melody by trying to list its elements. We must instead listen to the melody as a whole and concentrate on its organization.

Let us consider another example offered by the Gestaltists. When we recognize a friend, we recognize him all at once. We don't stop to compare his eyes with our memory of his eyes, his nose with our memory of his nose, his mouth with our memory of his mouth, and so forth. According to the Gestalt point of view, we recognize our friend by comparing the whole organization of elements before us with an equivalent organization in our memory; this recognition of our friend's identity is primary and basic and does not depend on the analysis of what we see into particular elements. If we do analyze our recognition into elements, said the Gestaltists, we do it after it occurs, not before.

The Gestalt psychologists realized that subjective judgments of qualities depend on relationships and patterns of organization. (For instance, the headlights of an oncoming car seem very bright at night when the surroundings are dim, but they seem less bright in the daytime when the surroundings are bright. The important determinant of the brightness of the headlights as we experience it is not the constant intensity of the headlights themselves, as structuralism might lead us to believe, but rather the relationship of that intensity to the intensity of the surrounding light. In other words, the total organi-

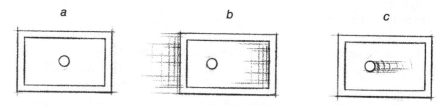

Figure 1.15 *Duncker's experiment with "induced movement." (a) Spot of light within a frame in a dark room. (b) Experimenter moves frame slowly to the right, but (c) subject reports seeing spot move slowly to the left.*

zation is what we experience.) Consider this experiment by the Gestalt psychologist Karl Duncker (1903–1940). In a dark room, the subject was shown only a spot of light located within a square frame. The frame was then moved while the spot was kept still. But the subject always thought that the spot moved within an immobile frame (Figure 1.15). Duncker called the apparent movement of the spot "induced movement." The Gestalt psychologists saw this experiment as proof that movement is seen subjectively in the relationships of an object (the spot) with its environment (the frame) and not in terms of isolated sensations.

The Gestaltists also objected to certain aspects of the dualism of the psychology of their time. They believed that there were not two separate sets of laws, one for the physical brain and another for the mind, but that one set of laws, molar in character, applied to both.

The Gestalt psychologists were mentalists, to be sure, but they broke with tradition on an important point. Although they were studying the mind and although they maintained that the mind could influence behavior (as indicated by arrow Y, Figure 1.3), they also maintained that there were no uniquely mental processes. Recall the structuralist view: The mind receives isolated sensations, then (on the right side of the dotted line in Figure 1.3), these sensations are combined by the process of association—a mental phenomenon—that takes place in the mind but not necessarily in the brain. The Gestaltists denied the existence of such unique mental processes. According to them, consciousness is isomorphic to (has the same form as) processes in the brain. But if we have no separate conscious processes, if everything we think of or are aware of has a physical counterpart in our brains, how can we explain those instances where our consciousness does not reflect the real world? For instance, how can we explain the misperception of movement in Duncker's experiment (as illustrated in Figure 1.15)? Previous mental psychologists would have said

Background

that the misperception occurs in the mind, but the Gestalt psychologists explicitly denied that anything could occur in the mind without a counterpart in the brain. If we see the spot of Duncker's experiment as moving, its representation in our brains must be a moving representation, and the representation of the frame must be standing still. When the perception of things differs from reality, the distortion occurs, not only in our minds, but in internal physical processes as well. The Gestalt psychologists went on to postulate certain physical processes in the brain that they believed might explain some of the phenomena they had discovered.

In the early twentieth century physicists had begun to study electromagnetic fields. The Gestalt psychologist Wolfgang Köhler (1887–1967) thought that many of the processes of electromagnetic fields had parallels in human perception of form and motion.

Physical Molarism

The influence of the Gestalt psychologists was not limited to their attack on the structural doctrine of the mental psychologists. The Gestaltists' idea that the best way to study any process is to look at the organization of that process as a whole was extended to the behavior of the body as well as that of the mind, as other psychologists, studying behavior in terms of discrete movements, began to question whether they could ever explain very complex behavior.

Let us consider how reflexologists might try to explain the path taken by Mr. X, who walks to work every morning. From the time he kisses his wife goodbye to the time he greets his co-workers, X's behavior can be described as a series of movements—of steps, left turns, right turns, stops, and starts—that might well be interpreted as a series of reflexes learned by constant repetition.

Yet suppose one morning there is construction on the street X usually takes, and that he must detour through a completely strange back alley. If he is a reasonably clever man, his detour will be successful and he will end up once more on the familiar street with the construction behind him. How could X have possibly made this detour if his behavior was running off mechanically as a series of reflexes, each triggered by a familiar stimulus? Some psychologists reasoned that such behavior could not be satisfactorily explained in terms of the kind of simple reflexes that the physiologists Sechenov and Pavlov studied. They claimed that X has, in fact, never acquired such reflexes, but rather that he has learned a *strategy*, an overall plan for getting to work, a sort of complex set of instructions to himself that takes into account, before they happen, the various possible environmental obstacles. What exactly the learning of such complex contingencies consists of remains a matter of dispute.

Some psychologists would say that the unifying theme of X's behavior is his purpose—getting to work—and that we must therefore study behavior in terms of purposes. They would contend that meaningful laws of behavior will never be expressed in terms of discrete reflexive actions—but always in terms of aims and goals. X's ordinary path and his detoured path have one thing in common—their destination. Change his destination and you will change his behavior in a fundamental sense; keep his destination the same and all paths to the destination can be studied as a single kind of behavior.

Still other psychologists see X's detour as evidence that explanations of behavior in purely physical terms will never succeed—that we must study man in terms of his mental life. What X acquires when walking to work is a cognitive or mental map of the path to work, and his detour is made with reference to the map that he has learned and carries around in his mind. One need not talk about his purpose in walking to work, these psychologists argue, for he would have acquired this mental map even while strolling aimlessly around the neighborhood.

The Gestalt psychologists themselves would have claimed that X's successful detour was a product of *insight*. One characteristic of conditioned reflex behavior is that it is gradually acquired by repeated pairings. Yet, according to the Gestaltists, the man's solution to the problem of the detour on his way to work was sudden and immediate. Insight is not something that is gradually learned by repeated pairings, but comes about by looking at a situation in a novel way, so as to grasp the structural and functional relationships of the problem.

Köhler, the Gestalt psychologist whose field theory of the brain we previously mentioned, was detained during World War I on Tenerife, an island that possessed a colony of apes for scientific study. Köhler performed a series of experiments with these apes that mainly consisted of setting problems for them and observing their solutions. Köhler almost invariably found that when they were given complicated problems the apes would persist in an incorrect solution or merely do nothing until they suddenly would perform the correct act without hesitation. Köhler ascribed this sudden change in the apes' behavior to insight—the seeing of a relationship between the elements of the problem. For instance, when a banana was hung out of reach of the chimpanzees in a room containing only an open box placed on the floor,

All six apes vainly endeavoured to reach their objective by leaping up from the ground. Sultan [one of the apes] soon relinquished this attempt, paced restlessly up and down, suddenly stood still in front of the box, seized it, tipped it hastily straight toward the objective, but began to climb upon it at a horizontal distance of half a meter, and springing upwards with all his force, tore down the banana. About five minutes had elapsed since the fastening of the fruit; from the momentary pause before the box to the first bite into the banana, only a few seconds elapsed, a perfectly continuous action after the first hesitation. Up to that instant, none of the animals had taken any notice of the box; they were all far too intent on the objective; none of the other five took any part in carrying the box; Sultan performed the feat single-handed in a few seconds. [Köhler, 1925, p. 40]

In Figure 1.16, we observe an ape faced with a somewhat more difficult problem.

Drawing by W. Steig. © 1968. The New Yorker Magazine, Inc.

Figure 1.16

The Gestaltists' objections to the analysis of behavior into discrete elements convinced most contemporary psychologists that although it was useful and important to study reflexes in the way that Sechenov and Pavlov had studied them, reflexes could not be regarded as the simple building blocks of all behavior (the behavior of Köhler's apes for example). Something more than the conditioned reflex was needed to account for truly complex behavior. It thus seemed necessary to modify radically the concept of the reflex or even to abandon it altogether as a basic mechanism of complex behavior.

The "Gestalt revolution" in psychology was only partially successful. Its negative purpose succeeded, for it demonstrated the inadequacy of a structural account of all behavior. However, its positive purpose failed, for it did not produce a completely molar account of behavior. Most psychologists see the value of both structural and molar analysis and are convinced that behavior can be understood on many different levels.

Functionalism

We have seen how Gestaltism, with its emphasis on the study of molar behavior, brought into question the premises of both physiological and mental structuralism. We now come to an even more influential doctrine, that of *functionalism*, which has flourished in the United States. The functional and molar revolutions in psychology overlapped considerably. Which came first is difficult to determine. Both made headway slowly, by fits and starts; the ultimate origins of both may be traced to historical arguments within philosophy and the physical sciences.

Functionalism stems from the theory of evolution put forward by the biologist Charles Darwin (1809–1882) a little over one hundred years ago. Darwin's theory, in capsule form, is that those organisms that are best able to survive in their environment tend to increase in number, and those that are least able to survive in the environment tend to decrease in number. Because organisms within a species naturally vary in physical qualities and behavior patterns, those organisms that are better able to survive than others will survive and reproduce—and their distinct adaptive qualities will tend to become preponderant; by this process the whole species will gradually change so as to become better fitted to cope with its environment.

Let us consider one common illustration of the action of evolution: the origin of the extreme length of the giraffe's neck. To begin with, (1) all giraffes, no matter how long their necks, depend on foliage for food, and (2) foliage is sometimes in short supply. In the course of natural variation, some early giraffes were born with longer-than-average necks—just as some humans are born very tall, even, occasionally, when they have parents of average height. Those giraffes with long necks were better able to eat leaves on the high trees in their environment and lived longer and produced more offspring. Those with short necks were unable to reach the leaves on the upper parts of the trees and tended to die earlier and to produce fewer offspring. Thus, as the generations went on, there were more and more offspring of long-necked giraffes, who tended on the average to be long-necked—just as the children of tall human parents tend on the average to be tall.

Darwin saw natural selection as a process similar to the artificial selection used by animal breeders; for instance, a race of plump chickens or turkeys can be created by breeding plump fowl and not breeding lean or stringy birds. Figure 1.17 shows how the process of natural selection works in the case of giraffes. Note that this process is contrary to the notion that (1) giraffes were constantly stretching their necks to reach the high leaves on trees, (2) this stretching made their necks longer, (3) they passed this trait on to their young.

A profound implication of the theory of evolution is that all living creatures share a common biological inheritance. After Darwin, species were no longer regarded as immutable; there was no longer a sharp boundary separating "higher animals" from "lower animals"—or even men from animals. In regard to human life, evolution meant that the traits humans possess must have evolved from traits their ancestors once possessed.

One of the first effects of this principle of *biological continuity* on psychology was the acceptance of the notion that because humans have minds and consciousness, then other animals also have minds and consciousness, although of a more rudimentary kind. This led psychologists who were studying the mentality of humans to become interested also in the mentality of animals. The evidence for mentality in animals had long rested on anecdotes about the clever actions of pets and farm animals. However, a group of American psychologists (the functionalists) began to investigate animal behavior in laboratories, especially at the University of Chicago. One of the tools they devised to study the mental processes of animals was the maze, and some of the first animals to be studied in mazes were rats.

In 1901, in a paper entitled "Experimental Study of the Mental Processes of the Rat," Willard Stanton Small (1870–1943) introduced the rat in the maze to psychology. Small's maze was modeled on the Hampton Court Maze, a garden maze created for the amusement of the English nobility. (These mazes are shown in Figure 1.18 and 1.19.) The object of Small's maze experiments was to determine the conscious state of an animal by observing its behavior. In the following description of a rat's behavior, Small's observations of behavior and his

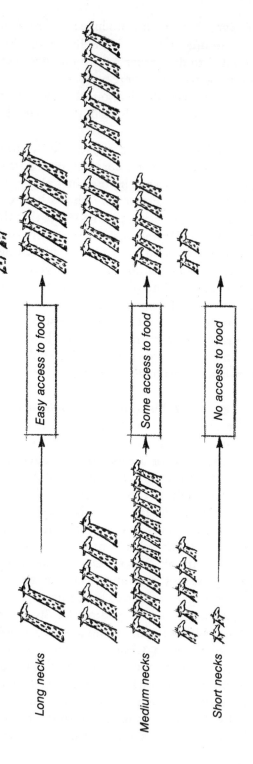

Figure 1.17 These graphs show how natural selection has altered the structure of the giraffe's neck. Leaves —the giraffe's food —have been in relatively short supply during the long history between the earlier and the later populations shown; thus the long-necked giraffes, which were able to reach higher leaves, had a better chance of surviving and reproducing than the short-necked giraffes. Since the offspring of long-necked giraffes had, on the average, longer necks than the offspring of the general population, there is a gradual increase in the proportion of long-necked giraffes. Note also the disappearance of the short-necked giraffe.

Long necks

Medium necks

Short necks

Easy access to food

Some access to food

No access to food

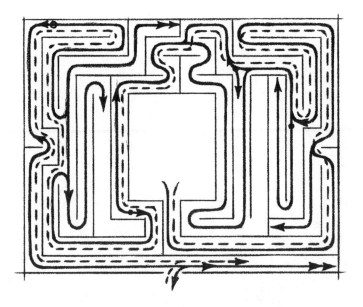

Figure 1.18 *Floorplan of Small's maze. Small studied the "mental processes" of rats with this maze, which he based on the maze in the gardens at Hampton Court Palace in England.*

conclusions about the rat's conscious states are italicized. It might be instructive for the reader to try to list those italicized words that seem to him to be direct observations of behavior—as opposed to those that seem to express conclusions drawn by Small about the conscious state of the rat.

Analyses of Results

In appreciating the results of this series of experiments, . . . the [following] . . . facts come into view. . . . *the initial indefiniteness of movement* and the *fortuitousness of success;* the just *observable profit from the first experiences;* the gradually increasing *certainty of knowledge* indicated by *increase of speed and definiteness,* and the *recognition of critical points* indicated by *hesitation* and *indecision;* the lack of *imitation* and the improbability of *following by scent;* the outbreak of the instincts of *play* and *curiosity* after the edge of *appetite* is dulled. In addition are to be noted the further observations upon the contrast between the *slow and cautious entrance* into, and the *rapid exit* from the blind alleys, after the first few trials; the appearance of *disgust* on reaching the end of a blind alley; the clear indication of centrally excited *sensation* (images) of some kind; *memory* (as I have used the term); *the persistence of certain errors;* and the almost *automatic character of the movements* in the later experiments.

View from above

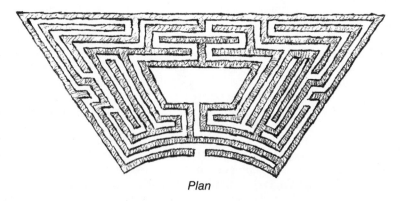

Plan

Figure 1.19 *The Hampton Court maze. [Crown copyright.]*

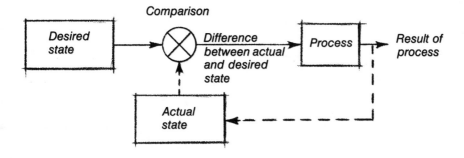

Figure 1.20 *A diagram of a simple feedback system.*

The historical importance for psychology of the notion of biological continuity is that it stimulated much research in comparative psychology—the study of the behavior of one species as compared to another species. At first the purpose of this research was to affirm or deny Darwin's theories by comparing the mental qualities of one species with those of another—to answer the question, for instance: Which animal has the higher developed mentality, the dog or the horse?—and to thereby rank the various species in terms of the properties of their minds. Contemporary comparative research ignores the relative "mental development" of species and concentrates more on the comparison of various complex behavior patterns.

The general principle that the process of natural selection embodies is critically important in modern psychology, as well as in other sciences; it is the principle of *feedback*. In a feedback system, a process is regulated through testing the actual state of the process against a selected potential state.

In Figure 1.20 the dotted lines represent a feedback loop whereby information about the actual state of an ongoing process is compared with information about a potential state of the process. In the case of the natural selection of long-necked giraffes, a potential state was signaled by the height of the leaves on the trees. Time after time, this potential state was compared with the actual state of the length of the giraffes' necks. The long-term result of this process was attainment of a new actual state: a population of long-necked giraffes.

Feedback is a very common process in everyday experience. Consider a household thermostat. In this case, a desired state is represented by the setting on the thermostat, say 72°. The actual state is the current temperature of the house, say 65°. The ongoing comparison of these two states controls a process—the burning of coal, gas, or oil to

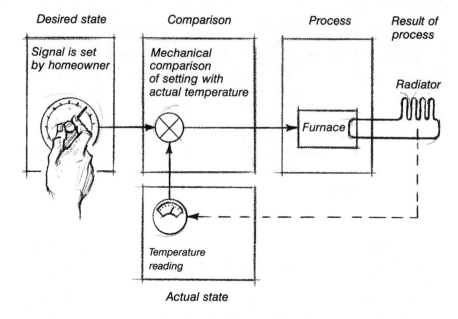

Desired state	Comparison	Process	Result of process

Signal is set by homeowner

Mechanical comparison of setting with actual temperature

Furnace

Radiator

Temperature reading

Actual state

Figure 1.21 *A diagram showing the operation of a household thermostat.*

warm the house. As soon as the difference disappears—that is, as soon as the house becomes as warm as the setting on the thermostat indicates it should be—the heater or furnace is turned off. Figure 1.21 shows such a thermostat mechanism.

Such self-adjusting systems embody simple *negative* feedback (a term borrowed from engineering usage). The feedback is called negative simply because the ongoing comparison tends to decrease the difference between the actual state of the system and the selected potential state of the system. Both the system of natural selection and the thermostat can eventually reach *equilibrium* when the actual and signaled states are identical, and the process terminates. However, it is possible to have other kinds of feedback. *Positive* feedback tends to amplify the difference between the actual state and the selected potential state, producing a runaway process. Suppose, for instance, that the thermostat we have been considering got connected by mistake to the air conditioner instead of the furnace. Then, the difference in temperature between the desired 72° and the actual 65° would activate the air conditioner, causing the actual temperature to drop further, increasing the difference. The thermostat feeds more power to the air conditioner, which in turn decreases the temperature still further, and so forth. Positive feedback in everyday situations often causes havoc. A young man, for instance, thinks that a young woman is cool to him because he is not forward enough, whereas the reverse is actually true. He increases his forwardness and finds her cooler. He interprets this continued coolness as a sign that he is still not forward enough, increasing his advances in proportion to the degree of coolness his very advances are generating. Such miscalculations between persons can result in something unpleasant, like a slap on the face. In the case of an international arms race, they could lead to disaster.

The feedback principle, showing how a process could be controlled by a desired end or function, formed the basis for functional psychology. The functionalists, inspired by Darwin's theory, believed that mental processes had evolved to serve various useful functions for organisms struggling to cope with their complex environments. According to the philosopher and psychologist William James:

> Mental facts cannot be properly studied apart from the physical environment of which they take cognizance. The great fault of the older rational psychology was to set up the soul as an absolute spiritual being with certain faculties of its own by which the several activities of remembering, imagining, reasoning, willing, etc., were explained, almost without reference to the peculiarities of the world with which these activities deal. But the richer insight of modern days perceives that our inner faculties are adapted in advance to the features of the world in which we dwell, adapted, I mean, so as to secure our safety and prosperity in its midst. Not only are our capacities for forming new habits, for remembering sequences, and for abstracting general properties from things and associating their usual consequences with them, exactly the faculties needed for steering us in this world of mixed variety and uniformity, but our emotions and instincts are adapted to very special features of that world. In the main, if a phenomenon is important for our welfare, it interests and excites us the first time we come into its presence. Dangerous things fill us with involuntary fear; poisonous things with distaste; indispensable things with appetite. Mind and world in short have been evolved together, and in consequence are something of a mutual fit. [James, 1893, p. 4]

Notice that the adaptation between our minds and environments is said to take place *in advance*. That is, our emotions and desires, which help us survive, are inborn, so that we are interested in an object that is important for our welfare "the first time we come into its presence." Furthermore, note that the locus of our sense that the object is important is said to be in the mind—considered a separate "organ" whose properties are as subject to the action of evolution as the length of the giraffe's neck, but which, like Descartes' concept, is still not to be found in the physical world (see Figure 1.3).

From the notion that the mind (1) is subject to evolutionary changes and (2) develops in response to the environment, it follows that complex behavior, which the mind controls, also must change with the generations of species, so that individuals cope better with their environments. This notion gave rise to research such as Small's, in which the complex behavior patterns of various organisms were studied with a view towards determining their mental qualities. To return briefly to the principle of biological continuity, recall that this principle implies that consciousness is not a purely human trait—that if it is possessed by humans, it must be possessed by other animals, at least to some degree. By 1912, some American psychologists had discovered the other side of the same coin. They observed that since both biologists and psychologists were studying animal behavior fruitfully without recourse to the notion of consciousness, then perhaps much of human behavior could also be explained without having to analyze or even refer to consciousness. The Russian reflexologists had previously abandoned the idea altogether as an explanatory concept. The important point for our discussion is not whether there really is such a thing as consciousness, but that when attention was no longer focused on consciousness, introspection lost its position as the prime method of psychological investigation.

John Broadus Watson (1878–1958) studied at the University of Chicago when the functionalist school of psychology flourished there. He was trained to perform animal experiments similar to Small's experiments with rats in a maze. Watson soon became convinced that he could separate his observations into (1) those that could be verified by other psychologists and (2) those that could not be so verified. In the former category, he placed observations of the overt behavior of animals—where and how they moved. Watson knew that such observations yielded general agreement. In the second category, he placed observations of the conscious states of animals. He knew that these observations consistently failed to yield much agreement. (In other words, Watson found it far more likely that three observers would agree on whether a rat turned left or right in a maze than on whether the rat was happy or sad while it was turning.)

Whereas some functionalists faulted each other's introspective training, Watson held that introspection itself was the source of the prevalent disagreement about animals' mental states. Watson declared that introspection should be banished from psychology and that psychological observations should be restricted, like other scientific observations, to overt behavior.

Because Watson focused on observable behavior, he called himself a "behaviorist" and broke away from the other functionalists at

Chicago. As Watson's position gained adherents, behaviorism emerged as a successor to functionalism. Both approaches share a common attitude toward biological continuity, and both stress the adaptive function of behavior, but whereas functionalism was devoted to examining the *mental life* of men and animals, behaviorism is devoted to examining their *overt activities*. As time has gone by, behaviorism has become predominant in American psychology.

Bibliography

The best way to get an idea of the history of psychology is to read the original sources. A good place to start is R. J. Herrnstein and E. G. Boring's *A Source Book in the History of Psychology* (Cambridge, Massachusetts: Harvard University Press, 1965). The material that introduces each section is particularly illuminating. Most of the quotations in the present volume come from selections in Herrnstein and Boring. From the source book one can go to more comprehensive original sources.

There are two classic history books of experimental psychology by E. G. Boring: *A History of Experimental Psychology* (New York: Appleton-Century-Crofts, 1950) and *Sensation and Perception in the History of Experimental Psychology* (New York: Appleton-Century-Crofts, 1942). The attitude toward the history of psychology in the present volume is basically that of Boring's two history books; the approach in these books is to follow the history of psychology from Descartes through the British associationists to modern psychology. For an approach centered around studies of behavior *per se*, see J. R. Kantor's *The Scientific Evolution of Psychology* (2 vols., Chicago: The Principia Press, 1963–1969). For a history of studies on the reflex, see F. Fearing's *Reflex Action* (New York: Hafner Publishing Company, 1930).

The material quoted in this chapter is from the following sources:

Descartes, René, *De Homine*. Leiden: 1662. Reprinted in Herrnstein and Boring, p. 269.

Fechner, G. T., *Elemente de Psychophysik*. Leipzig, 1860. Reprinted in Herrnstein and Boring, p. 75.

Hartley, David, *Observations on Man, His Frame, His Duty, and His Expectations*. London and Bath, 1749. Reprinted in Fearing, p. 86.

James, W. *Psychology*. New York: Henry Holt, 1893.

Köhler, W. *The Mentality of Apes*. Translated by E. Winter. New York: Harcourt, Brace and Company, 1925.

La Mettrie, J. O. de, *L'homme Machine*. Leiden, 1748. Reprinted in Herrnstein and Boring, p. 278.

Locke, John, *An Essay Concerning Human Understanding: in Four Books*. London, 1690. Reprinted in Herrnstein and Boring, p. 584.

Mill, J. S., *A System of Logic, Ratiocinative and Inductive, Being a Connected View of the Principles of Evidence, and the Methods of Scientific Investigation*. London, 1843. Reprinted in Herrnstein and Boring, p. 379.

Pavlov, I. P., *Pavlov: Selected Works*. Translated by S. Belsky. Moscow: Foreign Languages Publishing House, 1955.

Prochaska, George, *De Functionibus Systematis Nervosi*. Prague, 1784. Reprinted in Herrnstein and Boring, p. 294.

Sechenov, I. M., *Refleksy Golovnogo Mozga*. St. Petersberg, 1863. Reprinted in Herrnstein and Boring, p. 321.

Small, W. S., Experimental study of the mental processes of the rat. *American Journal of Psychology*, 1901, **12,** 218–220. Reprinted in Herrnstein and Boring, pp. 552–553.

2

Basic Procedures
and Techniques

The emergence of behaviorism in the early twentieth century brought fresh approaches to the question: How do organisms learn? There began a series of attempts to provide a systematic and thorough answer based on behaviorist principles. American behaviorists Edwin R. Guthrie (1886–1959), Clark L. Hull (1884–1952), Edward C. Tolman (1886–1959), and B. F. Skinner (b. 1904), among others, published influential works in which they tried to identify and fit together the pieces of this subtle and complex puzzle. We shall note in passing some of the experimental methods their systems have contributed to the study of behavior.

In general, contemporary behaviorists tend to set aside vast theoretical questions and to ask instead how a particular organism acquires a particular behavior. In their work, they make free use of one or another of the many methods developed by various theorists and innovators. In other words, psychologists seem to have abandoned—at least temporarily—the effort to systematize and unify their field of study; they favor piecemeal attacks on specific areas of behavior, for which they use whatever tools are convenient and effective.

The aim of this chapter is to give the reader an appreciation of the basic procedures and techniques that are the essential features of modern behaviorism. We shall first discuss *classical conditioning,* then we shall take up *instrumental conditioning.** We shall compare these two commonly followed procedures. Finally, we shall discuss techniques for measuring behavior in the laboratory.

CLASSICAL CONDITIONING

Pavlov's Experiments

Seven decades ago the Russian physiologist Pavlov was studying the salivation reflex in dogs when he discovered that systematic changes in the dogs' reflexes were clearly linked to his own pattern of behavior in the laboratory. Pavlov began to study this intriguing phenomenon and subsequently produced the first empirical reports on the conditioned reflex.

Pavlov had initially set out to investigate the physiology of the secretion of various fluids within the mouth and stomach. By ingenious surgical techniques he was able to implant tubes leading from various points along the dogs' digestive tracts out through the skin. Part of the secretion of fluids in the digestive tracts passed into the tubes and was collected and its amount was measured. In effect, the questions that Pavlov asked were, "If I give the dog some food to eat, how soon will the food, acting as a stimulus, cause the mouth and the stomach to secrete their various digestive fluids?" "What is the mechanism that links the insertion of food in the mouth and the secretion of saliva?" "What is the function relating the amount of food and the amount of saliva secreted?" "As the food reaches the stomach, how long does the stomach take to secrete the acids necessary to digest the food?" Such physiological questions seemed unrelated to psychology.

However, in the course of his research Pavlov began to be plagued by an annoying phenomenon: as dogs became familiar with the experimental situation, they would often begin to salivate and secrete

---

*Other names for classical conditioning include *Pavlovian conditioning,* and *respondent conditioning.* Instrumental conditioning is also known as *instrumental learning* and *operant conditioning.* Some psychologists distinguish between instrumental conditioning, instrumental learning, and operant conditioning on the basis of the kind of response (locomotor versus nonlocomotor) or the procedure (trial-by-trial versus continuous observation of behavior). There is more similarity than difference among these techniques, however, and we will treat them alike here under the rubric of *instrumental conditioning.*

stomach acids as soon as Pavlov walked into the room. Pavlov called these premature secretions "psychic" secretions because he believed at first that they resulted from the dogs' psychic (mental) activity. Later, he realized that these "annoyances" bore certain similarities to the physiological reflexes he had been measuring, and he decided to study them.

One of the first of Pavlov's experiments on psychic secretions is particularly instructive. A dog's secretion of stomach acids, following the introduction of food into its mouth, increases and then decreases over the course of four hours, as shown in curve (a) of Figure 2.1. This curve represents (1) whatever was secreted as a direct result of the stimulation of food in the stomach *plus* (2) whatever was secreted before food reached the stomach (the "psychic secretions"). Pavlov wished to measure these two components of the curve separately. In order to plot the curve of direct secretions only, Pavlov introduced food not through the dog's mouth, but directly into its stomach through a tube, called a fistula, which bypassed the normal routes from the mouth to the stomach. When food was introduced through the fistula into the stomach, the gastric secretion was much less than when food was eaten in a normal way. Curve (b) in Figure 2.1 shows the amount of secretion under this special condition. This, then, represented one component of the total secretion—the secretion that followed direct stimulation of the stomach by food. The second component of curve (a) was determined by a method called *sham-feeding*. The dog ate food in the normal way, chewing and swallowing it, but the food was not allowed to pass into its stomach; instead, the food was removed through another fistula before reaching the stomach. Despite the fact that no food reached the stomach, there was a secretion of stomach acids as shown by curve (c). Curve (d), which is the sum of curves (b) and (c), is similar to curve (a). Thus, the experiment confirmed Pavlov's suspicion that total stomach secretion derived about equally from direct stimulation and "psychic" stimulation.

Now let us turn to another of Pavlov's experiments. Pavlov knew that his dogs began to salivate when they merely saw food, just as a hungry man begins to salivate when he enters a restaurant or passes a bakery. Pavlov wondered whether such premature salivation was caused only by the sight of food in particular or whether *any* stimulus, such as the sounding of a tone, would cause this premature salivation if followed often enough by actual eating. To answer this question, Pavlov constructed the apparatus shown in Figure 2.2. A hungry dog was isolated from as many extraneous stimuli as possible. Then Pavlov struck a tuning fork, which produced a tone, and after half of a second,

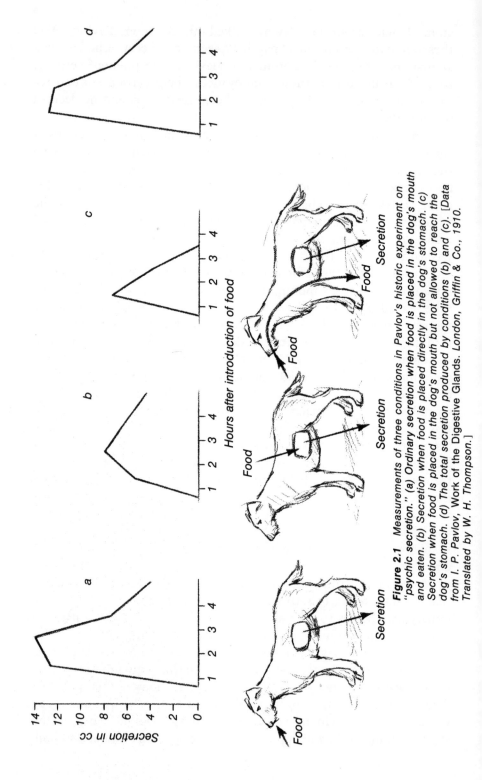

Figure 2.1 Measurements of three conditions in Pavlov's historic experiment on "psychic secretion." (a) Ordinary secretion when food is placed in the dog's mouth and eaten. (b) Secretion when food is placed directly in the dog's stomach. (c) Secretion when food is placed in the dog's mouth but not allowed to reach the dog's stomach. (d) The total secretion produced by conditions (b) and (c). [Data from I. P. Pavlov, Work of the Digestive Glands. London, Griffin & Co., 1910. Translated by W. H. Thompson.]

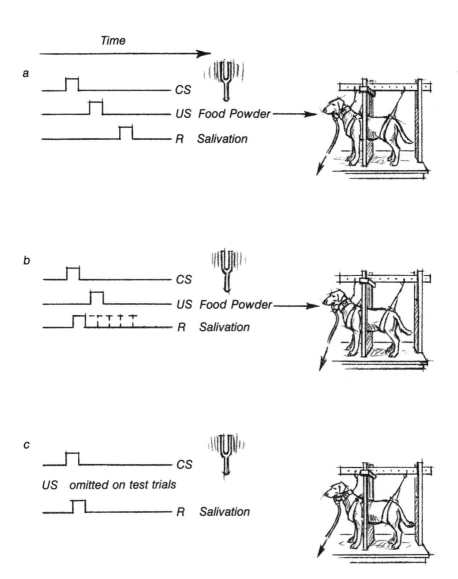

Figure 2.2 *Classical conditioning. (a) Procedure for the establishment of conditioning. (b) One test for conditioning: Does the response come to precede the US? (c) Another test for conditioning: Does the response occur in the absence of the US?*

fed the dog. He repeated these pairings of tone and food several times, measuring salivation all the while through a tube leading from the dog's cheek to a small container. At first, the dog salivated only after the food was inserted into its mouth. But it gradually salivated earlier and earlier in the procedure, until salivation finally appeared somewhat *before* the dog was fed, but after the tone. Pavlov found that such "psychic" secretions could be established in this manner for many kinds of stimuli.

It is important to recognize the difference between Pavlov's earlier experiment with sham-feeding and his later one with the presentation of a tone before feeding. In the first experiment, Pavlov observed a "psychic" secretion linked to food, a stimulus that had already been established and (for all Pavlov knew) could have been established even before the dog was born. In the second experiment, however, Pavlov observed a "psychic" secretion that followed a wholly new and arbitrarily chosen stimulus. This process—the forging of a connection between a new stimulus (like a tone) and an existing reflex (like salivation to food in the mouth)—Pavlov called *conditioning*.

Elements of Classical Conditioning

It is worth examining Pavlov's classical procedure more closely, in order to learn the traditional nomenclature for its various elements.

The first necessary element is an established reflex. A reflex consists of a stimulus and a response, when the response is reliably elicited by the stimulus. In Pavlov's experiment the response was salivation and the stimulus was the presence of food in the mouth. The stimulus part of this reflex—the presence of food in the mouth—is traditionally called the *unconditioned stimulus* or, more briefly, the US. The next requirement for classical conditioning is a neutral stimulus, anything that will not by itself cause the response before the experiment begins. This neutral stimulus is called the *conditioned stimulus* (CS). Besides tones, Pavlov used lights, pictures, and other objects as CS's. Indeed, Pavlov himself became a CS for his dogs. (This was the bothersome effect that launched Pavlov's research into conditioning.)

The US–response connection and the CS are the two basic components of any classical conditioning experiment. The schematic sketches in Figure 2.2 show how they are related in time.

The end result of the conditioning procedure is the *conditioned reflex*. The conditioned reflex in Pavlov's experiments was salivation in response to a previously neutral stimulus. Parts (b) and (c) of Figure 2.2 show two measurable effects of classical conditioning, both of which were studied by Pavlov. Part (b) shows the salivation response occurring progressively earlier until it occurs before the US; part (c) shows the occurrence of the response with the US omitted. In order for the response to occur with the US omitted, the sequence in (a) is presented repeatedly—except that, according to a prearranged schedule, the US is occasionally omitted. As the experiment progresses, the usual observation is that the response without the US becomes almost, but not quite, as large in magnitude as the response with the US. Measurement of the effect shown in (b) emphasizes the latency of the response; measurement of the effect shown in (c) emphasizes the *magnitude* of the response. (As classical conditioning proceeds, one finds that the latency of the response to the CS becomes shorter and its magnitude becomes larger.)

Pavlov saw conditioning as the establishment of a new reflex by the addition of a new stimulus to the group of stimuli that are capable of triggering a response.

Classical conditioning, Pavlov believed, shed new light on the process of association. In association, as studied by Ebbinghaus with nonsense syllables for instance, there are all the elements of classical conditioning. One syllable is presented to the subject first (the CS). Then another is presented to the subject (the US). These pairings are repeated, and, finally, the subject can say the name of the second syllable (the response) when he is presented with the first. Pavlov maintained that psychologists like Ebbinghaus who were studying association were really doing experiments in classical conditioning, but with the stimuli and responses not as well controlled as they were in Pavlov's laboratory.*

Although Pavlov's original experiments used the secretion of saliva to food in a dog's mouth as the basic reflex, to which a neutral CS was attached, the classical conditioning procedure has since been carried out with many other kinds of reflexes. Mild electric shock has often been used as a US because it produces a host of measurable responses. For example, after electric shock, the rate of breathing increases, the heart rate increases, and the part of the body being shocked is withdrawn. In one experiment performed by H. S. Liddell at Cornell University, sheep were shocked briefly on the foreleg, causing them to breathe faster and deeper and also to raise the leg (even though the wires delivering the shock were attached to it). The experimenters decided to set a metronome ticking a few seconds before the shock was

---

*Currently, even psychologists most involved in the study of mental events recognize that some processes in the brain must correspond to these events. But nowadays the mental processes studied are often so complex that it proves difficult to trace their relationship to simple classical conditioning procedures. Thus, cognitive psychology and physiological psychology are two separate disciplines. Psychologists in both disciplines hope that one day they may be unified with a common set of principles.

given. After this was done four or five times, a sheep would lift its leg and begin breathing faster as soon as the metronome started ticking. The shock was the US; the metronome ticking was the CS; the leg-raising and faster breathing were responses.

Extinction

So far we have been talking about conditioning as if it were a one-way process. We have noted, for example, that by a procedure such as that shown in Figure 2.2 we can condition a dog's salivation response to a tone struck on a tuning fork. The dog salivates when it hears a tone. Is that dog fated, then, for the rest of its life, to salivate when it hears the tone? No, it is not. Any response can be eliminated if the CS occurs a sufficient number of times without the US following. We recall that the CS was occasionally presented alone in the test trials of part (c) of Figure 2.2. However, it was isolated like an island amid a sea of conditioning trials, like those in part (a) of Figure 2.2. Suppose we arranged large blocks of trials in which the CS is always presented alone. What would happen to the response? We would find that the response would begin to decrease in magnitude so that eventually it would cease to appear. This process is called *extinction* of the re-sponse. A typical extinction curve is shown in Figure 2.3.*

The usual procedure for extinguishing a response is quite straightforward. The US is simply omitted from the normal conditioning procedure.

In order to clarify the nature of the process of extinction, let us pay an imaginary visit to Pavlov's laboratory. Suppose we bring a dog with us, one that has never been exposed to any laboratory conditioning procedure; if we prevail upon Pavlov to sound his tuning fork, our dog will not salivate. Suppose another dog, one of Pavlov's, was previously conditioned so that it salivated to a tuning-fork tone but that its response was subsequently extinguished. When Pavlov sounds his tuning fork, his dog salivates as little as ours. It seems as though the conditioning of Pavlov's dog has been "wiped away" by the process of extinction and that no one could ever tell the two dogs apart on the basis of their behavior.

---

*The galvanic skin response (GSR) of Figures 2.3 and 2.5 is a change in electrical resistance between one area of the skin and another. It is often measured between the front and the back of the hand (as shown in Figure 1.1). This change in resistance may be caused by sweating of the palm, but there is dispute as to whether sweatiness is the only factor involved. In any case the GSR reliably follows electric shock and other painful stimuli and is frequently the measured response in classical conditioning experiments with humans.

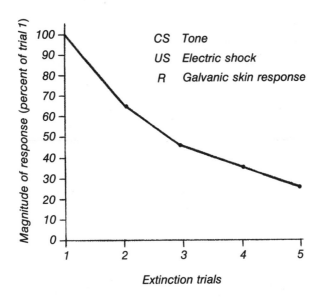

Figure 2.3 *Typical extinction curve. Each extinction trial is a presentation of the CS alone. In this case the curve shows the extinction of the galvanic skin response following 24 conditioning trials. Each point represents the average response of 20 human subjects.* [Data replotted from C. I. Hovland, "Inhibition of reinforcement and phenomena of experimental extinction." Proc. Nat. Acad. Sci. 22, 430–433, 1936.]

In fact, Pavlov found that he *could* distinguish between two such dogs if he presented the tone and then sounded a loud noise suddenly and unexpectedly. The dog with the extinguished response (Pavlov's, in our example) would salivate, and the other dog (ours) would not salivate. Pavlov reasoned that extinction did not simply "wipe away" conditioning but that it added another force equal and opposite to the force of conditioning. He called the force added by extinction an *inhibitory force.* He thought that the sudden loud noise somehow temporarily removed the inhibitory effect of extinction and allowed salivation to begin.

Pavlov had discovered that if the noise was sounded during conditioning it stopped salivation. In other words, the noise acted in the opposite direction to whichever process was going on. It could not do this if a response that had been both conditioned and extinguished was identical to an unconditioned response. Pavlov called the extinction process a form of *internal inhibition.* The action of the loud noise during extinction, which produced salivation, he called *disinhibition,*

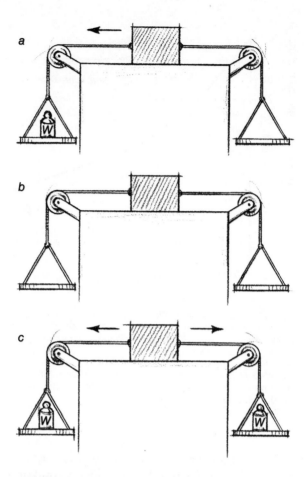

Figure 2.4 This system of weights shows how extinction might operate as either a negative or a positive process. (a) If conditioning is seen as the pull of a weight, extinction can be either (b) a negative process that simply removes the weight, or (c) a positive process that adds a new weight to the system to counterbalance the effect of conditioning.

or the release of inhibition. The action of the loud noise during conditioning, which inhibited salivation, he called *external inhibition*.

The process of internal inhibition may be compared to a system of weights and counterweights. Imagine a weight attached to a block of wood (as in Figure 2.4) and tending to pull it towards the left (assume the weight of the scales themselves is insignificant). There are two ways to stop the block from moving towards the left. One is to cut the string or otherwise remove the weight (an analogy to "wiping away" conditioning). Another way is to add another weight on the other side (an analogy to a force of inhibition). Both procedures produce a stationary block (extinction). If the weights and strings are hidden from view, how can you tell which system applies? You can distinguish between conditions (b) and (c) in Figure 2.4 by cutting one of the strings (an analogy to the disinhibitory effect of the loud noise). If this is done to the apparatus shown in (b), nothing will happen to the block. But if it is done to the apparatus in (c), the block will move suddenly in one direction (this is analogous to the reappearance of the response).

Generalization and Discrimination

There is bound to be some *generalization* in a process through which a new pattern of behavior is acquired. For instance, if a dog's behavior is modified in a laboratory so that the dog salivates when it hears a tone sounded by a tuning fork, another tone slightly higher or lower in pitch will also make it salivate. Generalization is also evidenced when a child, sometimes to the embarrassment of his parents, calls every man he meets "Daddy." Of course, the child will eventually learn to reserve the name "Daddy" for his male parent. When this occurs, we say he has learned to make a *discrimination*.

Let us consider an experiment performed in the United States in 1934 on the generalization of a classically conditioned response. The GSR (galvanic skin response) was conditioned in a group of college students; the US in the experiment was mild electric shock and the CS was a vibrating instrument applied to the skin. For some subjects the instrument was applied to the shoulder and for others it was applied to the calf. As training progressed the amount of GSR measured on test trials (when the CS was presented without the shock) was seen to increase. Then, on later test trials, the instrument was occasionally applied at places on the skin *other* than where conditioning was originally established. The farther away the instrument was applied on these later test trials, the less was the response. Figure 2.5 shows the magnitude of the response as a function of the distance from the original point of application. The kind of curve shown in Figure 2.5 is called a *generalization gradient.* *

Generalization gradients like the one in Figure 2.5 are by no means unalterable. Suppose we have a set of several similar stimuli, only one

---

*The specific spot at which the vibrating stimulus was applied was not important in determining the gradient; what was important was the distance from the original CS, wherever that CS may have been applied.

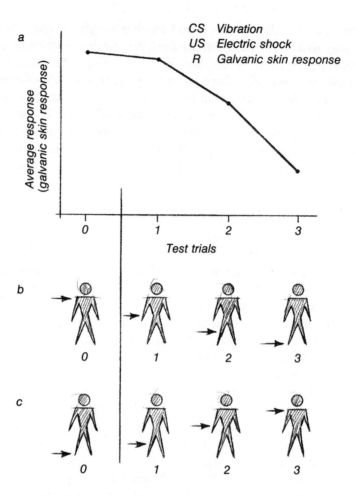

Figure 2.5 The generalization of a classically conditioned response. (a) This graph shows the decline of a galvanic skin response to vibration as the vibration is moved progressively farther from the original site of conditioning. (b) Some subjects were initially conditioned on the shoulder. (c) Some subjects were initially conditioned on the ankle. [Data from M. J. Bass and C. L. Hull, "The irradiation of a tactile conditioned reflex in man." J. of Comparative Psychology, 1934, 17, 47–65.]

of which we want to be a CS. Suppose that, even though we use only the desired stimulus as the CS in a classical conditioning experiment, we find that the subject generalizes and responds to the other stimuli too. How can we eliminate responses to these other stimuli but retain responses to the one we want to be a CS? We may try alternating

Basic Procedures and Techniques

conditioning trials that contain both the desired CS and the US with extinction trials that contain no US—only the unwanted stimuli. Our hope is that the organism will learn to discriminate the particular stimulus to which we want it to respond from the unwanted stimuli. This procedure works—but, significantly, it works only up to a point.

We know Pavlov's view that extinction is an active process of inhibition, not just a matter of "wiping away" old conditions but more like adding counterweights to a hypothetical system of weights (Figure 2.4). Keeping this in mind, consider the following experiment, performed by one of Pavlov's students, Shenger-Krestovnikova. She trained dogs to salivate by a method similar to Pavlov's except that instead of a tone she used a circle drawn on a card as the CS. She found that after the salivation response had been conditioned in the presence of a circle, the response generalized to the extent that the dogs would also salivate when they saw an ellipse, like those in Figure 2.6. In order to condition discrimination between (a) and (b), (a) was presented with the US and (b) was presented without the US. Following this procedure, the dogs would salivate in response to (a) but not in response to (b). Then the same procedure was repeated with (a) and (c), then (a) and (d)—(d) being an ellipse very much like the circle. According to Pavlov, this is what happened when (a) and (d) were discriminated:

> In this case, although a considerable degree of discrimination did develop, it was far from being complete. After three weeks of work upon this differentiation not only did the discrimination fail to improve, but it became considerably worse, and finally disappeared altogether. At the same time the whole behaviour of the animal underwent an abrupt change. The hitherto quiet dog began to squeal in its stand, kept wriggling about, tore off with its teeth the apparatus for mechanical stimulation of the skin, and bit through the tubes connecting the animal's room with the observer, a behaviour which never happened before. On being taken into the experimental room the dog now barked violently, which was also contrary to its usual custom; in short it presented all the symptoms of acute neurosis. On testing the cruder differentiations they were also found to be destroyed. . . . [Pavlov, 1927, p. 291]

One cannot help but draw a parallel to the behavior of humans when they are required to perform for long periods of time at the limit of their discriminative capacities. Humans can make just so many discriminations, until, like Pavlov's dogs, or rather like those of Shenger-Krestovnikova, they start making mistakes and are unable to perform tasks that were previously easy for them. In extreme cases they may develop the "symptoms of acute neurosis" to which Pavlov refers.

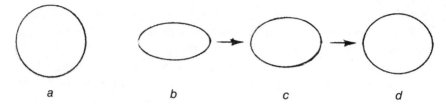

Figure 2.6 *Shenger-Krestovnikova's stimuli. Dogs were conditioned to respond to a circle (a). Their responses to an ellipse (b) were extinguished. As the ellipse was gradually changed to look more like a circle, as in (c) and (d), the dogs' ability to discriminate broke down, and, in Pavlov's words, their behavior "presented all the symptoms of acute neurosis."*

Noninstantaneous Stimuli and Responses

In most of Pavlov's conditioning experiments each stimulus and response was considered to be a fairly discrete event. A buzzer was sounded for an instant, or a light was flashed and an increase in salivation occurred for only 1 or 2 seconds. However, there is no need for the US, CS, or response to be instantaneous discrete events for the conditioning procedure to be effective. Indeed, the CS and the US may be ongoing processes. For instance, let us consider the relation between temperature and a dog's rate of breathing. These two processes are clearly correlated. (That is, temperature and rate of breathing tend to rise and fall together. When the temperature is high, dogs breathe fast; when the temperature is low, dogs breathe slowly.) In this case there is no reason to look for a specific stimulus for each breath—we merely consider the dog's rate of breathing as the response and the temperature to be a US. Let us add a CS to the situation: a light that signals high temperatures. In this case the response can be considered to be the *rate* of a series of fairly discrete events—after a while, to test the CS, we turn on the light without raising the temperature and observe the rate of breathing.

Here is another, similar conditioning experiment with dogs: the *rate* of buzzer sounds is correlated with *rate* of presentation of food, and the response is measured as the *rate* of salivation. All three events—buzzers, food presentations, and salivation—occur over the same time span. A high rate of buzzer presentation is used to signal a high rate of food presentations and a low rate of buzzer sounds is used to signal the reverse. Learning then consists of a dog's changing its rate of salivation in accordance with the rate of buzzer presentations. We can see how the concept of classical conditioning can be extended to familiar, everyday situations, in which behavior often adjusts to over-all rates of environmental events instead of to each separate event as it occurs.

INSTRUMENTAL CONDITIONING

The Law of Effect

In 1898, Thorndike laid the groundwork for a simple but important principle, which he named the "law of effect." Here is a paraphrase of his principle: one effect of a successful behavior is to increase the probability that it will occur again in similar circumstances. Thorndike based this conclusion on experiments in which cats, dogs, and chicks were confined repeatedly in puzzle boxes like the one shown in Figure 2.7. In order to escape from the box and get the food that was within view, the hungry animal had to step on a lever or pull out a bolt, or perform some other mechanical task. Thorndike found that the animal, in the course of its behavior in the box, would sooner or later make the correct movement and get out of the box. He measured the latency of the correct movement—how long it took the animal to escape—and continued to measure latency for each successive trial. Thorndike found that, in general, there was a negative correlation between the number of times an animal had escaped from the box and the length of time it took to escape—the more trials, the less time to escape. After many repeated trials, the animal would solve the puzzle and get out of the box almost immediately. (The graphs in Figure 2.8 show how latency decreased with repeated trials.)

Now let us consider the following hypothetical experiment, which is rather similar to Thorndike's and may further clarify the "law of effect." Suppose we construct a puzzle box like Thorndike's, except that we make the ceiling somewhat higher. And suppose that we now put a cat into the box, but that instead of letting it out after it solves a puzzle, we simply observe its behavior, particularly its jumping. (Thorndike reported that one common behavior of a hungry cat in a box is jumping.) If we measure the heights of the jumps and plot them as a distribution (see the lower left portion of Figure 2.9), the curve will probably be bell-shaped, showing some very low jumps and some very high jumps but mostly medium jumps. Suppose that we open the door to the box after each jump greater than some arbitrary height, a little above average, say 13 inches, and feed the cat before putting it back into the box. At first, we find the usual number of 13-inch jumps. But

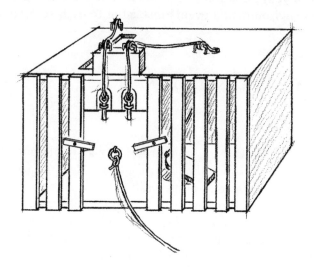

Figure 2.7 Thorndike's puzzle box. Cats that were placed inside this box learned to unbolt the door and then to press the door outward to escape. [From E. L. Thorndike, Animal Intelligence. New York, Macmillan Publishing Co., 1911.]

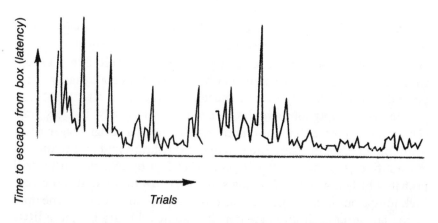

Figure 2.8 These two curves show the performances of two cats in Thorndike's box. [From E. L. Thorndike, Animal Intelligence. New York, Macmillan Publishing Co., 1911.]

as the experiment progresses, we find more and more jumps of 13 inches and above. In fact, the distribution will probably change to one resembling that on the lower right of Figure 2.9.

Thorndike's puzzle box experiments were comprised of the following steps: (1) The experimenter provided a stimulus to the organism and observed the organism's behavior in its presence. (2) If the behavior was "appropriate," in the sense that it conformed to criteria set by the experimenter, he rewarded the organism. (3) This, in turn, increased the likelihood of the behavior recurring and producing more rewards. (In this sense, a reward to the organism is said to *reinforce* its behavior.) Today, Thorndike's experimental procedure is considered a major variant of *instrumental conditioning*, so called to distinguish it from Pavlov's classical conditioning procedure, which was discussed previously.

It is important to realize the purpose of the highly artificial situation in which Thorndike put his animals. He believed that the "law of effect" was not limited to such artificial situations but was a general law of nature. In his view the environment usually sets the conditions of the "puzzle" for individual organisms. Thorndike reasoned that a fox learns how to enter a barnyard in the same way that he learns to get out of a puzzle box. The reason Thorndike built his puzzle box was to isolate the phenomenon of learning and measure its progress. The conditions he set in the laboratory were meant to parallel the conditions of the environment, but to be less complicated. If the puzzle box seems to be an artificial way to study behavior, we should remember that all experiments are inherently artificial because they isolate from the complexity of the environment those particular variables that are of interest to the experimenter.

Much as the physicist, when he studies the behavior of falling bodies, prefers to work with an approximation to a vacuum, where air resistance is eliminated, Thorndike tried to isolate the mechanism of the influence of reward by removing environmental distractions.

The early experiments of Thorndike are important for many of the same reasons as are the early experiments of Ebbinghaus, which we discussed in the first chapter. Unlike the casual observations of their predecessors, the experiments of Ebbinghaus and Thorndike were systematic enough to be replicable. Their experiments have been repeated; as long as the same procedures have been followed, similar results have always been obtained.

We turn now to the topic "learning and evolution." Thorndike, who helped lay the foundation of instrumental conditioning, saw a direct connection between individual adaptation—the selection of

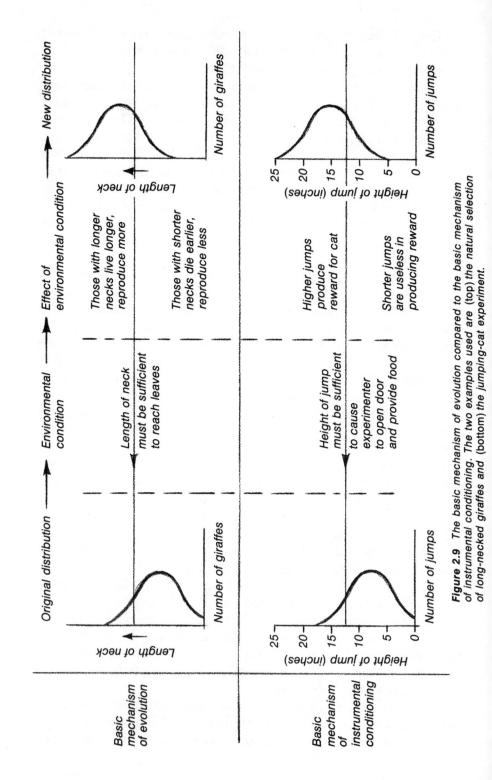

Figure 2.9 The basic mechanism of evolution compared to the basic mechanism of instrumental conditioning. The two examples used are (top) the natural selection of long-necked giraffes and (bottom) the jumping-cat experiment.

successful behaviors from an organism's repertoire—and species adaptation. Indeed, the "law of effect" is simply natural selection at work within the life history of a single organism.

Learning and Evolution

Both species structures and species behaviors evolve. If the environment changes slowly, and is the same for all members of the species, evolution from generation to generation works well. The spider's web-spinning and the social interaction of bees, ants and other insects are behaviors that have been brought about by natural selection.

But this evolutionary process, which takes generations to do its work, is too slow to solve some of the problems faced by some species. Take foxes for example. If a farmer devises a new fence for his barnyard, a particular fox must change its behavior to get past that particular fence. If the fence is too high to jump over, the fox must learn to climb over it or to tunnel under it or to gnaw through it. Since there are many foxes, many farmers, and many kinds of fences, there is little chance for the evolution of a whole breed of foxes whose specific "fence-climbing behavior" would be just suited to the peculiarities of any single fence. If such a breed of foxes did come into being, the farmer would replace the fence with another fence that the new breed could not climb over, and the process would have to begin again. In other words, given their relatively changeable environment, the only hope for foxes lies in individual adaptation rather than in species adaptation. Each fox must respond to its own specific environmental conditions. Individual adaptation, the ability of an organism to change its behavior in relation to changes in the environment, is nothing more or less than learning. This relatively rapid adaptability of individual behavior complements the more gradual adaptability of species structure and species behavior we find in the long-term evolutionary process and is, itself, a product and a part of that process.

Complex Behavior

Because an action cannot be rewarded or punished unless it occurs, the mechanism of the "law of effect" can only strengthen acts that *do already* occur. This being the case, how could a man teach a dog to run to the closet and fetch his slippers? The man would probably have to wait a long time before this rather complex behavior occurred fortuitously so he could reward it. Instead, he must begin by rewarding the dog for simple acts already within its repertoire. As these simple acts are strengthened, other acts will appear in the repertoire more like the desired final behavior. The "law of effect" works rather subtly and rather slowly in regard to complex patterns of behavior; these complex patterns evolve from simpler patterns, just as complex species structures evolve from simpler structures. In our hypothetical experiment with the jumping cat, we would have to wait a very long time for a jump over 20 inches to occur when the cat is first put into the box. Thus, if we tried to strengthen 20-inch jumps by rewarding them initially, we might not succeed. If, however, we first rewarded 12-inch jumps, we see from the revised distribution at the lower right of Figure 2.9 that 20-inch jumps would become fairly frequent. *Then*, if we rewarded 20-inch jumps we would be likely to succeed in strengthening them. By this method of *successive approximations* to our goal, we could finally train the cat to consistently jump at the very limits of its capacity.

So, it is clear that complex patterns of behavior can evolve within the life history of a single organism through the mechanism described by the "law of effect." Thorndike called such evolved patterns of behavior *habits*. He felt that the particular habits of an individual organism depend on the history of that organism. Thorndike believed that the complex patterns of behavior that enable one person, say, to operate a lathe and another person to quarterback a football team cannot arise wholly from inheritance but must be largely due to the unique patterns of experience of the two people.*

Kinds of Instrumental Conditioning

There are four basic principles used in instrumental conditioning, all of which are related to the evolution of individual behaviors. In capsule form, we can describe the four principles as *reward, punishment, escape,* and *omission.*

1. The principle of reward was stated in Thorndike's "law of effect"—a reward tends to increase the probability that the

---

*We must not neglect another source of complex patterns of behavior. Complex behaviors can also evolve gradually from generation to generation. Such behaviors, said to be *instincts*, are much the same from generation to generation and from organism to organism within an entire species. As organisms within the species mature, they acquire the complex behaviors that are specific to their species. Much of the complex behavior of species of insects, for example, consists of unvarying sequences of acts that are adaptive as long as relatively constant environmental conditions are not disrupted. Unlike foxes, however, a species of insect might essentially have only *one way* to solve a problem (to build nests, for example).

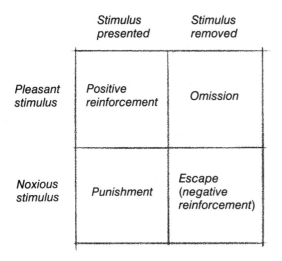

	Stimulus presented	Stimulus removed
Pleasant stimulus	Positive reinforcement	Omission
Noxious stimulus	Punishment	Escape (negative reinforcement)

Figure 2.10 Four basic kinds of instrumental conditioning are classified by the consequences of a specific act. For example, if a specific act is followed by the presentation of a pleasant stimulus (a reward), the instrumental conditioning is classified as positive-reinforcement.

response to which it is related will recur.* In conditioning experiments, reward is called *positive reinforcement.*

2. The principle of *punishment* is the inverse of Thorndike's law—an aversive, or noxious, stimulus tends to decrease the probability that the response to which it is related will recur.

3. In what is called *escape conditioning*, a particular response is related to escape from an aversive stimulus. Escape from an aversive stimulus increases the probability that the response will recur. For example, Thorndike found that his cats would often learn to solve the puzzle in the box even when they were not fed afterwards. In other words, they learned to respond solely in order to escape confinement. This type of conditioning is also called *negative reinforcement.*

4. *Omission* of reward occurs when the absence of a reward, otherwise present in the environment, is related to the response. Like punishment, the omission of a reward tends to decrease the probability that the response will recur. This type of conditioning is also called *negative punishment.*

Figure 2.10 is a diagram showing basic relationships among the four kinds of instrumental conditioning.

(Later in this chapter, when we discuss the aversive control of behavior, we shall have something to say about which of these methods can best be used in a given situation to increase or decrease the occurrence of various kinds of behavior.)

---

*Thorndike would have replaced the phrase "to which it is related" by "which it follows," but we use the more general term.

CLASSICAL AND INSTRUMENTAL
CONDITIONING COMPARED

How are classical conditioning and instrumental conditioning related? No definitive answer to this question is generally accepted by modern behaviorists. Without going into the details of the theoretical disputes in this area, we can observe that classical conditioning and instrumental conditioning are two closely related but distinguishable phenomena.

Differences between classical and instrumental conditioning experiments can be found (1) in the organism's influence on reinforcement and (2) in the way behavior is classified by the experimenter.

The Organism's Influence on Reinforcement

Let us take food as an example of a reinforcer. In a classical conditioning experiment, the organism's influence on the appearance of food is negligible. The experimenter decides the time for the delivery of food. By contrast, instrumental conditioning experiments are arranged so that the organism can produce food by a particular response. In Pavlov's experiments food was presented on each trial, whatever the organism did. If one of Pavlov's dogs had been trained with food withheld until salivation occurred, the classical conditioning experiment would have been transformed into an instrumental conditioning experiment.

If we consider the organism to be a single unitary system, we find that there are three elements in both the classical and instrumental conditioning procedures that cross the boundary of this system. (See Figure 2.11.) Because the US in classical conditioning and the reward in instrumental conditioning are corresponding elements, they share a common name—reinforcement. In both procedures the presence of reinforcement serves to determine conditioning and its absence serves to define extinction. (In instrumental conditioning, we speak of the response as being reinforced. We say "The dog was rewarded for opening the latch" or "The latch-opening response of the dog was reinforced" not "The dog was reinforced" or "The response was rewarded."). When reinforcement is mentioned in connection with classical conditioning, the speaker is referring to the US. Thus, in classical conditioning, an unreinforced trial is either a test trial, as in Figure 2.2b, or part of a block of extinction trials.

Whether reinforcement in classical conditioning acts functionally in a manner similar to reinforcement in instrumental conditioning is a

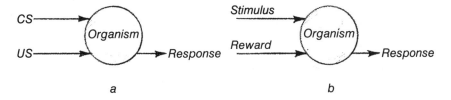

Figure 2.11 *Classical conditioning and instrumental conditioning compared with respect to inputs to the organism and outputs from the organism. (a) Classical conditioning. (b) Instrumental conditioning.*

question about which there is some dispute. Although Figure 2.11, which shows the organism as a system, reveals a similarity with respect to the inputs and outputs of the system, the difference between the two methods lies in the interaction between the organism and conditions in its environment. Figure 2.12 shows the system in Figure 2.11 with the environment also diagrammed. The difference between the two parts of Figure 2.12 is the dotted feedback loop in the instrumental conditioning diagram. In classical conditioning the temporal relation between the CS and US is determined by the experimenter in advance, and nothing the subject does will change it. In any classical conditioning trial the CS and US are both always present. Reinforcement is always present. In instrumental conditioning, on the other hand, reinforcement is *not* given every time the stimulus is presented. It is only given when the response is made. In some early experiments on conditioning this critical difference was not realized. Consider the following two experiments diagrammed in Figure 2.13. In both experiments, a tuning fork is sounded and electric shock is delivered to the dog's paw. In one case, the circuit is arranged so that lifting the paw serves to break the circuit. In the other, lifting the paw does not break the circuit. The procedure shown at the bottom of the figure is instrumental conditioning: the subject's behavior here serves to determine the presence or absence of the shock. The procedure sketched at the top is classical conditioning: the subject's behavior has no effect on the shock, but the pairing between the tuning fork stimulus, the shock, and the withdrawal of the leg is always maintained.

We discussed extinction previously in relation to classical conditioning. Extinction consisted in eliminating the US (the reinforcement). Extinction in instrumental conditioning also consists in eliminating the reinforcement. In order to extinguish an instrumentally conditioned response, we stop rewarding the animal for making the response. The results are the same for classical and instrumental conditioning—the probability that the response will recur decreases.

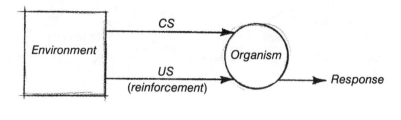

a

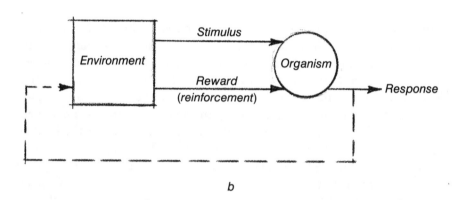

b

Figure 2.12 *Classical and instrumental conditioning compared with respect to interaction between the organism and its environment. (a) Classical conditioning. (b) Instrumental conditioning.*

We have spoken of the *probabilities* that responses will recur. One difference between classical and instrumental conditioning can be seen in the different contingencies involved. A contingency is a set of conditional probabilities, the probability that, given one event, another event will occur. A contingency table that could apply for a classical conditioning experiment is shown in part (a) of Figure 2.14. It shows that when the CS is presented, the probability of the US is 1.0 and that when the CS is absent the probability of the US is zero; that is, the US (the reinforcement) is completely dependent on the CS. With instrumental conditioning the contingency set by the experimenter is between the response and the reinforcement. The table in part (b) of Figure 2.14 says that when a response is made, the probability of reinforcement is 1.0 and that when no response is made the probability of reinforcement is zero; that is, the reinforcement is completely dependent on the response. The reinforcer is omitted during extinction of both kinds of conditioning, and all the terms in the first column of the table would be zero.

Basic Procedures and Techniques

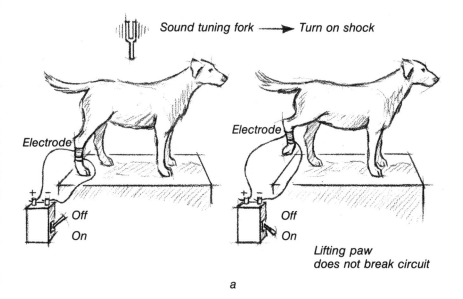

Sound tuning fork ⟶ Turn on shock

Electrode

Electrode

Off

On

Off

On

Lifting paw
does not break circuit

a

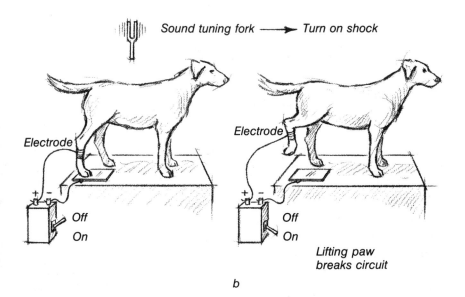

Sound tuning fork ⟶ Turn on shock

Electrode

Electrode

Off

On

Off

On

Lifting paw
breaks circuit

b

Figure 2.13 *The difference between classical conditioning and instrumental conditioning illustrated by a minor change in an electric-shock circuit. (a) Classical conditioning. (b) Instrumental conditioning.*

	US	No US
Presence of CS	1.0	0
Absence of CS	0	1.0

a

	Reinforcement	No reinforcement
Presence of response	1.0	0
Absence of response	0	1.0

b

	Elevator arrives within 2 minutes	Elevator doesn't arrive within 2 minutes
Pushes button	0.8	0.2
Does not push button	0.4	0.6

c

Figure 2.14 *Contingency tables (a) for a standard classical conditioning experiment, (b) for a standard instrumental conditioning experiment, and (c) for elevator arrivals versus button pushing. The values in the tables are conditional probabilities. In (c), for instance, 0.8 is the probability that a certain elevator will arrive within 2 minutes of pressing the button.*

One advantage of this way of formulating the two types of conditioning is that other, nonzero and nonunity values may be put in the table and their effect on conditioning studied. In everyday life we rarely find the complete dependencies shown in parts (a) and (b) of Figure 2.14. Responding that usually produces reinforcement sometimes fails to work and nonresponding that usually fails to produce reinforcement sometimes produces reinforcement. Occasionally, pushing the button and waiting fails to bring an elevator and occasionally elevators arrive without any button-pushing at all. The contingency of elevator arrivals on button-pushing might be as shown in Figure 2.14c. Clearly, pushing a button makes elevator arrivals more probable, but it by no means makes them certain.

Classifying Behavior

The ever-changing pattern of events that comprise an organism's behavior are sometimes analyzed into relatively large chunks (like "sleeping," "resting," and "eating") and sometimes into relatively small bits (like "heartbeats," "breaths," "blinks," and "nerve impulses"). Obviously there is no single correct way to classify behavior. How one classifies the behavior of a particular organism depends largely on one's point of view and on the degree of one's interest in the organism.

For most of us, a man's eye movements in his sleep is a detail scarcely worthy of note; we are content with the observation that the man seems to be asleep. On the other hand, if we were studying the nature of sleep, we might attempt to keep a careful record of such bits of behavior, and eye movements and other muscular spasms might turn out to be significant classifications of behavior within the context of our study.

If we observe someone, say a businessman, for a considerable period, how should we group the events we observe? Our businessman is always doing something, always breathing for instance. Will that form an important part of our description? Should we describe in detail the nervous mechanism involved in each breath? or should we ignore his breathing entirely and concentrate on molar actions, like his work or his eating? We also face the problem that at any given time our subject may be doing *many* things—breathing, writing, working, earning money, digesting his food, advancing his career, biting his upper lip, blinking, hoping, thinking, and sitting.

Consider how different observers might describe what the businessman did in a single day. Some descriptions might be relatively molecular in the sense that they go into some detail about bits of his behavior. Some might be more molar in the sense that they divide his behavior into relatively large chunks, but all could be fairly consistent and reasonable ways to look at what he is doing. The businessman's associates may describe his behavior in terms of his business activities. His wife may describe his behavior in terms of his domestic activities. His doctor, his insurance agent, his banker, will each have a particular outlook. Each will describe the behavior of the man in terms of his interest in the man. As psychologists, though, where do *we* draw the line? How can we bring some organization to this complex ongoing process? (Indeed, how shall we classify *all* the possible behaviors of *all* possible organisms?) If we are interested in the *modification of behavior*, then we must find a way to classify behavior in terms of its modifiability.

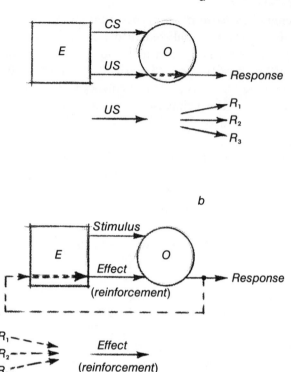

Figure 2.15 *Classification of behavior in terms of classical conditioning and instrumental conditioning. (a) Classical conditioning. Any acts that are invariably elicited by a single stimulus can be grouped together. Thus we can identify "leg-withdrawal following electric shock," and distinguish it, as a category, from other muscular movements. (b) Instrumental conditioning. Any acts that produce the same effect can be grouped together. Such a category is called an* operant. *An operant could include such diverse actions as pressing an elevator button with one's thumb, one's forefinger, or one's elbow or even asking another person to press the button—in short, any action that moves the button.*

We have described two methods of modifying behavior—classical conditioning and instrumental conditioning. What do they tell us about how to classify the businessman's behavior (and behavior in general)? Figure 2.15 shows how the contingencies of reinforcement in the two methods aid in the classification of behavior.

In classical conditioning, reinforcement is the presentation of an unconditioned stimulus that invariably elicits a response. Thus, responses in classical conditioning must be grouped into a class, or category, on the basis of their common elicitation by a certain type of stimulus. (The stimulus thus defines the category.) As our hypothetical businessman goes through his day some of the things he does fall into such stimulus-defined categories.

For instance, when a light is turned on, the man's pupils contract, and there is some electrical activity in the cortex of his brain. When he hears a sudden loud noise, he withdraws from it, shows increased heart rate, and a group of other measurable phenomena. Each stimulus has a set of behavioral and physiological responses that follow it. With respect to classical conditioning, *the group of measurable phenomena elicited by a particular stimulus are classified together as the response to that stimulus.* Only a limited set of responses, however, can be so classified. Most of the man's behavior, especially that part that appears to be "voluntary" cannot be elicited by any particular stimulus. The techniques of classical conditioning are difficult to apply to such behavior. For instance, if our businessman were head of a construction company engaged in building a dam, we would be hard put to find any unconditioned stimulus that elicited the behavior of dam-building in the businessman.* The psychologist who is interested in classical conditioning does not talk about the response of dam-building. If he wants to describe dam-building at all in terms of classically conditioned behavior, he must break the entire process down into smaller responses such as the movements of certain muscles, each of which itself *can* be elicited by known stimuli.

In instrumental conditioning, on the other hand, we need not limit ourselves only to behavior known to be elicited by certain stimuli. We are free to work with any behavior that the organism will emit. The only requirement is that we be able to measure the behavior so as to reward or punish the organism when the behavior is emitted. The dam-building of our businessman can be measured, and reinforcement may be programmed for it. Dam-building is, thus, a legitimate category of behavior for instrumental conditioning.

In order to measure a given class of behavior, all the members of that class must have some common environmental effect. For instance, all dam-building behavior must potentially result in a completed dam. The businessman's contract, which determines the conditions of his reward, sets forth only specifications of the completed dam. How the dam is built is up to the businessman. There may be an infinite number of ways in which this contract could be fulfilled. Similarly, an experimenter might be training a rat to press a bar. He

---

*However, in the case of certain organisms like the beaver, dam-building may be an innate pattern of behavior capable of being elicited by certain stimuli.

programs reinforcement for bar-pressing, but he does not specify how the bar must be pressed. The rat may press the bar with its left paw, its right paw, its head, its tail, or in an infinite number of different ways. What these infinite different actions of the rat have in common is that they all change a certain portion of the environment in the same way—they all succeed in moving the bar through a certain angle, and they all may produce reward. Any class of behavior that produces such a common effect on the environment is called an *operant*. The term was coined by the American psychologist B. F. Skinner, who first proposed that instrumental behavior consists of *emitted* acts, which are classified according to their effect on the environment (as opposed to classically conditioned behavior, which consists of elicited acts, which are classified according to the stimulus that elicits them). In this chapter, we shall deal with several operants, including bar pressing, key pecking, door opening, the breaking of photocell beams, and even running from one place to another. All are operants in the sense that they are categories that describe an infinite set of individual acts having a common effect on the environment.

Classical and Instrumental Conditioning in the Same Experiment

In a given situation, both classical and instrumental responses may be reinforced simultaneously. In other words, Response A may be required to produce the reinforcement, and Response B may be elicited by the very same reinforcement.

An experiment by Gaylord D. Ellison and Jerzy Konorski produced classical and instrumental conditioning with the same reinforcer, and studied the two kinds of responses separately. Their method was to train a dog to press a lever during a light in order to produce, not food directly, but a buzzer (CS) followed by food. They could measure both lever presses and salivation during the light and during the CS. When the light was introduced, the dog had to press the lever nine times. This turned off the light and produced the buzzer. Eight seconds later the food was automatically presented.

This somewhat complicated procedure enabled Ellison and Konorski to measure rates of salivation (classically conditioned) and bar pressing (instrumentally conditioned) separately. First, they measured salivation and bar pressing before all of the nine presses were made. (At this point, bar pressing was the appropriate response since it was required to produce the reinforcement. Second, they measured

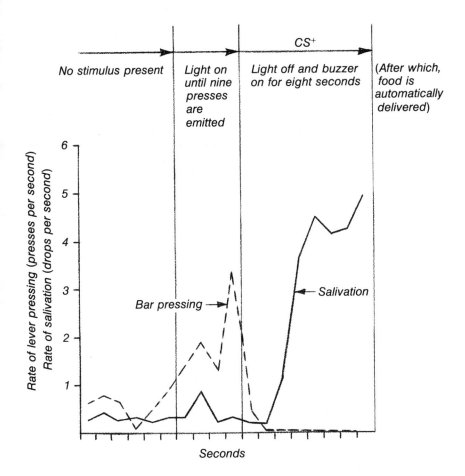

Figure 2.16 *An instrumentally conditioned behavior (bar pressing) and a classically conditioned behavior (salivation) occurring simultaneously in the same experiment.* [Data from G. D. Ellison and J. Konorski, "Separation of the salivary and motor responses in instrumental conditioning." Science, 1964, 146, 1071–1072. Copyright 1964 by American Association for the Advancement of Science.]

salivation and bar pressing after the nine presses were made (and after the CS was presented) but *before* the US (food) was presented. By then bar presses had no effect, but the CS produced salivation. Figure 2.16 shows their results. Barpresses, the instrumental response, were high during the light and low during the buzzer; salivation was high during the buzzer and low during the light. Thus, within a single experimental situation, both classical and instrumental responses can be measured separately and made to occur with maximum force at different times depending on the conditioning procedure that generated them.

Anatomical Correlates of Classical and Instrumental Conditioning

Some psychologists believe that classical and instrumental conditioning may be distinguished by the part of the nervous system in which they can act. Classical conditioning is said to work better with autonomic functions such as glandular secretions, and instrumental conditioning is said to work better with nonautonomic responses such as muscular movements. Ellison and Konorski's experiment provides an example of this distinction. The classical component was autonomic (salivation) while the instrumental component was muscular (lever pressing).

These anatomical boundaries, however, have been crossed many times. Classical conditioning experiments have been performed with muscular responses such as eyeblink, and Neil Miller and his students at Rockefeller University have recently instrumentally conditioned autonomic responses. For instance, when an animal's heart rate is measured and it is given reward (feedback) only when its heart rate varies within a certain range, the heart rate tends to stay within that range more than it does if rewards are delivered randomly. Apparently, the characteristic of autonomic behavior that normally makes instrumental conditioning difficult is lack of feedback to the behaving organism.

This area of research holds practical promise since it implies that people can learn to keep blood pressure, stomach acidity, and so forth, at nonharmful levels provided they have feedback informing them of the state of these autonomic functions. This is the goal of the emerging field of biofeedback, which uses electronic devices to enhance awareness and control of physiological processes.

PSEUDOCONDITIONING

Pseudoconditioning in Classical Experiments

Suppose we select a CS and a US and, after pairing them and testing the results as shown in Figure 2.2, find that the unconditioned response is now elicited by the CS. Can we safely assume that conditioning has taken place? Unfortunately, no. In some cases, the US presentation may change the state of the organism so that the CS produces the response by itself without any necessary connection to the US. Consider, for example, an experiment using electric shock as the US and a vibratory tactile stimulus as the CS (see Figure 2.17). First vibrations

Basic Procedures and Techniques

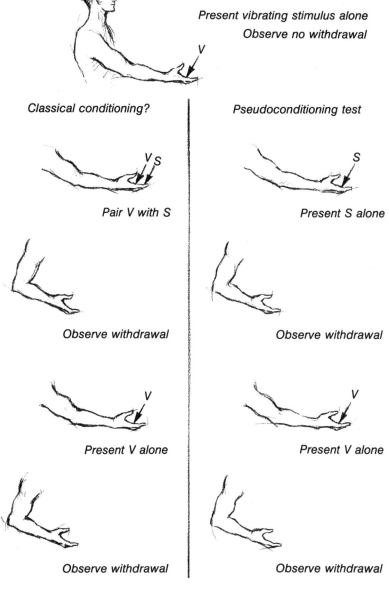

Present vibrating stimulus alone
Observe no withdrawal

Classical conditioning?

Pseudoconditioning test

Pair V with S

Present S alone

Observe withdrawal

Observe withdrawal

Present V alone

Present V alone

Observe withdrawal

Observe withdrawal

Figure 2.17 *An example of a test for pseudo classical conditioning. If the results of these two procedures (left and right) are withdrawals similar in latency and extent, then it is possible that none of the withdrawals is a classically conditioned response. However, if there is no withdrawal after the test procedure (bottom right) even though there is a withdrawal after the classical conditioning procedure (bottom left), then the response at bottom left is a genuine classically conditioned response. In this case, "V" stands for a vibration and "S" stands for a shock.*

are applied to one hand of a human subject. No effect is found. Then vibrations are paired with shock to the hand, and we observe a withdrawal of the hand. Then vibrations are applied alone, and again the hand is withdrawn. Is this effect the result of classical conditioning? The test is to get another subject, apply electric shock alone (unpaired with vibrations), then apply vibrations alone, and see if the hand is now withdrawn. If it is, we can be fairly sure that the shock merely made the hand more sensitive to the vibrations, and that we did not observe classical conditioning in the first subject.

A critical test of classically conditioned behavior is to determine whether the *relation of the CS and US* is necessary to produce the behavior. When we perform a classical conditioning experiment and observe what appears to be a conditioned response, but then find that the relation between the CS and US is not necessary to produce that response, we have merely observed *pseudoconditioning*. It is always important to test classical conditioning experiments to see if they can be explained on the basis of pseudoconditioning. Figure 2.17 shows the sequence of the pseudoconditioning test.

Pseudoconditioning in Instrumental Experiments

In instrumental conditioning, any response that would occur without *pairings of response and reinforcement* is a pseudoconditioned response. Consider the following hypothetical experiment. The experimenter puts a rat in a chamber, which has a bar protruding into it. Eventually, the rat, in the course of its normal movements about the chamber, will press the bar. When this happens the experimenter sprays the rat with a powder that makes it itch. As a result, the rat jumps vigorously about the chamber. Because of these vigorous jumps, the rat hits against the bar sooner than before and the experimenter records a reduced latency of bar pressing. After the second press, the experimenter again sprays in the itching powder, causing still more jumping about and, hence, an even faster rate of bar presses. This continues until the rat is exhausted. Can we say that itching powder is rewarding to the rat and that we have here a genuine case of instrumental conditioning of the bar-press response? We cannot, until we have tested for pseudoconditioning.

How can we perform such a test? In order to test for pseudoconditioning we have to find out whether the same response would occur without the critical element, the pairings, of response with reinforcement. In the case of the rat and the itching powder, it would be easy to prove that itching powder was not instrumentally conditioning bar

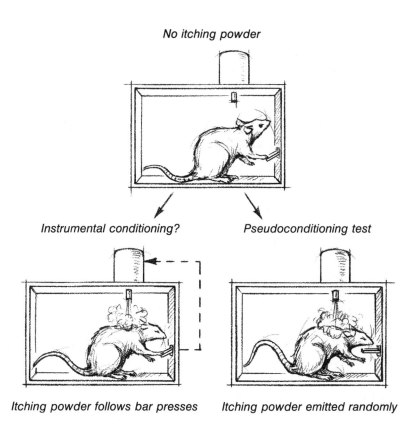

No itching powder

Instrumental conditioning?   *Pseudoconditioning test*

Itching powder follows bar presses   *Itching powder emitted randomly*

Figure 2.18 *A hypothetical example of a test for pseudo instrumental conditioning. At top, a rat's bar-presses are observed in the absence of reward or punishment. At bottom left, itching powder is sprayed on the rat whenever it presses the bar. At bottom right, itching powder is sprayed on the rat at random regardless of its bar-presses. The situation shown at bottom left may look like true instrumental conditioning—the rat seems to press the bar repeatedly to get sprayed by itching powder. However, the situation shown on the bottom right results in an equal increase in bar pressing, simply because the rat is agitated by the itching powder, thus revealing that the behavior at bottom left is not truly conditioned.*

presses. We would merely take another rat and place it in an identical chamber. This time we would ignore the bar. We would spray the second rat periodically with itching powder, just as we sprayed the first rat with itching powder. (Of course, the systematic relation of the spraying of itching powder and pressing the bar would be absent.) If this rat's rate of pressing increased as much as the first rat's (as it is likely to do), we could assume that the increase in pressing we observed for the first rat was not a result of the pairing of responses with reinforcement but merely an artifact of the reinforcement (in this case, the itching powder) itself. This, then, would be a case of pseudoconditioning. Figure 2.18 shows the procedure for testing for pseudoconditioning in instrumental conditioning experiments.

METHODS OF MEASUREMENT

Techniques for measuring behavior are the tools of the psychologist's trade; they are as important to him as a hammer and saw are to a carpenter. Indeed, at times they seem so important that psychologists become more interested in the operation of the tools themselves than in the functions they have been designed to perform. But it is important to have a general understanding of these tools and what they measure.

Techniques for measuring responses that have been classically conditioned are identical to techniques for measuring unconditioned reflexes. One obvious example is the fistula and receptacle Pavlov devised for measuring salivation. Other reflexes, such as the eyeblink, knee jerk, and GSR can be measured by specialized electronic devices.

Instrumental-conditioning responses are grouped according to their common effect on the environment. In the laboratory, this common effect is determined by the experimenter. Hence the problem of measurement in instrumental conditioning is not to *discover* the response to a stimulus, as it is in classical conditioning, but to *invent* a device that will be sensitive to changes in the organism's behavior produced by the learning process. The latitude for such inventions is great, and there have been many widely different kinds of apparatus used. We shall describe a few of the most common kinds of measurements here.

Latency

The latency of any sort of behavior is the time between some signal and the occurrence of the behavior. The latency of an instrumental response will depend on the condition of the subject as well as the reinforcement being presented. For instance, when a mother calls her little boy to dinner, he is likely to come faster when he is hungry than when he is not, faster for hamburgers than for liver, and faster on rainy days than on sunny days. Latency has been a popular dependent variable for instrumental conditioning experiments and was, in fact, the measure of learning used by Thorndike in his original instrumental conditioning experiments. Thorndike measured the interval from the time the animal was put into the puzzle box until it solved the puzzle and got out. (One difficulty with the puzzle box is that it is impossible to specify exactly *when* the response occurs. At what instant is the puzzle solved?—when the animal starts to pull the bolt out of the latch? or when it finishes?)

Since Thorndike's time, puzzle boxes have been simplified. One modification of the puzzle box has been the shuttle box invented by Neal Miller and O. Hobart Mowrer. A form of this device is a box with a barrier in the center. Instead of solving a puzzle and escaping to freedom and food, the animal jumps over the barrier from one side of the box to the other. The experimenter may put food in the other side of the box or he may put some aversive stimulus in the side with the animal. The most common aversive stimulus is electric shock. When electric shock is used, the animal jumps over the barrier into, say, the right side of the box to escape the shock on the left side, and the experimenter is able to measure the time between the onset of the shock and the jump. Then the animal is shocked on the right and the time between shock and jump is measured again. One would expect an animal to become experienced with this procedure and jump faster and faster to escape shock. This is exactly what happens. In fact, if a signal precedes the shock, the animal does not wait for the shock to come on, but eventually learns to jump at the signal so that it avoids the shock altogether.

The shuttle box has two big advantages over the puzzle box. First of all, the behavior of the animal can be measured without the experimenter handling the animal between trials. (When the experimenter handles the animals he is likely to affect their behavior.) Secondly, the response of jumping is fairly discrete, in the sense that the response takes only a split second, so the latency from a signal to the beginning of the jump is about the same as the latency to the end of a jump.

Another isolation chamber in which latency can be measured is the lever box, or Skinner box, invented by B. F. Skinner (see Figure 2.19). Here, instead of shuttling over a divider, the animal presses a lever to escape shock. In a Skinner box, the response takes even less time than in the shuttle box. A further convenience of the Skinner box is the fact that the lever can be connected to a switch automatically delivering food or stopping electric shock.

Rate of Response

In many forms of behavior, each response is preceded by a signal (or stimulus). The running of a race, for instance, is formally started by the sound of a gun. In that case, the proper measure of responding is the time between the signal and the completion of the response. Some-

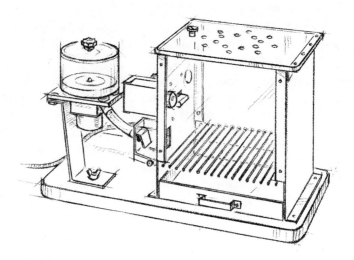

Figure 2.19 *A lever box, or Skinner box. [Courtesy of Ralph Gerbrands Co., Arlington, Mass.]*

times, however, a certain form of behavior is repeated many times in the presence of a single signal. For instance, suppose that the little boy in our previous example has finally come home to dinner. He begins to eat, lifting a forkful of food. The signal for this first forkful is a plate of food, which remains present during repeated instances of the same response. Although we can measure the latency of his first forkful of food, we must turn to *rate of response* if we want to quantify the rest of his eating. His rate of eating (like his latency in coming home) may be expected to vary with his hunger and his food preferences. When he is hungry he needs no coaxing to eat heartily, but when he is not hungry he is likely to eat listlessly or not at all.

Perhaps the simplest way to measure rate of response in the laboratory is to measure the speed with which an organism gets from one point to another. One device used for this purpose is called a *straight alley* and is, indeed, nothing but an alley with a box at either end. The animal runs from one box to the other, and its rate of running (its speed) can be measured automatically as it interrupts the light beams of a series of photocells. The straight alley is good for measuring the speed with which an animal runs toward a goal or away from a painful stimulus. However, if we were interested in continuously measuring an animal's running speed 1, 2, and 3 hours after an injection of a drug such as caffeine, we would need an impossibly long straight alley to allow a rat to run as far as it could. In order to measure rate of running over such long periods we use a device called a *running*

Basic Procedures and Techniques

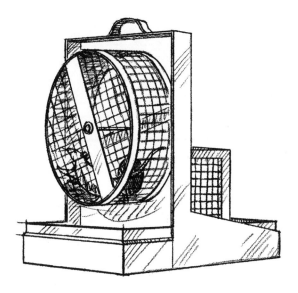

Figure 2.20 *A running wheel. [Courtesy of Wahmann Manufacturing Co., Baltimore, Md.]*

wheel (Figure 2.20). As far as the animal (usually, a rat) is concerned, the running wheel is an infinitely long straight alley; its convenience for the experimenter is that no matter how fast or far the rat runs, it remains in the same place. The rat's speed of running is easy to obtain by timing the wheel's revolutions.

The Skinner box is frequently employed to study rate of responding as well as to measure latency. To use this device to measure rate of responding, we leave the signal on continuously and stipulate that, while the signal is on, pressing the lever will be reinforced. Figure 2.21a shows a record of lever-presses by a rat when each lever-press was followed by a pellet of food. We can get a better picture of the changes in rate of response if we plot the responses cumulatively as in the Figure 2.22. In such a cumulative record, a steep slope represents a rapid rate of responding and a shallow slope represents a slow rate of responding. A machine for plotting cumulative records directly is shown in the Figure 2.23b.

Choice

Choice is a relative measure, a measure of *ratios* rather than *absolute values.* The devices by which choice is measured in the psychological laboratory will illustrate the point.

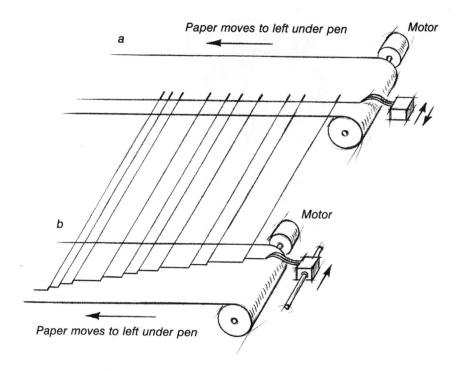

Paper moves to left under pen
a
Motor

Motor
b

Paper moves to left under pen

Figure 2.21 *(a) An event recorder. A pen makes a regular tick for each response. (b) A cumulative recorder. A pen moves in one direction along a slide for each response and automatically drops back to the starting position when it reaches the edge of the roll of paper.*

Small's maze embodied the principle of choice (Figure 1.18 in Chapter 1). Since Small's time, mazes for psychological experiments have become much simpler. One much-used maze is the T-maze shown at the top of Figure 2.24. The T-maze consists of a single central alley down which an animal (again usually a rat) runs until it reaches the cross of the T, where it must choose which of the two arms to run down next. This point is called the *choice point*. The two arms of the T are essentially two separate straight alleys that the rat can choose between. (Most of the devices that measure choice are, in fact, combinations of two or more rate-of-response devices.) At the choice point, the experimenter may provide the rat with a cue—for instance, a card, one side of which is painted red, and the other side green. At the ends of the arms lie two goal boxes, in which the rat may be rewarded or punished. Almost always, the events in the two goal boxes will be different. For instance, when the rat runs down the arm corresponding to the green part of the card it might be rewarded in the goal box with a

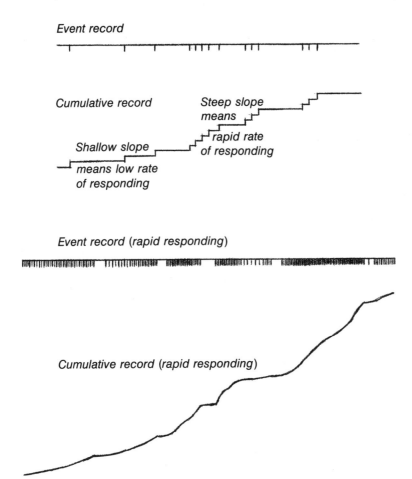

Figure 2.22 *Event records and cumulative records of responding. When responding is rapid compared to the speed of the paper and the size of the steps, the cumulative recorder draws a relatively smooth line whose slope is proportional to the rate of responding at any instant.*

pellet of food, and when it runs down the arm corresponding to the red part of the card, it might be punished in the goal box with electric shock. In this case, the experimenter would measure the number of trials required for the rat to learn always to run down the arm indicated by the color green. The green card could always be on the left, but it could also be shifted from left to right on various trials.

With a device such as the T-maze, the experimenter can measure the ability of an animal to respond differentially to various stimuli at the choice point, that is, to discriminate between two stimuli by

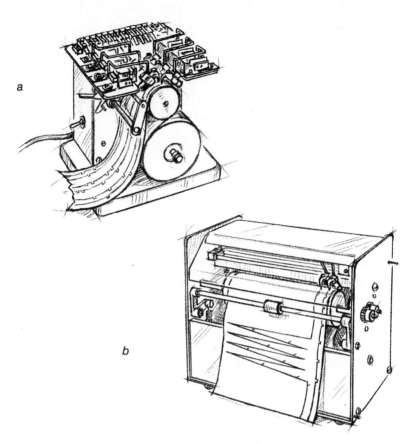

Figure 2.23 *(a) An event recorder. (b) A cumulative recorder. [Courtesy of Ralph Gerbrands Co., Arlington, Mass.]*

always running down the arm corresponding to one of them. For instance, if the rat in the above example were color blind, it might never learn to run down the arm corresponding to green. The greater the rat's ability to discriminate between the stimuli at the choice point, the more quickly it could be expected to learn always to choose the arm corresponding to the preferred reward.

The experimenter could also determine the priorities of various rewards or punishments for the rat. For instance, suppose the rat was given twice as much food in Goal Box A as in Goal Box B, but was also shocked in Goal Box A, whereas no shock was given in Goal Box B. Which would it choose? Would its choice depend on how long it had been since the rat last ate? These kinds of questions can be answered with the help of a T-maze.

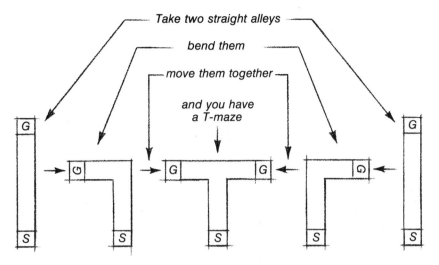

Take two straight alleys

bend them

move them together

*and you have
a T-maze*

where choice can be measured

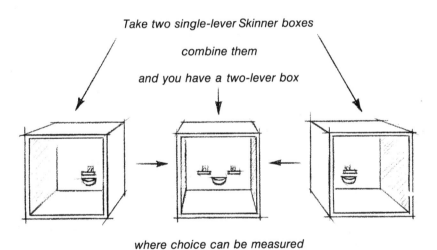

Take two single-lever Skinner boxes

combine them

and you have a two-lever box

where choice can be measured

Figure 2.24 *In principle, each of these two-choice devices combines two simpler rate-of-response devices.*

Because the T-maze measures Behavior A *relative* to Behavior B, the kind of psychological data that the T-maze produces is called a *behavior ratio*. The behavior ratio is simply the percentage of trials that the animal goes to one side or the other. (For instance, if food is in the left goal box of the T-maze while the right goal box is empty, the animal will learn to choose the left alley on 100 percent of the trials. Thus, the behavior ratio is 100 percent. If the animal were indifferent between the left and right, the behavior ratio would be 50 percent; if it always chose the right, the behavior ratio would be 0 percent with reference to the left goal box.)

A fairly obvious example of a combination of two rate-of-response devices into a single device that will measure choice is the Skinner box containing two response levers instead of one. Pressing one lever might cause food to be delivered, and pressing the other might cause water to be delivered. With one lever, the relevant measure of behavior is the rate at which the lever is pressed. With two levers, the relevant measure is again a behavior ratio. Whatever percentage of the total number of presses are made on one lever determines the behavior ratio with respect to that lever. As with the T-maze, behavior ratio varies anywhere from zero to 100 percent.

We do not know at present which is more important, absolute measures (such as latency or rate of responding), or relative measures (such as choice measured by the behavior ratio). In common experience, sometimes one and sometimes the other is the most useful. (A candidate for public office may need a certain absolute number of signatures on a nominating petition. But, in order to be elected, he needs more votes than his opponent regardless of the absolute number of votes. The techniques for obtaining nomination may, in fact, be different from those for getting elected simply because of the absolute versus relative requirements of the two endeavors.)

Another device often used to measure choice is called the Lashley jumping stand (Figure 2.25), invented by Karl Lashley around 1938. A rat is placed on the jumping stand, in front of which is a vertical wall in which two cards are inset. If the rat jumps at the correct card, the card gives way and the rat lands on another platform, where it may be fed. If the rat jumps at the wrong card, the card does not give way and the rat falls into a net. When this device is used discriminations between two given stimuli (for instance, vertical versus horizontal stripes) are learned more rapidly than with the T-maze. It is worth examining the differences between the two devices for clues as to why this should be so. There are three essential differences between the devices: (1) In the Lashley jumping stand the animal must look at the patterns to be discriminated because it must look where it is jumping. (2) With the jumping stand, reward or punishment immediately follows choice. In the T-maze, the animal must take the time to run down an arm of the maze before it reaches the consequences of its choice; on the jumping stand, it has but to jump. The principle at work here is *delay of*

Basic Procedures and Techniques

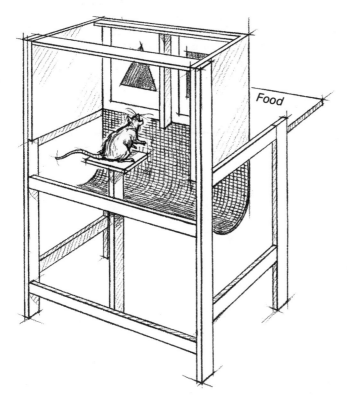

Figure 2.25 *The Lashley jumping stand.* [*After K. S. Lashley, "The mechanism of vision, XV. Preliminary studies of the rat's capacity for detailed vision."* J. of Gen. Psych., *1938,* 18, *126.*]

reward: the longer that rewards are delayed following responses, the less effective they tend to be. (3) In the jumping stand procedure, there is an immediate aversive consequence of jumping at the wrong door. There is usually no such built-in punishment for the wrong response in the T-maze. In the usual T-maze discrimination, one box contains food, the other, nothing. It is interesting to note that when rats are punished for entering the wrong goal box in a T-maze (as well as rewarded in the right goal box), they learn to discriminate more rapidly.

Bibliography

Pavlov's works have received excellent translations, are easy to read, and ought to be fully comprehensible to beginning students. I. P. Pavlov's *Conditioned Reflexes*, originally published in English in 1927 by Oxford University Press, is available as a paperback (New York: Dover, 1960). An introductory learning text with an approach similar to the one taken here is J. R. Millenson's *Principles of Behavioral Analysis* (New York: Macmillan Co., 1967). Another introduction to operant conditioning techniques, excellent within its limited area, is G. S. Reynolds's *A Primer of Operant Conditioning* (Glenview, Illinois: Scott, Foresman & Co., 1968).

A comparison of instrumental and classical conditioning can be found in G. A. Kimble's *Hilgard and Marquis' Conditioning and Learning,* Second edition (New York: Appleton-Century-Crofts, 1960). Two recent books contain much material discussed in this and subsequent chapters. One, edited by J. A. Nevin and G. S. Reynolds: *The Study of Behavior: Learning, Motivation, Emotion, and Instinct* (Glenview, Illinois: Scott, Foresman & Co., 1973), consists of a series of chapters written by different authors. The chapter on "Classical Conditioning" by H. S. Terrace is both thorough and well written. It would be a good place to look for material on this subject after reading the present volume. Another recent text is N. J. Mackintosh's *The Psychology of Animal Learning* (New York: Academic Press, 1974). This book provides an excellent up-to-date account of the issues in the field. It is detailed, but literate and fair.

A brief overview of learning theories can be found in E. R. Hilgard and G. H. Bower's *Theories of Learning* (New York: Appleton-Century-Crofts, 1975). One can start from Hilgard and Bower, but the best way to find out about a theoretical outlook is to read the original source. Here are some works by behavioral theorists:

Guthrie, E. R. *The Psychology of Learning.* Revised. New York: Harper & Row, 1952.

Hull, C. L. *A Behavior System: An Introduction to Behavior Theory Concerning the Individual Organism.* New Haven: Yale University Press, 1952.

Skinner, B. F. *The Behavior of Organisms: An Experimental Analysis.* New York: Appleton-Century-Crofts, 1938.

Tolman, E. C. *Purposive Behavior in Animals and Man.* New York: Appleton-Century-Crofts, 1932.

The experiment of Ellison and Konorski that used classical and instrumental conditioning together may be found in G. D. Ellison and J. Konorski's article "Separation of the salivary and motor responses in instrumental conditioning" [*Science, 146* (No. 3647), 1071–1072, 1964]. Konorski has also written a book about conditioning from a physiological viewpoint called *Integrative Activity of the Brain* (Chicago: University of Chicago Press, 1967).

The various items of apparatus described in the section "Methods of Measurement" are more fully described in J. B. Sidowski's *Experimental Methods and Instrumentation in Psychology* (New York: McGraw-Hill, 1966).

3

Reinforcement and Punishment

One of the principal functions of science is to make valid predictions. Astronomers predict positions of heavenly bodies; physicists predict the behavior of physical objects; chemists predict the products of various combinations of elements. Science, to be meaningful, must go beyond the explanation of events after they have happened and make predictions about future events.

Since the very heart of the conditioning process is reinforcement, psychologists have concerned themselves with predicting whether a given stimulus will reinforce a given behavior. We have been talking loosely about positive reinforcers such as food for hungry organisms or water for thirsty organisms, but we have not specified any characteristic that food and water have in common to make them reinforcing. If we knew what this characteristic was we could make true behavioral predictions; we would predict that a new stimulus with the characteristic would be reinforcing (that it would increase the probability of behavior it followed), while a new stimulus without the characteristic would not be reinforcing.

Theories of reinforcement are attempts to specify this characteristic. Let us consider a few of them.

THEORIES OF REINFORCEMENT

Four of the more influential theories of reinforcement that have emerged from the prolific speculation about the relation of reinforcement to organism are these: (1) *Need reduction.* This theory says that every reinforcer ultimately satisfies some vital need of the organism and "reduces the need" (that is, reduces the amount of the substance or thing needed) through a process of negative feedback. (2) *Tension reduction.* The tension-reduction theory says that every reinforcer ultimately lessens some tension in the organism through a process of negative feedback. (3) *Brain stimulation.* According to this theory, every reinforcer ultimately stimulates certain parts of the brain. (4) *Response as reinforcement.* This theory holds that responses are reinforced by the ability to make other responses, for example, that bar pressing is reinforced by the act of eating.

Before we discuss these four theories, we should note that each seems to contain at least a grain of truth but that none has succeeded, by itself, in accounting for all of the ways in which a response can be reinforced.

Need Reduction

Organisms need certain things to survive—food and water, for instance, oxygen to breathe, and specific temperature ranges outside of which they will perish. It is argued that all reinforcers must ultimately reduce one or the other of these physiological needs. (In other words, if the psychologist wants to know whether a certain substance is rewarding to a certain organism, it would seem that all he has to do is call up the biology department of his university and ask whether the substance satisfies a physiological need. If so, then it must be rewarding. If the biologist tells the psychologist that a platypus needs the chemicals found in bananas in order to survive, then bananas must be rewarding to the platypus.) Unfortunately, this theory is inconsistent with several well-known facts. Take the case of saccharine. There is no question that artificial sweeteners such as saccharine can be reinforcing. Rats will learn to run down the alley of a T-maze leading to a goal box with a saccharine solution in it although they have plenty of water available. Rats will learn to press a bar to receive a saccharine solution and humans will gladly put a dime in a slot to receive a cupful of carbonated water mixed with artificial flavoring and saccharine even when a water fountain is nearby. Yet, such artificial sweeteners are passed through the body virtually unchanged. This is but one of many reinforcers that do not appear to satisfy any vital need.

Tension Reduction

Another theory, one closely related to "need reduction," is that anything that immediately lessens tension of some kind in the organism is a reinforcer. Hunger, for instance, can be seen as a kind of tension that is lessened by eating. The trouble with this theory is that many things that seem to immediately increase tension are reinforcing. For instance, it may seem like cruel and unusual punishment to allow a male rat to copulate with a female and then to remove him before he has a chance to ejaculate. Nevertheless, male rats will repeatedly run down the alley of a T-maze leading to such treatment as opposed to lacking female rats altogether. Animals of all kinds will work hard at tasks which lead to no more startling reward than the sight of another animal or the opportunity to do a more complex task. For instance, monkeys will press a bar repeatedly to open a window that allows them to see activity in the laboratory. Monkeys will also solve puzzles with no reward involved other than the solution of the puzzle. It is difficult to classify all of these rewards in terms of tension reduction. If anything, presentation of some rewards seems to increase tension.

Of course, a tension-reduction theorist could argue that *immediate* tension reduction is not necessary for reinforcement. All that is necessary is *eventual* tension reduction. Then he could trace each reinforcement to its eventual tension-reducing act. But the problem with such theoretical maneuvering is that when a theory is stretched and stretched—even to cover cases like these—it becomes nebulous, does not allow us to make predictions, and does not advance our understanding a great deal.

Brain Stimulation

In 1954, two physiologists, James Olds and Peter Milner, found that rats would press a lever in order to deliver a mild electric shock to a certain area of their brain, the midbrain generally. The experiment is shown in Figure 3.1. The rat was enclosed in a cage with a lever attached to an electrical switch that sent current through a wire to certain areas of its brain. Each time the rat pressed the lever, a very mild current (of about 1/10,000 ampere) was turned on for less than half a second. Olds found that rats would press the bar thousands of times an hour for periods of 12 hours or more to receive this stimulation. Evidently the current in the rat's brain was reinforcing. This experiment led to the speculation that perhaps a common element in all rewards is an ability to stimulate certain locations in the brain. Olds called these areas "pleasure centers," reasoning that anything that stimulated them resulted in the feeling of pleasure.

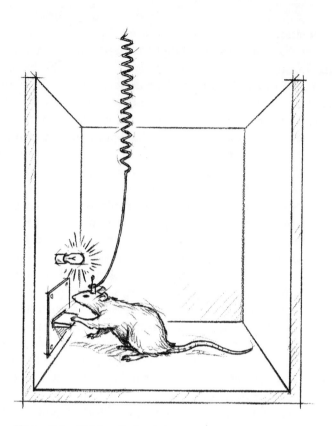

Figure 3.1 *Olds' self-stimulation experiment. [After "Pleasure Centers in the Brain," by James Olds. Copyright © 1956 by Scientific American, Inc. All rights reserved.]*

The brain is so complicated and knowledge of its functioning so vague, that we cannot tell whether any given stimulus branches to the pleasure center or not. In other words, we still have no operation that will predict what will or will not be reinforcing. While Olds' experiment seems to promise an eventual answer, it may be a long time before the promise is fulfilled.

Response as Reinforcement

Although it is convenient to call a stimulus *a reinforcer*, some psychologists argue that it would be more accurate to designate responses with this term. (Thus they might prefer to say "eating the pudding is a reinforcer" to "the pudding is a reinforcer.") This theory, that reinforcement lies in the *act* of consuming a needed substance,

Reinforcement and Punishment

rather than in the substance itself is called a *consummatory-response* theory. According to this theory, certain acts and the sensations involved in performing these acts are said to be innately reinforcing to organisms. The reason that bar-presses of a hungry rat will increase when they are followed by food is not because the bar-presses produce food but because they give the rat the opportunity to eat. Thus, *eating* and *drinking* are sources of reinforcement, as opposed to food and water themselves.

This theory, unlike the need-reduction theory, is consistent with the reinforcing powers of substances like saccharine, since the act of consuming saccharine and the sensations involved therein are the same as the act of consuming other substances that do reduce needs. While sugar and saccharine are different with respect to their *need-reducing* powers, they are similar with respect to their *consummatory response*.

Another response theory of reinforcement, proposed by the psychologist David Premack, is called the *prepotent-response* theory. This theory is similar to the consummatory-response theory in the sense that responses are said to be reinforced only by the opportunity to make other responses. It differs from the consummatory-response theory, however, because it postulates no innately reinforcing responses (like eating and drinking). Instead, any response may be reinforcing. The power of one response to reinforce another is determined only by the relative strength of the two responses, the stronger response being capable of reinforcing the weaker. Relative strength, in turn, is measured by the relative time that the organism spends performing the acts if both acts are continuously available. One of Premack's experiments illustrates the point. He allowed several children free access to candy and to pinball machines. He found that many of the children spent a greater proportion of time playing the pinball machines than eating candy. He reasoned that, for these children, playing with the machines was a stronger response than eating the candy. According to his theory a stronger response should reinforce a weaker one. When he tested this by allowing the children to play with the machines only after they had eaten a certain amount of the candy, he found that eating candy increased. In other words, playing with pinball machines reinforced eating. Note that this is a reversal of the usual situation where eating is the reinforcer and some other act is reinforced.

Two advantages of Premack's theory are (1) that it takes the relative nature of reinforcers into account. It treats reinforcement as a *relation* between behavior and its consequences rather than an absolute fact, and (2) it provides an independent measure of reinforcing power by observation of the relative time an organism is engaged in the reinforcing and to-be-reinforced acts.

The argument against both the consummatory-response theory and the prepotent-response theory is that reinforcement often can be achieved by by-passing any response. Normally, when food is used as reinforcement, the presentation of food and eating of the food go together. It is possible, however, to separate them. When food is delivered without eating, by injecting it directly into the stomach, the food is still reinforcing. Rats will learn to press a lever that results in the injection of food into their stomachs. Also, animals will learn to press a lever to get a higher proportion of oxygen to carbon dioxide in the air of a stuffy room despite the fact that more oxygen in the air causes less breathing—in other words, less responding (whether consummatory or prepotent). We must conclude, then, that animals can be rewarded in other ways than by making a response.

Premack might reply to this objection that, as opposed to all the other theories, his is not a physiological theory at all but a behavioral theory. His theory relates (a) a choice test between two responses and (b) the reinforcement paradigm (that is, the power of one response to reinforce the other). When a response is bypassed by injecting food directly into the stomach, the event is not a choice test nor does it fit into the reinforcement paradigm. If an animal presses a bar to inject milk into its stomach, the entire sequence, consisting of bar press plus milk injection, would be considered by Premack to be one consummatory response. This sequence, as a whole (because it now contains a response), fits both the choice-test model and the reinforcement paradigm vis-à-vis another response.

Which Theory Is Correct?

The above are only a few of the many theories about how positive reinforcers function. Even within the area of positive reinforcement, however, we have not been able to arrive at a simple classification. Theories help to give us insight about how to choose reinforcers in specific instances, since they are all correct up to a point, and, between them, they cover most of the reinforcers we have so far found. The point to be remembered here, though, is that none, by itself, is sufficient to account for all known reinforcers. This means that the best way to tell if a stimulus is reinforcing is to try it out in an instrumental conditioning experiment.

One consolation for the lack of a unifying principle that would enable us to predict the things that are reinforcing is the general consistency in the way reinforcers act once they are known to be reinforcing. A reinforcer for one response will generally be a reinforcer for other responses of the same organism. If you can teach your dog to give you his paw by rewarding him with a dog biscuit, you probably can also teach him to roll over with the same type of reward. But whether dog biscuits are rewarding in the first place can only be determined by trying them out.

REINFORCEMENT SCHEDULES

One of the earliest experiments relating to schedules of reinforcement was done more-or-less by accident by B. F. Skinner around 1932. In order to study the eating behavior of rats, he trained them to press a lever to receive a pellet of food and measured their rate of pressing, hence, their rate of eating, after various periods of food deprivation. One day, Skinner found that his supply of pellets was low. This inspired him to set up the apparatus so that instead of every press producing reinforcement, only one press a minute would be reinforced, no matter how many times a rat pressed the lever.

Not only did the rats keep pressing the lever but their rate of pressing was considerably higher than when every press was reinforced. This increase in rate of responding is evidence against the notion that less reinforcement would simply produce less responding. Skinner inferred that the schedule (or rule) according to which reinforcement is presented could be a powerful way to control behavior and is a worthwhile subject of study in and of itself. The name for the particular reinforcement schedule used by Skinner is a "fixed interval" schedule. Let us now consider a method for expressing the requirements of Skinner's schedule and the animal's performance with this schedule in graphic form.

Fixed-Interval Schedules

In order to diagram fixed-interval (FI) schedules of reinforcement, we construct a graph with number of presses on the vertical axis and time on the horizontal axis, as in part (a), Figure 3.2. Furthermore, we represent the conditions of reinforcement by a line on the graph. In Skinner's experiment, the requirement is that one minute elapse since

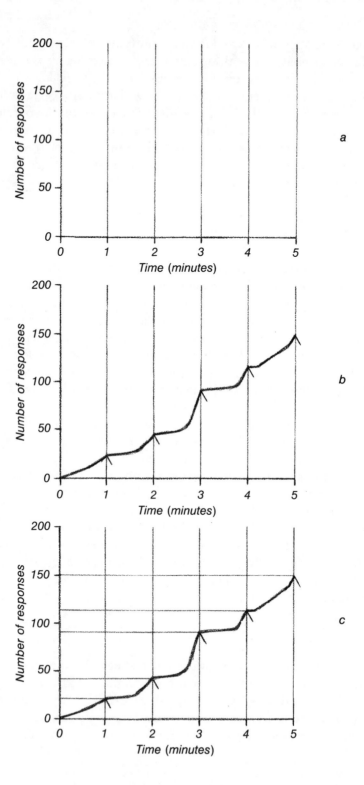

Figure 3.2 *Cumulative record of lever presses by a rat reinforced on a one-minute fixed-interval schedule. (Ticks mark reinforcements.) (a) The vertical lines mark the locus of each reinforcement; reinforcement is available once at the end of each minute no matter how many times the rat presses the lever. (b) Cumulative record of responding, showing reinforcements received by the rat. (c) Projection of the results to the vertical axis. The distances between the horizontal lines show how many responses occurred for each reinforcement.*

the last reinforcement. Assuming that the rat presses the lever often enough, one response would be reinforced every minute. This could be represented by a vertical line at each minute on the horizontal axis. Starting at the origin, then, we can draw a cumulative record, as in part (b), Figure 3.2, of the responses until they reach the required interval. Each response raises the cumulative record another step. The width of the step is the time between responses. When the first minute is reached, reinforcement is given (represented by a downward slash on the graph) after the next response and so on for the other intervals. If we project the slashes across to the vertical axis, as in Figure 3.2c, we get a picture of the number of responses between reinforcements. In a one-minute fixed-interval schedule (an FI-1' schedule) the organism has only to respond once every minute to receive the maximum reward. Any additional responses during the minute have no effect. The kind of behavior often observed with fixed-interval schedules, and shown by the cumulative records of Figure 3.2, is a pause after reinforcement and then an increase in rate of responding until a high rate is reached just as the interval is about to end. This pattern (called scalloping) is found with many organisms and many responses. (An example of human behavior which conforms to the same pattern might be the frequency with which one looks at a pot of water when one is impatient for it to boil, or the frequency with which the oven door is opened to test the turkey while a hungry family is waiting.)*

Fixed-Ratio Schedules

Another kind of schedule much studied in the laboratory is the fixed-ratio (FR) schedule. Here, the organism is rewarded only after making a certain fixed number of responses. For instance, a rat may be rewarded for every fourth press instead of for every press. Figure 3.3a shows a cumulative record of a pigeon rewarded with three seconds of

---

*Recent experiments have shown that in many fixed-interval schedules the change from pausing to rapid responding is quite sudden.

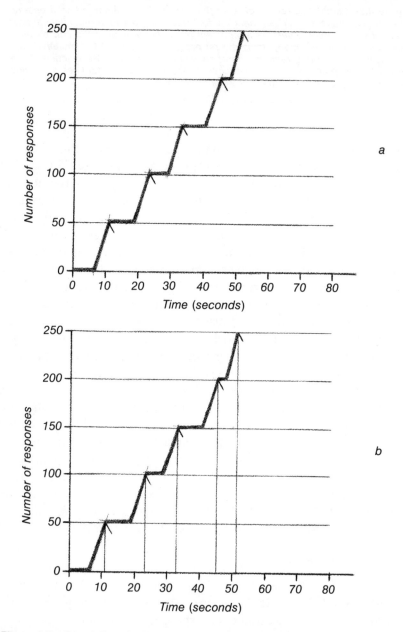

Figure 3.3 Cumulative record of pecks by a pigeon reinforced on a fixed-ratio schedule of one reinforcement for each 50 pecks. (a) Cumulative record with horizontal lines marking the locus of each reinforcement and ticks representing actual reinforcements. (b) Projection to the vertical axis, showing time between reinforcements.

access to food for every 50 pecks on an illuminated disk. (This is called an FR-50 schedule.) The lines showing the locus of reinforcement are horizontal instead of vertical, reflecting the fact that fixed numbers of responses rather than intervals of time determine the availability of reinforcement. Each response raises the cumulative record a small step. When the step is reached corresponding to the ratio, reinforcement is given; reinforcement is represented by a slash on the graph. If we project the slashes downward to the horizontal axis, as in Figure 3.3b, we get a picture of the rate of reinforcements in time. If the reinforcements are close together, they are coming rapidly; if they are far apart, they are coming slowly. Note that after each reinforcement the pigeons pause before beginning to respond again. This pattern of a rapid burst of responding which fulfills the ratio and then a pause after reinforcement is found for pigeons pecking a disk, rats pressing a lever, monkeys pressing a disk, humans tapping a telegraph key and innumerable other responses.

Compound Schedules

The basic fixed-interval and fixed-ratio schedules may be combined in various ways. In the fixed-ratio, a certain *number* of responses must appear before reinforcement occurs. In the fixed-interval, a fixed time must elapse. Suppose we specify that a fixed number of responses must occur *or* a fixed time must elapse before reinforcement. This type of schedule is diagrammed in Figure 3.4a. The patterns of behavior shown by the two cumulative records would be rewarded at points (p) and (q). Pattern (p) would be rewarded sooner, but at the cost of more responses; pattern (q) would be rewarded later, but with fewer responses.

If we were to stipulate that both the interval *and* ratio requirements must be met for reinforcement to occur we would have the situation diagrammed in Figure 3.4b. The same patterns of responding would not be reinforced at (p) or (q), where only the ratio or interval requirements are met, but at (r) or (s) where both requirements are met.

A third, and more complex kind of compound schedule is the interlocking schedule diagrammed in Figure 3.4c. For this schedule, the requirement is that a certain *sum* of responses and seconds must occur before a response can be reinforced. This schedule works on the same principle as a taximeter, which adds the time of the ride to the distance travelled to determine the fare. In the schedule, the time is added to the number of responses. When they reach a certain sum, reinforcement will be available at the next peck.

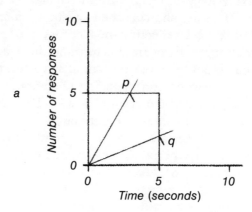

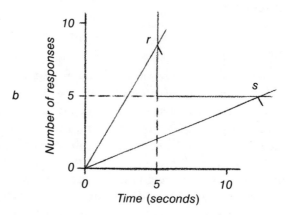

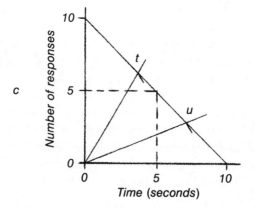

Figure 3.4 *Compound schedules of reinforcement. (a) Locus of reinforcement for 5 responses or a 5-second interval. At p, behavior is reinforced after 5 responses in less than 5 seconds. At q, behavior is reinforced after 5 seconds and fewer than 5 responses. (b) Locus of reinforcement for 5 responses plus a 5-second interval. At r, behavior is reinforced after more than 5 responses in 5 seconds. At s, behavior is reinforced after 5 responses in more than 5 seconds. (c) Locus of reinforcement for 10 responses or 10 seconds or any number of responses and seconds totalling 10. At t, behavior is rewarded for 6 responses in 4 seconds. At u, behavior is rewarded for 3 responses in 7 seconds.*

Variable Schedules

The fixed patterning of responses that occurs when fixed-interval or fixed-ratio schedules are imposed does not appear with variable-interval and variable-ratio schedules. A variable-interval (VI) schedule makes reinforcement available sometimes after short intervals and sometimes after long intervals. Figure 3.5 shows cumulative records of pigeons pecking a key for variable-interval and variable-ratio schedules of reinforcement. When we refer to a fixed-interval schedule of one minute (FI-1'), we mean that each reinforcement is made available after a one-minute interval. When we speak of a variable-interval schedule of one minute (VI-1'), we mean only that the *average* of the intervals used in that schedule is one minute.

When variable-interval and variable-ratio schedules are used, responses usually occur at a fairly constant rate. Note that the rate of responding with the variable-ratio schedule in Figure 3.5 is quite a bit faster than the rate for the variable-interval schedule. Because of the slow steady rate of responding on variable-interval schedules, these schedules are often used as baselines to gauge the effects of other variables on behavior. A rat on a variable-interval schedule, for instance, responds more rapidly after being given an injection of dexedrine, a stimulant, than after begin given an injection of pentobarbital, a depressant.

Extinction After Partial Reinforcement

We know that the withdrawal of reinforcement from an instrumental response extinguishes the response. In other words, it gradually comes to be no longer emitted. We might ask how extinction of responses that have been conditioned under various schedules of reinforcement we have discussed compares with extinction of responses conditioned under a schedule of constant reinforcement (where each response is reinforced). Our line of thinking might run as follows: The more reinforcement for a response, the stronger that response should be. The stronger a response is, the better it should resist extinction. The better

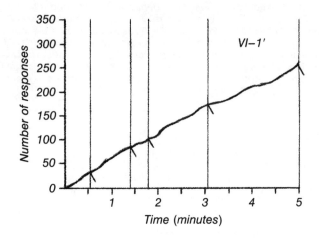

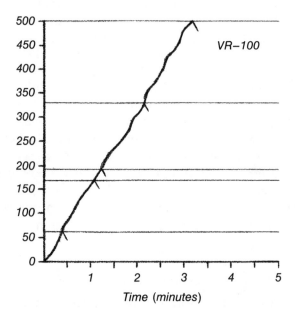

Figure 3.5 *Loci of reinforcements and cumulative records for variable-interval and variable-ratio schedules of reinforcement of a pigeon's pecking. (Ticks mark reinforcements.) VI-1': This graph shows a variable-interval schedule in which a reinforcement is available at the average rate of once per minute. VR-100: This graph shows a variable-ratio schedule in which a reinforcement is available at the average ratio of one per 100 responses.*

a response resists extinction, the more responses one should observe after reinforcement has been withdrawn. This line of reasoning seems logical, but, as a matter of fact, exactly the opposite holds true. When a response has been constantly rewarded, extinction is usually much faster than when the same response has been rewarded only part of the time. This result so surprised psychologists that they called it "Humphreys' paradox" (after Lloyd G. Humphreys, the man who first demonstrated it experimentally). Yet, this seeming paradox is a most reliable, reproducible, and significant effect.

Perhaps we can gain an insight into Humphreys' paradox from this example:

There are two hypothetical Coke machines. One, in Building A, produces a drink for every dime inserted. The other, in Building B, is partially broken. Occasionally, when a dime is inserted, nothing happens. The people in Building B complain repeatedly but ineffectually about the situation, but they seem to be willing to lose their dimes once in a while as long as they eventually get a Coke. Now, suppose both machines break down completely. Which one will receive more dimes before the dimes stop altogether? Probably the machine in Building B, which has been only partially reinforcing the "dime-inserting behavior." It will take a while before the people in Building B realize that the machine is completely inoperative. The people in Building A, on the other hand, will immediately realize that there is something wrong and stop inserting dimes.

To be more general, the Coke-machine example shows that organisms must learn to discriminate between conditions of reinforcement and conditions of extinction, and that anything that helps them to do this will speed up extinction. Partial reinforcement on some schedule is more like extinction than is constant reinforcement and, hence, harder to tell from extinction. To the extent that conditions of reinforcement resemble conditions of extinction, there will be more responses during extinction.

But when we say that an organism responds to conditions, that the conditions of extinction must be discriminated from the conditions of reinforcement, what do we mean? Simply that organisms can discriminate between general situations as well as between particular stimuli. Once more, this is the problem of molecularity versus molarity. At the beginning of this chapter we discussed the problem of categorizing an organism's behavior. Let us return to this problem and consider the following example: Two people might describe the behavior of the same man as "building a house" or as "laying bricks" depending on their point of view. One continuum upon which these descriptions could be located is that of molarity–molecularity. The molar view is broad and encompassing; the molecular view is narrow and detailed. In the same way that the experimenter (or the environment) may react to the molar or molecular behavior of the subject, so the subject may react to molar or molecular aspects of the environment. If a person moves from Alaska to Florida, he probably does not do so because it happened to snow in Alaska one day, but he might do so because it is generally snowy in Alaska. He is more likely to react to the *rate* of snowing than to an individual snowstorm. Similarly, any animal may react to the *rate* of reinforcements, or some other collective property of reinforcements rather than to each reinforcement as it occurs.

More direct evidence that the problem of extinction is actually one of discriminating between conditions of reinforcement and conditions of extinction is that, when cues are provided during extinction, the extinction process is speeded up. For instance, in a Skinner box, if the color of the illumination of the test chamber is changed when reinforcement is withdrawn, extinction is faster. Any signal that is present during extinction and not present during conditioning will speed up extinction. Another piece of evidence is the fact that extinction is faster for fixed-interval and fixed-ratio schedules than for variable-interval and variable-ratio schedules. In the fixed schedules, disruption of the pattern of regular reinforcements signals extinction; in the variable schedules, there is no pattern to disrupt.

The assumption in the original reasoning that led to Humphreys' paradox is that strong conditioning of a response would produce more responses in extinction. This assumption is based on the notion that latency of response, magnitude of response, and resistance to extinction are all measures of the same thing, namely, the "strength" of the response. Apparently responses in extinction are not exclusively determined by the "strength" of a response—but also reflect a failure to discriminate between conditions of extinction and conditions of reinforcement. Where enough cues to this discrimination are provided, there are relatively few responses after reinforcement is withdrawn.

SECONDARY REINFORCEMENT
AND CHAINS OF BEHAVIOR

It may have occurred to the reader by now that there are few human actions that are directly reinforced by primary reinforcers such as food. "Man does not live by bread alone," the saying goes. But then, what *does* he live by? At the risk of impiety, behaviorists must answer: Man lives largely by *secondary reinforcers.*

The idea of a secondary reinforcer is really quite simple and is based on common sense. In classical conditioning, a neutral stimulus (which becomes the CS) is always followed by primary reinforcement. In instrumental conditioning a neutral stimulus will always be followed by primary reinforcement, provided the correct response is made in its presence. Thus from the subject's point of view it is sufficient to obtain the neutral stimulus in order to be sure of eventual primary reinforcement. If a child is fed (primary reinforcement) whenever he is seated in a certain chair (the neutral stimulus) he will soon learn to climb into the chair when he is hungry and will direct his efforts to sitting in the chair. To a visitor who did not know that the child was fed in that chair it would seem as if the chair itself was reinforcing. The visitor would see the child strain to climb into it and cry until he was placed in it. In this sense, the chair is a secondary reinforcer. (If the child's mother eventually stopped feeding him there, the chair would lose its secondary reinforcing properties.)

Secondary reinforcement bridges the gap between laboratory procedures and complex human and animal behavior. It is a process by which things and events that formerly did not reinforce behavior can become apparently reinforcing. A newborn baby's rewards are easy to enumerate: milk, a change of diapers, and a certain amount of fondling by its parents. As the baby grows up, the list of things that he will work to produce may be enlarged to include praise, money, fame, achievement, and so forth. A dollar bill may not be as rewarding to a baby as a shiny dime. As he grows older, though, the dirty green piece of paper may become relatively more sought after. It is reasonable to explain this change as a case of secondary reinforcement—the dollar has become linked to other reinforcements.

Wolfe's Experiment

An illuminating study of how secondary reinforcement becomes effective was done by John B. Wolfe in 1936. Chimpanzees, like babies, are initially quite indifferent to money, but Wolfe showed how money could come to reinforce behavior. The "money" used by Wolfe in his experiment consisted of poker chips. In a corner of the chimpanzees' cage, there was a vending machine that provided a grape every time the chimpanzees inserted a poker chip. After the chimpanzees learned to put a chip in the slot for the grape, Wolfe found that he could teach them to do other tasks, such as pressing a lever, or pulling on a string in

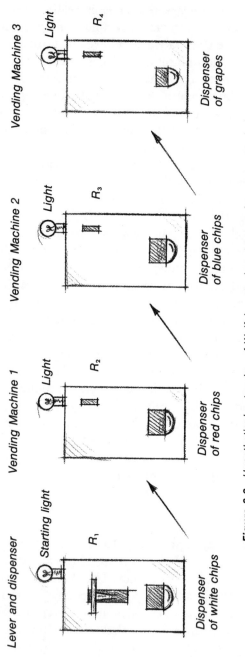

Figure 3.6 Hypothetical extension of Wolfe's experiment to produce an extended chain of behavior. The light on the dispenser at left signals a chimpanzee that a white chip is available. The chimp responds (first response, R_1) by pulling a lever. The light on Vending Machine 1 signals the availability of a red chip. The chimp now responds (R_2) by inserting the white chip in Machine 1. When the light on Vending Machine 2 comes on, he responds (R_3) by inserting the red chip in the machine. He receives a blue chip that may then be inserted (R_4) in Vending Machine 3 when its light signals that a grape is available.

order to receive poker chips. Thus, the poker chips, to which the chimpanzees were initially indifferent, took on the properties of reinforcement. In fact, even when the vending machine was not present, the chimpanzees would continue to work to accumulate chips that they could use to operate the machine later.

One can think of various ways of extending Wolfe's experiment. Suppose the vending machine only produced a grape if a blue chip was inserted. We could install another vending machine that would produce blue chips—but only if a red chip were inserted. We could install still another machine that would produce red chips if white chips were inserted. It is likely that the chimpanzees could then learn still another task to get the white chips. By such means highly complex instrumental behaviors are established.

The entire sequence, starting with the response that earns the white chip and ending with the response that earns the grape, is called a *chain of behavior*. We could reinforce each response in the chain only under certain specified conditions. For instance, the vending machines could be made inoperative except when a light is on above the slot. Then the chimpanzees would have to insert chips in slots only when the light is on above them. Figure 3.6 is a diagram of such conditions. While this particular chain is discontinuous, with each step clearly signaled by a specific stimulus and clearly delineated from the step before, chains of behavior may become quite continuous. (For instance, the sequence of movements involved in playing the piano eventually take on a continuous quality.)

The important rule in establishing chains is to start with the last response—the one that is rewarded with primary reinforcement. Wolfe *first* taught his chimps to put a token in the slot for the grape and *then* taught them to work for the tokens. If you want to teach a dog to fetch your slippers and drop them in front of you, *first* teach him to drop the slippers and *then* teach him to fetch them.

Extinction of Chains of Behavior

If the final primary reinforcement is eliminated from the chain, the entire chain of behavior will often disintegrate and eventually cease to occur. But what happens if the chain is interrupted in the middle? In other words, what happens if one of the secondary reinforcements is eliminated? In Figure 3.6 suppose that the lever and Vending Machine 1 remained operative but that Vending Machine 2 got clogged so that even when its light went on, depositing a red chip produced nothing but the loss of the chip. Our own experience in such situations tells us that the chimpanzee, after hitting the machine or shaking it or sticking his finger as far into the slot as it will go, will eventually stop depositing red chips. Soon after, he will stop operating the lever to produce the white chips. In other words, all behavior leading to the point at which the chain is broken will be extinguished. But what about the behavior after the point at which the chain is broken? This, generally, will remain intact. If, after the above extinction process were carried out, we gave the chimpanzee a red chip he would probably reject it. But, if we gave him a blue chip, he would be likely to operate Vending Machine 3 with it, showing that his behavior after the point of the interruption of the chain was not extinguished.

Do Secondary Reinforcers Acquire the Properties of Primary Reinforcers?

We implied that in the case of the child who cries to be put in his chair, the chair serves as a substitute for food and that it thereby takes on reinforcing properties. It is time now to examine this implication more closely.

We have to be careful before we attribute the properties of primary reinforcers to secondary reinforcers. In general, secondary reinforcers (reinforcers that have attained their power to strengthen the behavior that produces them because they, in turn, lead to primary reinforcement) will lose this power gradually if the primary reinforcer is withdrawn. The child's chair in our example is like a promissory note for food. As long as the promise is eventually fulfilled, or as long as it is fulfilled in a reasonable percentage of the cases, the chair will be sought after as if it were primary. However, if the child is no longer fed in the chair, his pleas to be put in the chair will eventually be extinguished. Similarly, we will drop only so many dimes into a broken Coke machine before we give up.

As a further illustration, let us suppose that there are two hotels identical in all respects except for one thing. In Hotel A each meal is invariably preceded by a dinner bell. In Hotel B the same meals are served, each preceded by a dinner bell, but the man who rings the dinner bell overdoes his job and frequently rings the bell between meals as well as before each meal. In both hotels the same meals are served, but in Hotel B there are many more dinner bells. Given experience with both hotels, which hotel do people prefer? Surely Hotel A. Meals are primary reinforcers for people, and since each meal in both hotels is always preceded by a dinner bell, dinner bells must be secondary reinforcers. In Hotel A there are fewer of these secondary

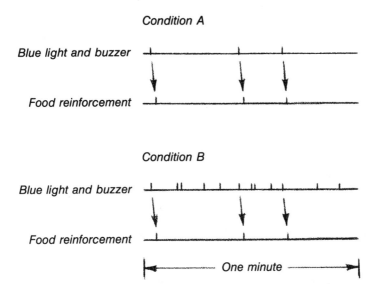

Figure 3.7 *Examples of the two conditions between which pigeons chose in Schuster's experiment. (All reinforcements are shown by ticks.) Condition A = each reinforcement preceded by a secondary reinforcement. Condition B = each reinforcement preceded by a secondary reinforcement plus extra secondary reinforcements.*

reinforcers than in Hotel B. While it is reasonable to assume that in Hotel B people spend more time walking toward the dining room, one might expect people to prefer Hotel A where dinner bells reliably precede meals. In other words, one might expect that secondary reinforcement (dinner bells) is reinforcing in this case only insofar as it is followed by primary reinforcement (meals).

A recent experiment by Richard Schuster with pigeons parallels the situation of the two hotels.

Schuster allowed his pigeons to choose between a few minutes of exposure to either of the following two conditions:

A. A condition where pecking a key occasionally (on a variable-interval schedule) produced a blue light and buzzer followed by food (corresponding to Hotel A).
B. A condition identical to the first (where pecking produced the blue light and buzzer followed by food) except that, in addition, pecking sometimes produced extra pairs of blue lights and buzzers that were not followed by food (corresponding to Hotel B).

Figure 3.7 illustrates the choice the pigeons were required to make.

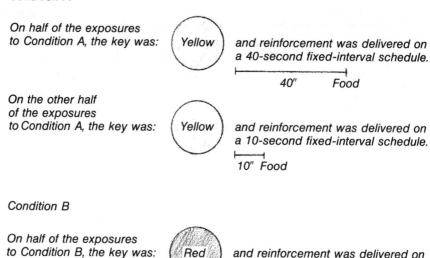

Condition A

On half of the exposures
to Condition A, the key was: Yellow and reinforcement was delivered on
a 40-second fixed-interval schedule.

40″   Food

On the other half
of the exposures
to Condition A, the key was: Yellow and reinforcement was delivered on
a 10-second fixed-interval schedule.

10″ Food

Condition B

On half of the exposures
to Condition B, the key was: Red and reinforcement was delivered on
a 40-second fixed-interval schedule.

40″   Food

On the other half
of the exposures
to Condition B, the key was: Green and reinforcement was delivered on
a 10-second fixed-interval schedule.

10″ Food

Figure 3.8 *Bower, McLean, and Meacham's experiment on the value of knowing when reinforcement is due. Pigeons chose between Conditions A and B.*

Suppose, on a given exposure to Condition A for one minute the pigeon pecked the key 60 times, and three of those pecks were followed by a blue light and a buzzer, followed in turn by reinforcement. Thus, there were three primary reinforcements each preceded by a secondary reinforcement. Suppose on a given exposure to Condition B for one minute, the pigeon also pecked the key 60 times. In Condition B suppose fifteen of the pecks produced a blue light and buzzer, but only on three occasions were the blue light and buzzer followed by food. Thus, there were again three primary reinforcements, each preceded by a secondary reinforcement, but there were twelve extra secondary reinforcements.

Schuster reasoned that if the buzzer and blue light had the properties of primary reinforcers, the pigeons should prefer Condition B, in which there were more of them, but if they were only reinforcing to the extent that they signaled, or promised, food, the pigeons should be indifferent or actually prefer Condition A, where the promise was more reliably fulfilled. Schuster found that although the pigeons pecked more during Condition B, they preferred Condition A (when they were given the opportunity to choose between the two conditions), indicating that the buzzer and light were only reinforcing to the extent that they reliably indicated that food was to come.

One useful way to characterize secondary reinforcers is not in terms of some reinforcement value that they acquire by association with primary reinforcers, but in terms of their power to give the subject information about the coming of a primary reinforcer. We may talk figuratively here about "promissory notes," "cues" and "signals," but there is a more exact way of specifying how much information a certain event in the environment conveys to a subject—that is, in terms of the degree to which that event reduces uncertainty.

There is some evidence that organisms prefer situations where uncertainty about reinforcement is low to situations where uncertainty is high even though the two situations involve the same reinforcement. (Schuster's experiment is one instance.) A study by Gordon H. Bower, Jim McLean, and Jack Meacham was called, "The value of knowing when reinforcement is due." They had pigeons choose between two identical reinforcing conditions. Their experiment is illustrated in Figure 3.8. In Condition A reinforcement was delivered on one of two fixed-interval schedules, a fixed-interval 10-second (FI-10") schedule or a fixed-interval 40-second (FI-40") schedule. Which of these schedules was in effect was determined randomly. The key was yellow during both schedules and there was no signal to indicate which of the two FI schedules was in effect. In Condition B reinforcement was also delivered on one of two fixed-interval schedules, and which of these two schedules was in effect was also determined randomly. However, if the pigeons chose Condition B, the key turned red when the FI-40" schedule was in effect and green when the FI-10" schedule was in effect.* The experimenters argued that the pigeons were choosing between an informative and a noninformative situation. Condition A provides no information about the schedule in effect while Condition B provides information. In other respects the two conditions are identical. The pigeons showed a strong preference for Condition B, the one with more information about reinforcement.

It is to the extent that secondary reinforcers convey information about reward that they, themselves, can be reinforcing.

---

*Choice in the Bower, McLean, and Meacham experiment (and in Schuster's experiment) was measured by pecking during still another condition when two responses were available, one leading to Condition A and the other to Condition B.

DELAY OF REINFORCEMENT

What happens when the temporal relation between response and reinforcement is varied so that reinforcement is delayed? The answer is that in almost all cases a delayed reinforcement is worth less than immediate reinforcement during acquisition of a habit. Let us first consider the power of delayed reinforcement to strengthen an individual response. Then we will consider choice between long and short delays of reinforcement.

Learning With Delayed Reinforcement

The main problem for an experimenter is to define experimentally the delay interval and its attributes. He must decide what sort of thing he wants to happen during the delay period. One point of view says that nothing at all should happen during the delay. But, if nothing happened, if in a strict sense all motion of any kind were suspended and all processes halted, then by definition delay could have no effect. Any effect it would have must be the result of some process (be it "forgetting" or "interference by other responses") during the delay period. In other words, to say that nothing must happen during the delay period is to say that the delay period can have no effect. It is as if you were instantly to freeze the universe in its motion for the delay period and then allow it to move again when the delay was over.

Another alternative would be to allow many events of all kinds during the delay period. For instance let us go back to the chain of responses illustrated in Figure 3.6. Suppose we consider the first response in the chain, pressing the lever to receive a white chip, as a response which is ultimately reinforced by the grape delivered at the end of the chain. The other responses, the placing of the various chips in the slots, would be merely ways of filling up the delay period between the lever press and the reinforcement. One criticism that has been made of this kind of experiment is that there really would be no delay of reinforcement even for responses at the beginning of the chain. The various poker chips would serve as secondary reinforcers which could effectively signal the coming of the food. Since poker chips had been repeatedly associated with food, the chimpanzee's behavior would be reinforced as much by the sight of the poker chips as it would have been by the sight of the food. The chimpanzee in this situation is much like the television quiz show winner who is presented with a check instead of prizes. Although the check is only a piece of paper, the recipient is as rewarded as the person who receives a refrigerator or television set because he will be able to cash the check and get the prizes in the future. In terms of information theory, we may say that the poker chip reduces uncertainty about whether food will be presented. Even should we cause a delay between acquisition of the poker chip and its insertion in the machine, the chimpanzee still has the poker chip (the promissory note) in his hand during the delay period. When Wolfe did cause such a delay (Figure 3.9b) the chimpanzees responded just as fast to get poker chips as when there was no delay. However, when Wolfe caused a delay between insertion of the poker chip and delivery of the food (Figure 3.9c), when the chimpanzee has to wait during the delay period with no poker chip in his hand, responding for poker chips fell off sharply.

Experimenters have tried to eliminate secondary reinforcement from delay-of-reinforcement experiments. G. Robert Grice (1948) provided food to rats in a device similar to a T-maze. The floor of one arm was white and the floor of the other arm was black. The arms were reversed occasionally so that the white and black arms were not consistently associated with the left and right sides. After running down either arm, the rats were kept in one of a pair of identical grey delay boxes for periods which varied for different groups of rats. Then they were allowed into a goal box. If they had originally run down the white arm, they were then fed in the goal box. If they had originally run down the black arm, they were not fed. Figure 3.10 is a diagram of Grice's experiment. When there was no delay, the rats learned fairly easily to go in the direction corresponding to the white arm. However, when the delay was longer than five seconds, none of the rats in the delay group could learn to run consistently down the white arm to food.

Like the chimps in Wolfe's experiment (Figure 3.9c), the rats in Grice's experiment (Figure 3.10b) had nothing during the delay period that signaled reinforcement to come. When Grice provided one delay box following a choice of white and another, distinctly different box following a choice of black (Figure 3.10c), the performance of the rats improved considerably, even with longer delays than the original five seconds.

The reason the rats in the conditions of Figure 3.10b did not learn the maze is that no stimulus in the grey delay box was reliably correlated with either alley. An organism could, however, provide such correlated stimuli by its own actions.

A human child in similar circumstances to those shown in Figure 3.10b might learn to put his hands in his pockets whenever he turned in the direction of a white passageway and keep them there until he

Normal sequence

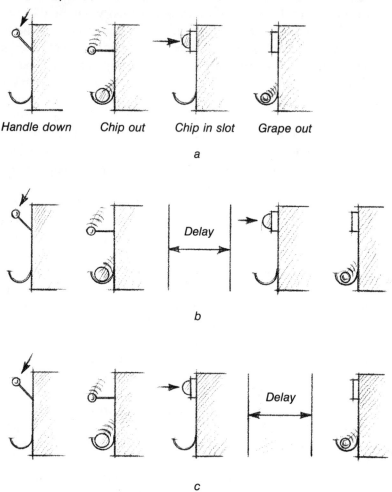

Handle down   Chip out   Chip in slot   Grape out

a

b

c

Figure 3.9 *How the point of delay affected lever pressing in Wolfe's experiment. (a) Normal sequence without a period of delay. (b) Delay between collecting chip and inserting it in slot. In this sequence, the chimp has the chip during the delay, and the delay does not slow down the chimp's lever pressing. (c) Delay between placing poker chip in slot and collecting grape. In this sequence, the chimp has no chip during the delay, and the delay does slow down lever pressing.*

was finally permitted to enter the goal room. Correspondingly, he could put his hands on his head whenever he turned down the black passageway and keep them there until he entered the goal room. He would soon learn that he was rewarded whenever he had his hands in

Reinforcement and Punishment

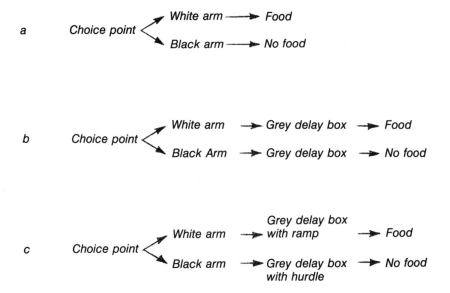

Figure 3.10 *Grice's experiment. (a) No-delay group, which learned to go to the white arm. (b) Delay group, which could not learn to go to the white arm when delayed longer than 5 seconds. (c) Secondary-reinforcement group, which learned to go to the white arm.*

his pockets and unrewarded whenever he had his hands on his head. This mediating response would serve to connect the situation at the choice point with that in the goal room and enable him to make the correct response easily. In other words, he could provide differential cues for himself like those Grice provided for some of his rats (Figure 3.10c).

Most of the mediating responses that humans use to bridge gaps between response and reinforcement are verbal. Instead of putting our hands in our pockets or on our heads we would probably solve the problem by saying to ourselves "I'll go to the white side now" or "I'll go to the side opposite to the white now." If, when reinforcement came, we had been saying some such phrase, we would be likely to remember what we were saying the next time we reach the choice point and use the phrase to guide our choice behavior. The use of repeated verbal responses is a common technique for bridging gaps in time. The shopping list repeated over and over again by a child as he walks to the store or the phone number repeated over and over again between the telephone book where we have looked it up and the telephone where we dial it are examples.

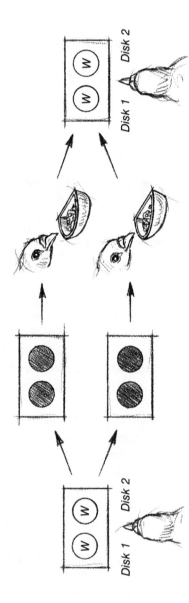

Pecks on Disk 1 occasionally produced a blackout of 8 seconds, (VI–I' schedule)

followed by 3 seconds access to grain reinforcement

followed by a return to the initial conditions

Disk 1   Disk 2

Pecks on Disk 2 occasionally produced a blackout of X seconds, (VI–I' schedule)

followed by 3 seconds access to grain reinforcement

followed by a return to the initial conditions

Figure 3.11 Diagram showing the procedure used by Chung and Herrnstein to study delay. Pigeons could peck at either or both illuminated disks.

Choice Between Short and Long Delays

The choice in the Grice experiment was between a delayed reinforcement and no reinforcement at all. Grice was interested in whether an animal could learn to make a response when reinforcement was delayed. Another question we might ask is: After a response is learned, to what extent is a short delay of reinforcement preferred over a long delay of reinforcement? In this case, we are interested not in the acquisition of a response, but in the choice between two conditions of reinforcement. The difference between the two questions is like the difference between the questions: (1) To what extent is it easier to learn to drive a car with automatic than manual shift? and (2) After learning both automatic and manual driving, which is preferred, and how much is it preferred? We have just discussed the first kind of question, and we found that it is easier to learn a task when the reinforcement is immediate than when it is delayed.

The second kind of question was asked by Shin Ho Chung and Richard Herrnstein (1967). These experimenters studied the pecking of pigeons in a box containing two disks, both illuminated with white light. Figure 3.11 illustrates the procedure. When the pigeons pecked on either of these disks (Disk 1 or Disk 2) they were rewarded on a one-minute variable-interval (VI-1') schedule. That is, on the average of once a minute a peck on either disk would produce three seconds of access to grain. If the pigeons pecked at both disks, they would receive an overall average of reinforcement every 30 seconds (once a minute from each of two disks). A pigeon pecking at two disks is somewhat like a farmer who has two chickens who each lay an egg every 24 hours on the average. The farmer will collect from his two chickens an average of two eggs a day.

The significant aspect of Chung and Herrnstein's experiment is that the peck that produced reinforcement was not followed immediately by reinforcement. Instead, all illumination in the box was turned off. Illumination was restored and reinforcement was presented to the pigeons after a period of delay. For Disk 1, this delay period was always eight seconds. For Disk 2, this delay period varied between 1 second and 30 seconds. Sometimes then the delay was longer for Disk 1 than for Disk 2 (when the Disk 2 delay was 1 second) and sometimes the delay was longer for Disk 2 than for Disk 1 (when the Disk 2 delay was 30 seconds). Under these conditions, all of the pigeons pecked at both disks. The question asked by Chung and Herrnstein was: What percentage of the total pecks were made on each disk as the delay of reinforcement for pecking on Disk 2 varied? (i.e., What was the behavior ratio?) The answer is that the pigeons always pecked more

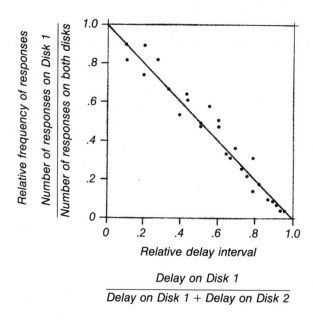

Relative frequency of responses

Number of responses on Disk 1

Number of responses on both disks

Relative delay interval

$$\frac{\text{Delay on Disk 1}}{\text{Delay on Disk 1} + \text{Delay on Disk 2}}$$

Figure 3.12 *Proportion of pecks on Disk 1 as a function of the relative delay on that disk.* [*From S. H. Chung and R. J. Herrnstein, "Choice and delay of reinforcement."* J. Exp. Analysis Behavior, *1967, 10, 69.*]

frequently on whichever disk represented shorter delays of reward. The curve of Figure 3.12 is a quantitative expression of the degree of preference for shorter delays. The 45° straight line drawn through the points shows that the relative frequency of responding on Disk 1 is inversely proportional to the relative delay on that disk. In other words, pigeons will always choose to get their food sooner than later, and the degree of their choice is proportional to how much sooner. If Disk 1 delivers food twice as soon as Disk 2, then Disk 1 will be pecked twice as often as Disk 2.

The purpose of this discussion of delay of reinforcement has been to provide an example of the kinds of questions that one can ask regarding the major variables that in combination determine the character of reinforcement. It represents only one part of the study of one such parameter, delay of reinforcement. Similar kinds of investigations have been made into such parameters as rate of reinforcement, and amount of reinforcement, and the degree to which presentation of reinforcement depends on occurrence of a response.

We have not nearly exhausted the kinds of questions that can be asked about delay of reinforcement alone. We have simply asked whether a response could be learned as well when reinforcement is delayed as when reinforcement is immediate. The answer is: No. We have also asked to what extent short delays are preferred to long delays. The answer is that preference varies directly in proportion to the relative shortness of delay. We could have asked: What effect does delay have on rate of responding, or on extinction of a response? How does delay interact with rate or amount of reinforcement?

Note that we have not asked how delay of reinforcement affects the strength of a response. As Humphreys' paradox revealed, "response strength" is an ambiguous notion. (See the third paragraph on page 118.) After all, we could argue that immediately reinforced responses are "stronger" than others because organisms quickly learn to recognize immediate rewards and prefer them to delayed rewards. However, we could also argue that responses that are acquired when rewards are delayed and only loosely correlated with responses (as is true of pushing buttons for elevators) are, in another sense, "stronger" because they are far more difficult to eradicate.

PUNISHMENT AND NEGATIVE REINFORCEMENT

So far, in our discussion of reinforcement, we have been dealing mostly with positive reinforcers, stimuli or objects that most organisms will approach, such as food, water, and sexual partners. These are shown in the top two boxes of Figure 2.10 where the types of instrumental conditioning are diagrammed. The bottom boxes of the figure show processes using aversive stimuli, stimuli which most organisms will escape from or avoid. Control of behavior with such aversive stimuli can be just as effective as control with positive stimuli. If we spend less time on aversive control it is because we have already covered basic principles applicable to both aversive and positive control, not because aversive control is unimportant.

Before we begin a discussion of experimental findings, let us repeat a few definitions made earlier. Figure 3.13 shows in a highly diagrammatic form a particular way of looking at the behavior of an animal in a laboratory situation. Suppose the animal is a rat in a Skinner box with a lever. The entire large circle represents all the behavior of which the rat is capable: scratching, biting, jumping, and so forth. The small white circle within the large one represents a particular portion of the total—presses of the lever. This portion is what we have previously defined as an operant—it represents, small as its area in the diagram is, a class of still smaller kinds of behavior, all of which somehow depress

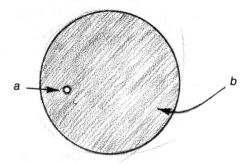

Figure 3.13 *Specific and nonspecific definitions of behavior. (a) A specific behavior, like pressing a lever. (b) All other potential behavior.*

the lever. If pressing the lever is followed by aversive stimulation the process is called punishment. If anything the animal does *except* pressing the lever is followed by aversive stimulation, the process is called negative reinforcement. For example, referring to Figure 3.13, if we shocked the rat for behavior included in the small white circle (after each lever press), we would be punishing the lever-pressing behavior. If we shocked the rat for all behavior included in the large grey part of the circle (that is, *except* after a lever press), we would be negatively reinforcing the lever press. Punishment will tend to decrease the rate of lever pressing and negative reinforcement to increase it. According to common usage, when we refer to positive reinforcement, we frequently just say "reinforcement" while when we refer to negative reinforcement we always say "negative reinforcement." (A similar convention exists with respect to positive and negative numbers. We often say "three" for "plus three" but we always say "minus three.") If we shocked the rat for all behavior in the big circle including that in the small circle, we would be delivering shock independently of the behavior of the rat.

The problem of defining an aversive stimulus is symmetrical to the problem of defining the nature of positive reinforcement, and the attempted solutions have also been symmetrical. Just as there is a need-reduction theory of positive reinforcement, there is a need-increase theory of aversive stimulation. Just as there are response theories of positive reinforcement, there are response theories of aversive stimulation. Defining aversive stimuli as "painful" and positive reinforcers as "pleasurable" does not help. Such definitions suffer from the same drawbacks as other mentalistic concepts, they give us no guidelines to tell what is painful or pleasurable to another organism.

It would be pointless to trace through a series of "aversive-stimulation theories" because our conclusion would be symmetrical to the one we reached about positive reinforcement: There is no unifying principle that would enable us to predict the things that are aversive. Our consolation, however, is also the same; a stimulus that proves to be aversive in one situation will generally be aversive in others. If beating a dog with a rolled-up newspaper is an effective punishment for defecating in the house, chances are it will also be effective punishment for jumping on the laps of guests. If electric-shock punishment reduces the rate of bar pressing in rats, it will also reduce the rate of wheel-running.

Punishment

Just as positive reinforcement tends to increase the rate at which a behavior is emitted, punishment tends to decrease the rate. Figure 3.14a shows a cumulative record of the lever-presses of a rat in a Skinner box where lever-presses have no effect. The low slope of the line means that the rat occasionally presses the lever, even with no positive reinforcement, but the rate of pressing is very low. Figure 3.14b shows a cumulative record of presses that are *positively* reinforced according to a variable-interval schedule. The steep slope of the line shows that the rate of pressing is much more rapid for positive reinforcement than for no reinforcement at all. Figure 3.14c shows cumulative records when lever-presses are rewarded *and* punished. In this case, the punishment was a brief electric shock following each press. The particular intensity of punishment used caused a slow-down, or suppression, of the rate of pressing shown by a slope intermediate between the rate of pressing for reward only, and the rate of pressing for neither reward nor punishment. The amount of suppression depends on the intensity of punishment. Figure 3.15 shows how the intensity of punishment determines the suppression in the rate at which pigeons peck a key. At higher intensities of shock, the rate of responding can be suppressed to zero.

Is Punishment a Form of Instrumental Conditioning?

In the last chapter, we discussed pseudoconditioning. We introduced pseudoconditioning in instrumental conditioning experiments with the hypothetical example of itching powder as a reinforcer for bar pressing in a rat. The test of itching powder as a pseudoreinforcer is whether the same increases in bar pressing occur when the injection of

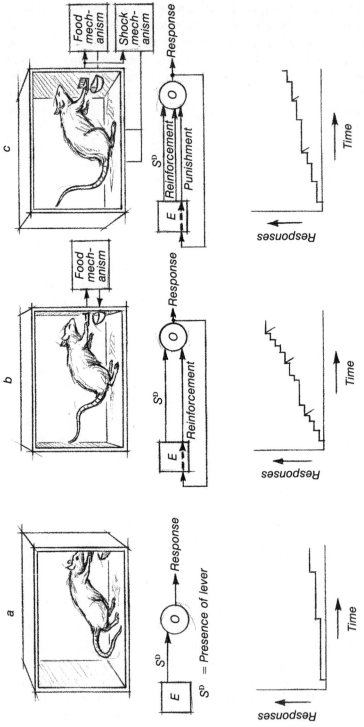

Figure 3.14 The effect of punishment on a rat's rate of bar pressing for food. (Ticks in cumulative records, at bottom, mark reinforced responses.) (a) Lever presses have no effect on reinforcement. (b) Lever presses are positively reinforced on a VI-1' schedule. (c) Lever presses are positively reinforced on a VI-1' schedule, and each press is punished with an electric shock.

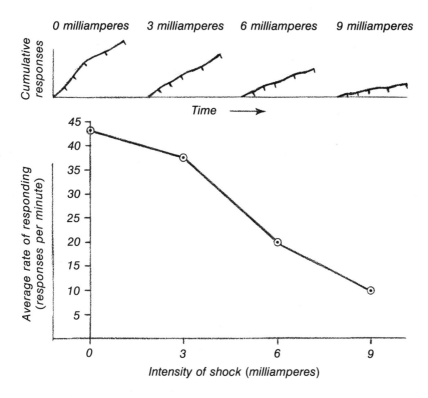

Figure 3.15 *The effect of punishment on the rate of key pecking in pigeons. Top,* cumulative records of pigeons pecking a key for reinforcement on a VI-1' schedule. (Ticks mark reinforcements.) *The graph at left shows a no-shock condition; the second graph shows the effect of a 3-milliampere shock; the third graph shows the effect of a 6-milliampere shock; the fourth graph shows the effect of a 9-milliampere shock.* At bottom, *a function showing that the rate of responding decreased as the intensity of the electric shock increased.*

itching powder is dependent on, and independent of, a bar-press. If the powder causes just as many bar-presses when it is delivered randomly as when it follows each bar-press, then we do not have a case of instrumental conditioning.

It is also possible that the process of punishment may not be a form of instrumental conditioning. With positive reinforcement we are trying to train the animal to *do* something. With punishment we are trying to train the animal *not* to do something. When a hungry animal is presented with food, the behavior that one observes is eating. In order to get the animal to perform some act other than eating (like pressing a bar), the food must be made dependent on the bar-press. When an animal is shocked, the behavior that one observes is jumping or running, or freezing in position, but *not* bar pressing. In other words, shock can itself produce "nonperformance" of bar pressing, the very effect we are trying to condition. In order to get the animal to *stop* pressing a bar, all one needs to do is shock the animal. But we said previously that true instrumental conditioning must involve a *relation* between responding and its consequences, not simple presentation of those consequences. It is at least conceivable that to reduce responding there may be no need to shock the animal in any relation to its responses.

The question then becomes: Will aversive stimulation delivered independently of responding suppress behavior as much as aversive stimulation delivered only when a response is made? If it does, then punishment does not have the properties of instrumental conditioning. If it does not—if aversive stimulation must follow responding to have its maximum effect—then punishment does have the properties of instrumental conditioning. Many experiments have been performed to answer this question, and their answer has been almost unanimous—aversive stimulation delivered independently of responding has some suppressive effect to be sure, but nowhere near as much as when it follows immediately after each response. To the extent that there is a difference, then, between the effects of response-produced aversive stimulation and response-independent aversive stimulation, punishment is a form of instrumental conditioning.

Curve B in Figure 3.16 shows rate at which a pigeon pecked a key where pecks were reinforced with food on a one-minute variable-interval schedule, and inescapable shocks were delivered twice per second. As the intensity of shock increased, the rate of pecking decreased slightly. Curve A in Figure 3.16 is a repetition of Figure 3.15, showing the rate at which another pigeon pecked a key when pecks were reinforced with food on the same schedule but shock was delivered only when the pigeon pecked the key. As the intensity of shock increased, the rate of pecking decreased drastically. The difference in the slopes of these two curves shows the instrumental effect of shock.

What implications can we draw from these empirical findings with regard to human behavior? Does it mean that our grandfathers were right when they said "Spare the rod and spoil the child"? Is modern child-rearing, with its deemphasis on punishment, all wrong? Not necessarily. There is no question that punishment works—the trouble with punishment may be not that it doesn't work but that it works only too well. A single intense shock to a pigeon following a peck on a key can suppress key pecking permanently without disturbing other behavior. If we severely punish a child for "being fresh" we must ask

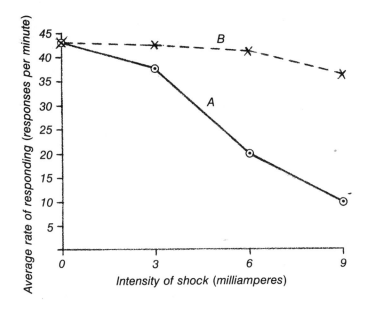

Figure 3.16 *Curve A is repeated from the bottom portion of Figure 3.15, showing the rate of response as punishment increases. Curve B shows the rate of response under the same conditions of reinforcement but with the shocks delivered independently of the responses. The rate of delivery of the independent shocks was 120 per minute.*

ourselves whether we want to suppress his outspokenness completely and permanently. Another implication to be drawn from this research is that random presentation of aversive stimulation has little positive effect. Consider the mother who is constantly spanking, shaking or slapping her child for reasons that are only tenuously related to his specific acts. She will never understand why he is so naughty despite her constant attempts at discipline. If a child is to be spanked, he should be spanked immediately after the offense. Otherwise, any acts performed between the offense and the spanking are liable to be suppressed along with or instead of the act the mother intends to suppress. If a child is innocently reaching for a lollypop at the moment it occurs to his mother that he ought to be punished for something he did an hour before, and she suddenly slaps his hand, it may be a long time before he again reaches for a lollypop.

Furthermore, one must be certain that "the punishment fits the crime." The classic example of an inappropriate punishment is spanking a child for crying. The spanking generates still more crying, which, in turn, is punished by still more spanking, and so on, until the child or the parent becomes exhausted. (Such "vicious circles" indeed may be responsible for some otherwise inexplicable cases of child abuse by parents.)

In general, with regard to both reward and punishment, the more specific and discrete the response, the more likely it is that reward and punishment will work. Punishment of a child for "being a bad boy that day" or reward for "being a good boy that day" will be much less effective than an immediate punishment for carelessly breaking a vase or an immediate reward for saying "please." When you want a specific response from a fellow organism, it is far more effective to reward the occurrence of the behavior than to punish its absence. When you want an organism *not* to do something specific, it is more effective to punish the occurrence of the behavior than to reward its absence. Referring to Figure 3.13, it is more effective, usually, to apply either reward or punishment to the operant represented by the small white area of the circle rather than to the large grey area. When reward and punishment are applied to the grey part, it is hard for the organism to distinguish the situation from one in which reward and punishment are applied to white and grey together—in other words, a situation in which reward and aversive stimulation are independent of any response. In the next sections, on escape and avoidance, we will look at what happens when punishment is applied to large, general classes of behavior such as those represented by the large grey part of Figure 3.13.

Escape (Negative Reinforcement)

In the typical escape-conditioning experiment, an aversive stimulus is presented and the experimenter waits until the subject performs some act that the experimenter has specified in advance. When the act is performed, the aversive stimulus is removed. For example, a dog may be placed in a shuttle box (one with a hurdle in the middle that the dog can leap over). When the dog is on one side of the box, he may be shocked until he leaps over the hurdle. Dogs in such situations quickly learn to jump over the hurdle.

Negative reinforcement is a synonym for escape. Although the word "escape" vividly describes what is happening in a typical negative reinforcement experiment, we shall use the phrase "negative reinforcement" to remind us of the relation between this process and that of positive reinforcement. Both kinds of reinforcement will strengthen whatever acts they follow. Positive reinforcement reinforces by adding a positive stimulus; negative reinforcement reinforces by taking away a negative stimulus. The line between these two processes is not always easy to draw. (Is turning on the heater on a cold day reinforcing because it gives us warmth or because it removes our feeling of cold?)

One theory of reinforcement (the need-reduction theory that we mentioned previously) holds that all reinforcement is negative reinforcement. The eating of food, for instance, is thus "escape from hunger," and the drinking of water is "escape from thirst."

Nevertheless, the behavior of animals when exposed to aversive stimuli is different from that of animals who are deprived of food or water. A pigeon who is being shocked will jump around the area in which it is confined and flap its wings violently; a pigeon deprived of food will engage in more deliberate searching and pecking motions. It may be that one difference between an aversive stimulus (such as electric shocks or loud noises) and such feelings as hunger or thirst is that the former originate suddenly outside the organism while the latter originate gradually within it. Because of the violent behavior generated by aversive stimuli, it is difficult to train an animal to perform delicate, subtle or complicated acts to escape them. It is difficult, for instance, for organisms to react nonviolently to aversive stimuli even though, in many cases, nonviolence may be the best means of escaping it. Only a great deal of self-control and previous training enables people in a crowded auditorium to keep from running to the exits to escape a fire. Similarly, although it is easy to train a pigeon to peck a key to obtain food, it is difficult to train a pigeon to perform the same act to escape from electric shock. (On the other hand, it is easy to train a pigeon to flap its wings, to run around a cage or to raise its head to escape electric shock.)

A great deal of patience is required to train an organism to react to aversive stimuli in nonviolent ways. One must find the precise value of intensity that will be aversive enough to facilitate escape, yet not so intense as to trigger violent reactions. In everyday life, we are often faced with similar problems. Perhaps prisons should be aversive enough relative to the outside world so that people do not want to stay in them, yet not so aversive that prisoners become more bitter or violent than they were before their incarceration.

It is possible to train an animal to perform an act it would not ordinarily perform under aversive stimulation. For example, the cockroach will ordinarily run away from light, yet this photonegative insect can, in the course of repeated trials, learn to go to a dark box situated under a light. Figure 3.17 diagrams the experiment. The roach is placed in one end of an alley with a very weak light above a covered box at the other end. In order to get to the box, which is in complete shade, the

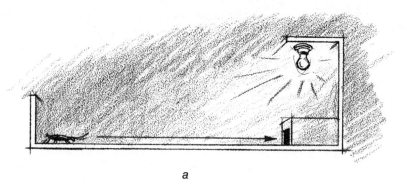

a

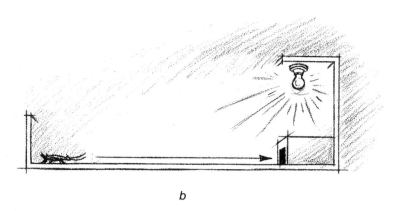

b

Figure 3.17 *Teaching a cockroach to approach a bright light. (a) The roach learns to go to the dark box. The intensity of the light is gradually increased over many trials until (b) the roach goes to the dark box in spite of a bright light.*

roach must move toward the light. If the light is made very bright initially, the roach will stay at the end of the alley where it is put, and not move. However, if the light is very dim, the roach will adapt to the light and move down the alley and find the dark box. Once the roach learns to run to the dark box when the light is dim, the intensity of the light can be increased slowly. The roach will eventually learn to approach a bright light to get to the dark box.

Avoidance

An experiment by Richard Solomon and L. C. Wynn illustrates the relation of avoidance to escape. They trained dogs in the shuttle box diagrammed in Figure 3.18. When the dogs were in Side A, they were

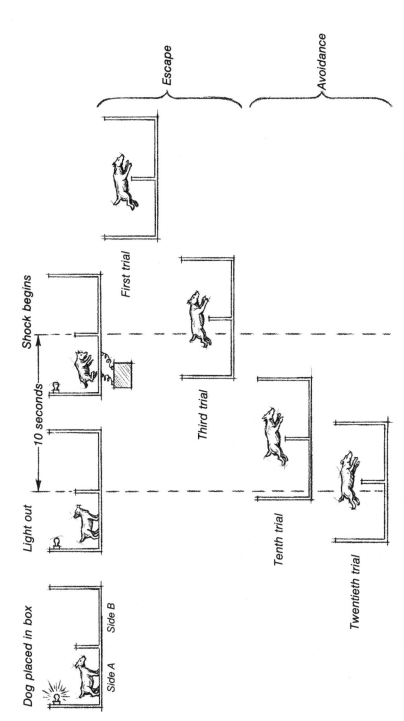

Figure 3.18 Solomon and Wynne's avoidance experiment. First trial: Dog jumps over barrier long after shock begins. Third trial: Dog jumps immediately after shock begins. Tenth trial: Dog jumps between signal and shock. Twentieth trial: Dog jumps immediately after signal starts.

severely shocked. The electricity remained on until the dogs jumped to Side B. However, 10 seconds before each shock, a light in the box went out. Gradually, the dogs were conditioned to jump when the light went out, *before* the shock came on, thus avoiding the shock altogether.

The relation between avoidance and escape bears a certain similarity to the relation between secondary reinforcement and primary reinforcement.

In secondary reinforcement experiments we concluded that one of the values of secondary reinforcers is that they signal to the organism "when reinforcement is due." Avoidance procedures perform a similar function; they tell the organism when aversive stimulation is due. In both secondary reinforcement and avoidance situations the signal makes a certain kind of behavior appropriate. Secondary reinforcing signals are part of a chain culminating in positive reinforcement. Avoidance signals are part of a chain culminating in nonpresentation of an aversive stimulus.

If we look upon organisms as reacting to overall molar features of the environment, we can see how avoidance behavior may easily come about. One man may react to the fact that the sun is shining and dress accordingly, while, on the same morning, another may react to the fact that it is the month of April and hence carry an umbrella even if the sun is shining at that particular moment. If a man reacts to the fact that the month is April and carries an umbrella despite the sunny weather at the moment, he is, in essence, avoiding getting wet, just as Solomon and Wynne's dogs avoided shock by responding even when shock was not present at the moment. For some of Solomon and Wynne's dogs, the transition from escape of shock (reaction to the shock itself) to avoidance of shock (reaction to the stimulus that indicated shock was to come) was rapid (Figure 3.19: Dog A); for other dogs this transition was more gradual (Dog B).

The invariable correlation between the light-out signal and the shock in Solomon and Wynne's experiment is not always paralleled in everyday life "avoidance situations." Just because it is April, it will not necessarily rain. Sometimes the man who responds to the more molecular aspects of his environment, who leaves his umbrella home on sunny days, even in April, is better off than his more foresighted brother. People obviously have to strike a general balance between a molecular and molar view of life, and sometimes this can be difficult.

It is generally true that children find it difficult to respond to the molar conditions of their environment. As we grow older we sometimes have difficulties in the other direction. The man who can never take a vacation, for instance, or the woman who worries and cannot

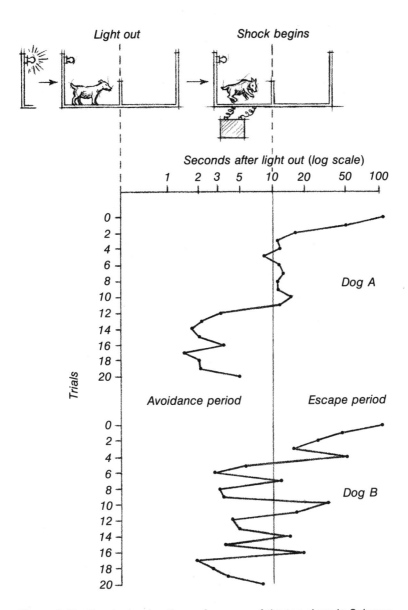

Figure 3.19 *Graph showing the performance of the two dogs in Solomon and Wynne's experiment. (Each point represents a jump over the barrier.) Dog A shifted rapidly from escape to avoidance. Dog B shifted gradually from escape to avoidance.* [Data from R. L. Solomon and L. C. Wynne, "Traumatic avoidance learning: Acquisition in normal dogs." Psychol. Monogr., 1953, 67 (No. 354)]

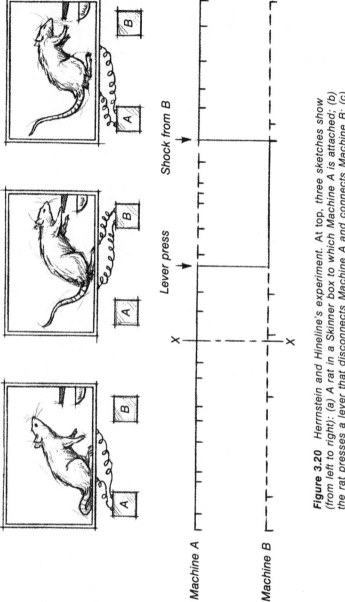

Figure 3.20 Herrnstein and Hineline's experiment. At top, three sketches show (from left to right): (a) A rat in a Skinner box to which Machine A is attached; (b) the rat presses a lever that disconnects Machine A and connects Machine B; (c) the rat receives a shock from B, which now disconnects B and connects A. At bottom, two horizontal lines with vertical ticks show the electric shocks programmed by Machine A and Machine B. Solid line shows which machine was connected to the box at a given time and thus which shocks were actually received. (This means, for instance, that if the rat had pressed the lever at point X—X, it would have been shocked immediately.)

enjoy herself while her children are away at camp are examples of people who are responding to aversive molar aspects of their environment at the expense of the molecular. To put it another way, there are those who cannot see the forest for the trees and those who cannot see the trees for the forest.

An experiment that illustrates how rats can avoid electric shock by responding to molar rather than molecular aspects of their environment was done recently by Herrnstein and Philip Hineline, who used rats in a Skinner box containing a lever and a grid floor (see Figure 3.20). There were two machines that could deliver shock to the rat through the grid floor, but only one was connected at a time. The shocks delivered by each machine were fairly intense, very brief, and came at irregular intervals. The only difference between the two was that Machine A produced shocks at a fairly rapid rate and Machine B produced shocks at a fairly slow rate. In other words, the probability of shock at any time was greater for A than for B. If we stretch our imaginations to conceive of snowstorms as analogous to shocks, it is as if one machine produced the snowstorms of January (a high rate of snowstorms) while the other produced the snowstorms of November (a low rate). Ordinarily, Machine A, which produces shocks at a high rate is connected, and Machine B is not connected. A press of the lever, however, disconnects Machine A and connects Machine B, which stays connected until a shock is received and then it is disconnected, and Machine A is connected. It is as if someone who disliked snowstorms could press a lever during January to restore the conditions of November which lasted until a November snowstorm occurred and then reverted to January. It is possible under these conditions that immediately after pressing the lever, Machine B would produce a shock (this would happen if the rat had pressed the lever at X—X in Figure 3.20). Just as, if one could switch from January to November, there would be no guarantee it would not snow the next day—even in November. Thus, pressing the lever did not avoid shocks completely. All it did was to change conditions so that the overall rate of shocks was less. In the Herrnstein and Hineline experiment, all the rats learned to press the lever for such molar negative reinforcement.

Extinction of Escape and Avoidance

When extinction of escape and avoidance is carried out in a way parallel to extinction of positively reinforced behavior, the reinforced response disappears quite rapidly. For instance, suppose one of Solomon and Wynne's dogs learned to jump over a barrier to escape—and then to avoid—shocks. Suppose we want to extinguish this behavior. During extinction the jumps would no longer be reinforced by escape or avoidance—we would shock the animal no matter what it did. When this procedure is followed, the jumps eventually stop. In fact, responses extinguished in this manner are often extinguished so thoroughly that it is difficult to get the animal to respond again, even when extinction is discontinued and conditioning is reinstated.

There is another procedure that one may follow in an attempt to reduce the rate of avoidance behavior that produces exactly the opposite results. Suppose again that an animal has learned to jump over a barrier to avoid shocks, as in the Solomon and Wynne study. Then, suppose the experimenter maintains the same conditions—the same box, the same signal, and the same jump before the shock comes on—except that the shock apparatus is unplugged. When Solomon and Wynne tried unplugging their electrical apparatus, they found that the dogs kept jumping; the dogs would jump literally hundreds of times after shock had been discontinued. Eventually, the avoidance behavior will slow down and stop under these conditions, but the process is a lengthy one, especially as compared to the normal extinction procedure. It is easy to understand why the second extinction process was so inefficient if we remember what was said about extinction of positively reinforced responses: *The easier it is to discriminate the reinforcement situation from the extinction situation, the faster extinction will be.* In the case of the two extinction processes for avoidance, the first is easily distinguished from reinforcement. As soon as the dog makes the previously reinforced jumping response, and the shock is maintained nevertheless, the conditions of reinforcement are obviously at an end. However, in the second procedure, when the dog jumps and is not shocked, the conditions are identical to those of reinforcement. With the second method of extinction, as long as the reinforced response is maintained, the conditions of reinforcement and extinction are identical.

Even when the previously reinforced response is prevented by physical restraint, it is not extinguished by this method. (With respect to chains of behavior, we noted that a conditioned response in the chain will be preserved even though other responses preceding it are extinguished. This is true for responses that are restrained as well as for responses that are not made because the signal for their occurrence is never given.)

To illustrate the two methods of extinction, consider the behavior of two children who learn to hit or otherwise interfere with the pleasure of other children in order to prevent the other children from taking their toys. One child is then put among older children who will take his toys regardless of how aggressively he behaves. The other child is put among younger children who will not take his toys, no matter how meekly he behaves. It is reasonable to suppose that the aggressive behavior of the first child will stop while that of the second child will continue; a model example, perhaps, of how a neighborhood bully is created. In fact, the slow, inefficient extinction of avoidance is seen by some behavioral therapists as a major parameter in much adult human neurotic behaviors. As children, people learn many avoidance behaviors. Sometimes, as adults, they continue to perform these behaviors even though the sources of aversive stimulation have long been absent. For instance, if a boy is punished in his youth for open displays of emotion, as an adult he is likely to inhibit such display, perhaps inappropriately, to the detriment of his relations with his wife and children. In this case, a therapist might encourage his patient to express his emotions openly in a permissive atmosphere in the hope of extinguishing the heavy-handed childhood conditioning.

Bibliography

Books on the nature of reinforcement usually have the word "motivation" in the title. The sections on motivation and reinforcement in the books by Kimble, Mackintosh, and Nevin and Reynolds (all previously cited) are excellent. A book by D. Bindra, *Motivation* (New York: Ronald Press, 1959), gives an overview of the various topics usually collected under this rubric. A book by R. Bolles, *Theory of Motivation* (New York: Harper and Row, 1967), covers the topic thoroughly. A collection of the classic articles on reinforcement is available in a paperback edited by R. C. Birney and R. C. Teevan, *Reinforcement* (Princeton: Van Nostrand, 1961).

The parameters of reinforcement: schedule, delay, secondary reinforcement, and so forth, are discussed in detail in the Kimble and Mackintosh books, and in a collection of original essays by students of B. F. Skinner: W. K. Honig, ed., *Operant Behavior: Areas of Research and Application* (New York: Appleton-Century-Crofts, 1966). Punishment and aversive control are treated only sketchily in the Kimble book but are more fully covered in the Mackintosh book and in the Honig collection. I particularly recommend the article "Punishment" by N. H. Azrin and W. C. Holz (in Honig's book). A systematic account of the investigation of parameters of reinforcement and punishment can be found in a paperback by F. A. Logan and A. R. Wagner, *Reward and Punishment* (Boston: Allyn and Bacon, 1965).

Schuster's experiment with secondary reinforcement is available in D. P. Hendry (Ed.), *Conditioned Reinforcement* (Homewood, Ill.: Dorsey, 1969). The Bower, McLean, and Meacham experiment called "The value of knowing when reinforcement is due" appears in the *Journal of Comparative and Physiological Psychology* (62, 1967, 184–192). The Wolfe and Grice experiments are described in Kimble's book, but it is instructive to read Wolfe's own descriptions of his experiments to be found, unfortunately, only in J. B. Wolfe, "Effectiveness of token-rewards for chimpanzees," *Comparative Psychology Monographs*, 12, No. 60, 1936. The Chung and Herrnstein experiment is from the *Journal of the Experimental Analysis of Behavior* (10, 1967, pp. 67–74). The Solomon and Wynne experiment has been reprinted extensively and is described in most texts on learning. The original source is *Psychological Monographs* (67, No. 354, 1953). The Herrnstein and Hineline experiment, "Negative reinforcement as shock-frequency reduction," appears in the *Journal of the Experimental Analysis of Behavior* (9, 1966, 421–430).

4

Limits of Behavior Change

It is tempting to assume that conditioning occurs automatically whenever environmental and behavioral events are properly correlated. If this were the case, an experimenter could pick any conditioned stimulus and any unconditioned stimulus (for classical conditioning) or any response and any reward (for instrumental conditioning) and by correlating their presence and absence produce an association between them according to the general rules of conditioning. Unfortunately, no such regularity exists, even for the simple stimuli and responses dealt with in the laboratory. The experiments described in this chapter demonstrate vividly the limits of behavior change.

DIFFERENCES IN RECEPTIVITY

After a duck is hatched, there is a period of a few days, called a *critical period,* when it will attach itself faithfully to almost any large moving object. In nature this object is almost always its mother—which explains the strings of ducklings trailing after their mothers around a pond. But the duckling will follow the moving object if it is a goose or even a human being, instead of a duck. Ducklings tend to follow round objects more readily than square objects, but they will follow square objects too. In laboratory experiments ducklings have even followed painted blocks of wood. Whatever the duckling follows during its first few days it is likely to continue to follow, rejecting all other followable objects. If a duckling once starts to follow a human being, it will usually continue to follow that same person even though other people or other animals, including its natural mother, are available. This phenomenon, called *imprinting,* was first identified and studied extensively by the ethologist Konrad Lorenz. Lorenz found that if a duckling was imprinted with a goose during the early critical period and then after several weeks removed and put among other ducks, the next year it would direct its mating activity towards geese (the species with which it had been imprinted) rather than ducks, its own species, with which, moreover, it had spent all of its life except the first few weeks.

Some of these observations about imprinting fit neatly into the conditioning paradigms discussed previously. The first few days of life are bound to be upsetting, to say the least, and it is not unreasonable to suppose that any behavior would be reinforced that provides environmental stability (visual and otherwise). This would include, presumably, a duckling following its mother so as to maintain a single object in its visual field. When, as in nature, this object is also associated with food and warmth, it is not hard to understand why following occurs early in life, why the object followed is a source of reinforcement, and why the reinforcement might be expected to be strong and persistent. What is difficult to explain in terms of conditioning is why the critical period is so rigidly limited to the first few days and why this particular source of reinforcement and not any of the others subsequently experienced should determine future sexual behavior. In the nineteenth century, William James speculated that instincts and learning were inextricably intertwined. The facts of imprinting are a case in point.

The discovery of critical periods for animal learning has given rise to speculations that similar critical periods also exist for human learning. For instance, is there a critical period for the acquisition of language, prior to which language is impossible to learn and subsequent to which it is very difficult to learn? Does experience during some critical period determine once and for all whether we will be "basically" heterosexual or homosexual? As we have indicated previously, American psychology has been largely empiricist in orientation and has tended to answer these questions negatively. Acquisition of language, reading, sexual preferences, and other types of human behavior have been thought to be mostly due to experience—their predictability being attributed more to similar experience than to similar developmental processes.

After many years of comparative neglect, the work of the European ethologists is now having a strong effect on American psychology. This is probably because other limits of behavior change have been discovered by psychologists working within the American empiricist tradition, which have caused them to appreciate more the corresponding findings of their European colleagues. It is to these limits, discovered by the empiricists themselves, that we turn next.

DIFFERENCES IN MOTOR REACTIONS

Thorndike's experiments with cats in a puzzle box illustrate the sensorimotor aspects of *belongingness*. In most of his experiments Thorndike trained cats to pull strings or press levers to get out of the box. In one experiment, however, Thorndike trained a cat to yawn to get out of the box. This training proved to be exceedingly difficult. Finally, when Thorndike succeeded, the yawn produced by the cat was an artificial parody of what a yawn should be. The cat opened and closed its mouth but did not really yawn. Evidently yawning and getting out of a box do not "belong together." Thorndike met with similar failures in trying to train a cat to scratch itself to get out of the box. The problem may have been that Thorndike's cats did not naturally yawn or scratch when confined. Rather, they tended to explore the cage and poke their paws and noses into corners. Because the cats did not yawn or scratch Thorndike might have had difficulty teaching them these acts with *any* reward.

Negative Reinforcement

Since Thorndike, similar phenomena have periodically turned up in the psychological literature. Rats can be trained to jump forwards to escape shock to their rear paws and to jump backwards to escape shock to their front paws, but not to jump in the opposite direction, which in nature would be into instead of away from the place of danger. In avoidance studies it has been found easier to train rats to turn a wheel to avoid shock than to press a lever (Figure 4.1). Turning a wheel resembles the scrambling a rat would do to get out of the box, whereas pressing a lever involves orientation towards the source of the shock in the lower part of the box. The movements an organism would nor-

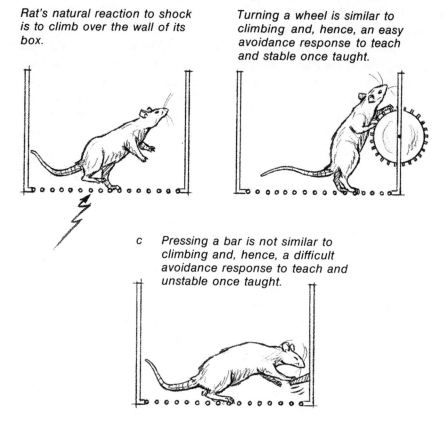

a

Rat's natural reaction to shock is to climb over the wall of its box.

b

Turning a wheel is similar to climbing and, hence, an easy avoidance response to teach and stable once taught.

c Pressing a bar is not similar to climbing and, hence, a difficult avoidance response to teach and unstable once taught.

Figure 4.1 *Why is it easier to teach a rat to escape and avoid shock by turning a wheel than by pressing a bar?*

mally make to escape from shock or other painful stimuli have been called, by the psychologist Robert Bolles, *species-specific defense reactions*. Each species has a repertoire of such responses ranging from freezing in place, to running away, to attacking. Bolles speculates that the responses corresponding to those the organism would normally emit in the presence of the aversive stimulus are the ones that can be taught as avoidance responses. If one attempts to teach an animal to avoid an aversive stimulus by making a response it would not ordinarily make in the presence of such a stimulus, the animal will learn the avoidance response only very slowly, the response will be unstable, and the performance of the response will look artificial, like the cat's yawning. When the response in an avoidance task is actually antagonistic to a species-specific defense reaction, it will be impossible or nearly impossible to teach. It is no accident, Bolles argues, that many avoidance studies deal with dogs or rats jumping over hurdles to avoid shock. Jumping over a hurdle is just what these animals would do naturally to escape a painful stimulus, so this is a convenient response to study. There is nothing wrong with this as long as it is realized that the association between jumping and avoidance of shock is far from arbitrary, and that any results obtained with this species-specific reaction must be scrutinized carefully before they can be generalized to other responses or other species.

It was once part of the lore of the animal conditioning laboratory that pigeons could not learn to escape or avoid aversive stimuli. What was meant was that pigeons could not be taught to escape or avoid shock by pecking an illuminated disk (called a key). Pigeons can avoid certain stimuli very effectively, as anyone can testify who has tried to catch one on the street. But pecking a key was a convenient response to use with positive reinforcement (we shall see why in a few pages when we discuss autoshaping), and there did not seem to be any reason that pigeons should not learn to escape or avoid shock as they had learned to obtain food. If instrumental conditioning were simply a matter of associating an arbitrarily chosen response with an arbitrarily chosen reinforcer, it would indeed be a mystery if pigeons could not learn to escape or avoid shock by pecking a key. But the mystery disappears as soon as it is realized that the typical species-specific defense reaction of pigeons to sudden, intense shocks, such as those used in escape or avoidance experiments, is running or flying away. Thus it was found that head raising (a movement preparatory to flying) could be taught to pigeons as an escape or avoidance response. Similarly, pigeons could be taught to escape shock by walking to the other side of the chamber. Pecking remained an impossible response to teach until shock was increased gradually instead of applied suddenly. When pulses of shock are introduced gradually, their intensity raised in slow steps from zero to the values usually used, the species-specific defense reaction of pigeons is different from the reaction to sudden, intense shock. With sudden shock the pigeons flee; with gradual shock they attack. When shock is introduced gradually it is in fact unnecessary to specifically train pigeons to peck a key to turn it off. If the key is suddenly illuminated after the shock reaches its maximum value, pigeons will attack the key. Figure 4.2 shows one pigeon pecking the key (actually a button illuminated and extended slightly into the chamber) and another hitting the key with its wings. Both of these responses occurred without any specific training. When the response in question is actually instrumental in turning off the shock it tends to occur earlier

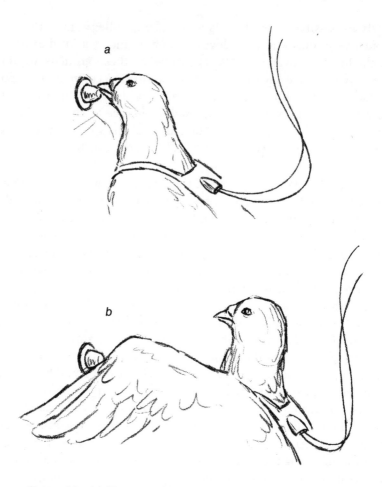

a

b

Figure 4.2 *(a) Pigeon pecking key to escape shock. (b) Pigeon hitting key with wing to escape shock.*

and earlier (at less intense shocks) and to be made more efficiently. Instead of attacking the key the pigeon now calmly brushes the key with its wings (if wing-flapping was the initial response) or calmly pecks the key (if pecking was the initial response). The response undergoes a metamorphosis from a natural species-specific defense reaction to an instrumental response that resembles the initial reaction only superficially (as the instrumental yawn of Thorndike's cats resembled a real yawn only superficially).

The species-specific defense reactions described by Bolles are a subcategory of what the ethologists call fixed-action patterns. The species-specific defense reactions are fixed-action patterns that occur in the presence of aversive stimuli. According to Bolles, any responses learned to escape or avoid aversive stimuli are derived from these fixed-action patterns. One need not accept entirely this strongly nativist view to recognize the significant role that fixed patterns of behavior play in negative reinforcement.

Positive Reinforcement

In positive reinforcement, fixed patterns of behavior also play an important role in determining what behavior can and cannot be modified. As in negative reinforcement, these patterns can help or hinder the process of conditioning, depending on whether the conditioning is or is not in harmony with the patterns. Let us first consider how fixed patterns of behavior may hinder conditioning.

Keller Breland set out, after receiving training at Harvard University in animal learning, to apply in a practical setting the principles he had learned. He and his wife Marian trained animals to do various tricks for advertising purposes and for exhibits at state fairs, shopping centers, and the like. The training was accomplished with the use of instrumental conditioning principles. For instance, one exhibit, activated by a customer putting a quarter into a slot, consisted of a chamber containing a chicken, a miniature basketball basket located a miniature foul-shot away from the chicken, and a short vertical tube a few inches in diameter located between the chicken and the basket. About a second after the chamber was illuminated, a continuous stream of air started from the tube and a ping pong ball popped out of the tube and hung suspended in the air stream. The chicken pecked at the ping pong ball and sent it in the direction of the basket, more often than not into the basket, scoring a point and receiving a short delivery of food from a hopper in the rear of the cage. After three points were scored, the chamber darkened and the show was over. After several such exhibitions the satiated chicken was retired for the day, and a hungry one replaced it. Tricks such as these, taught not only to chickens but also to reindeer, cockatoos, porpoises, and whales, helped confirm the principles discovered in animal laboratories.

In 1961, however, after about fifteen years of this sort of endeavor, the Brelands published a paper called "The Misbehavior of Organisms," in which they recounted some of their failures. The failures all took the same form: an animal would be taught some simple act and would learn the act quickly, but later another response would intrude into the act, becoming more and more frequent until it dominated the animal's performance so strongly that the food reward was delayed or not attained at all. For instance, consider the Brelands' description of the behavior of a pig:

> Here a pig was conditioned to pick up large wooden coins and deposit them in a large "piggy bank." The coins were placed several feet from the bank and the pig required to carry them to the bank and deposit them, usually four or five coins for one reinforcement. (Of course, we started out with one coin, near the bank.)
>
> Pigs condition very rapidly, they have no trouble taking ratios, they have ravenous appetites (naturally), and in many ways are among the most tractable animals we have worked with. However, this particular problem behavior developed in pig after pig, usually after a period of weeks or months, getting worse every day. At first the pig would eagerly pick up one dollar, carry it to the bank, run back, get another, carry it rapidly and neatly, and so on, until the ratio was complete. Thereafter, over a period of weeks the behavior would become slower and slower. He might run over eagerly for each dollar, but on the way back, instead of carrying the dollar and depositing it simply and cleanly, he would repeatedly drop it, root it, drop it again, root it along the way, pick it up, toss it up in the air, drop it, root it some more, and so on.
>
> We thought this behavior might simply be the dilly-dallying of an animal on a low drive. However, the behavior persisted and gained in strength in spite of a severely increased drive—he finally went through the ratios so slowly that he did not get enough to eat in the course of a day. Finally it would take the pig about 10 minutes to transport four coins a distance of about 6 feet. The problem behavior developed repeatedly in successive pigs.

The Brelands describe the interfering behavior of the pigs as *instinctive drift.* By this they mean that the pigs instinctively root (dig in the ground with their snouts), that the experimental situation with food and small wooden objects provided the conditions for exhibiting this behavior, and that the instinctive behavior came to predominate over the instrumentally reinforced behavior. We might call the rooting of the pigs a *species-specific appetitive reaction,* to parallel the species-specific defense reaction described by Bolles. Both the appetitive and defense reactions are subcategories of fixed-action patterns.

Now let us turn to situations where fixed patterns of behavior work for, rather than against, conditioning. In Chapter 2 we discussed the concept of instrumental pseudoconditioning. In the example cited there, itching powder delivered after each bar-press caused the rat to be more active and hence press the bar more often—so itching powder, although it increased bar-presses, may not have done so via the mechanism of instrumental conditioning. But suppose the reward used is truly rewarding (when tested against a pseudoconditioning control) but *also* elicits some behavioral pattern that enhances measured responding. This is often the case with food—the behavior elicited by feeding enhances the particular response that food is supposed to reinforce.

With pigeons, periodic free presentation of food generates pecking of one kind or another, usually pecking at the wall of the cage. If there is an illuminated key on the wall and periodic reinforcements are dependent on pecking the key (as with a fixed-interval schedule of reinforcement), many of the pecks on the key can be attributed to the periodic food presentations themselves rather than to the instrumental dependency of the food presentations on pecking. In other words, in many instrumental-conditioning situations a positive feedback process is at work. The food causes a pattern of behavior, which (as the experimenter has arranged) will produce more food, which in turn produces more of the behavior, and so on.

An experimental procedure that shows vividly how fixed patterns of behavior can interact with instrumental responding is the procedure called *autoshaping.* Autoshaping is a recent discovery and has not yet been defined precisely. But its basic message is clear: behavior can be "shaped" rapidly when species-specific reactions and associations are brought into play. Not only do pigeons tend to peck when food is presented freely, but they will also direct their pecks at a response key if illumination of the key is paired with food. In 1968 Paul L. Brown and Herbert M. Jenkins published the first report of the phenomenon. Their basic finding was that when a hungry pigeon was exposed to periodic free presentations of food, each preceded by a brief (3- or 8-second) illumination of the response key, most pigeons would peck the key after about 40 to 50 such presentations.

In ordinary instrumental conditioning experiments, animals are trained to respond by a process called "shaping." The experimenter observes the animal until it orients towards the response manipulandum, then presents food. This increases the probability of such orientation in the future. The next time the experimenter observes the orientation he withholds food until the animal comes somewhat closer to the manipulandum, then closer and closer in successive approximations until the desired response is emitted. Figure 4.3a shows how a pigeon's behavior is shaped to peck a key. Shaping is the same sort of procedure as previously described to train a cat to jump higher and higher. Figure 4.3b shows how autoshaping is used to get a pigeon to peck a key without observing the pigeon at all by automatically pairing the key illumination with food.

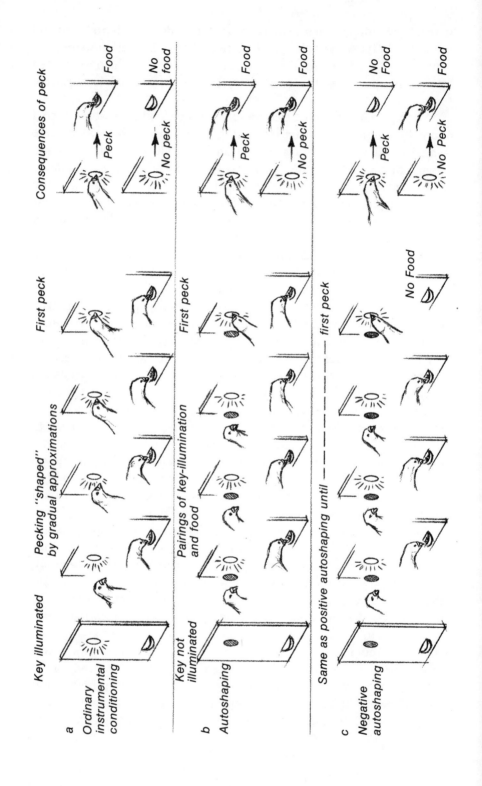

Figure 4.3 *Contingencies of acquisition and maintenance of key-pecking behavior in a pigeon with ordinary instrumental conditioning, autoshaping, and negative autoshaping.*

The process shown in Figure 4.3c is called *negative autoshaping.* It was first reported by David and Harriet Williams. Until the first peck at the key, the process is exactly the same as positive autoshaping shown above it. When the pigeon pecks the key, however, food is not delivered. Thus, there are two processes working in opposition in negative autoshaping. Pecking is stimulated by the autoshaping procedure, which acts as long as the pigeon does not peck. When the pigeon does peck, however, food is withheld—an instrumental contingency equivalent to *omission,* which tends to decrease pecking. The result of the negative autoshaping procedure is that pigeons peck (as they do with the positive autoshaping procedure) and continue to peck at a slow rate, sometimes going for many trials without food because they pecked the key. Evidently autoshaping is a strong process since it overcomes the omission contingency and keeps the pigeon pecking the key.

How does autoshaping work? The matter is in some dispute. At first, it was thought that successive approximations to a key-peck were being adventitiously reinforced by the food presentations. (The word "autoshaping" is derived from this theory. It connotes an automatic shaping of the response. We shall, however, use the word to refer to the procedure, not the theory.) But this simple instrumental-conditioning theory cannot really account for autoshaping because when the obvious test is made, of looking to see whether the pigeon is moving closer and closer to the key on successive trials, no such observation is made. There is also some evidence that the duration of the key-peck (the time that the pigeon's beak is in contact with the key) in autoshaping, especially negative autoshaping, is shorter than in regular instrumental conditioning. Another line of evidence against this theory is that in negative autoshaping pecking persists after the first peck. To explain such maintenance the adventitious instrumental reinforcement that is supposed to reinforce pecking would have to overcome the explicit instrumental omission contingency arranged to reinforce nonpecking. It seems unlikely to most experienced researchers that this could be the case. Whatever maintains pecking in this situation would have to be stronger than adventitious reinforcement would be.

A better explanation for the pigeons' behavior in this situation is an innate tendency to peck in a situation where food is probable. The onset of the key light just before food delivery provides a signal delineating the period of high food probability. This signal acts as what ethologists would call a *releaser* for the peck.* To some extent the signal is a *learned* releaser; in classical conditioning, a signal (a conditioned stimulus) by virtue of pairing with the unconditioned stimulus comes to cause a response ordinarily elicited by the unconditioned stimulus. This would explain the pigeon's tendency to peck during the signal (as it does at the food itself), but it does not explain why the pigeon directs its peck at the key. To some extent the onset of the key light must also be an *innate* releaser for pecking (provided there is an already established tendency to peck). The key itself perhaps resembles the food to some extent and releases pecks just as, in nature, the sight of a grain of food releases pecks.

Autoshaping, easy as it is to establish, depends on a number of conditions. (1) The pigeon should be hungry. Although autoshaping may work with relatively satiated pigeons, it works better with hungry ones. (2) Food should be presented occasionally in the situation. Turning the key light on and off does not work if no food is present. (3) The key light must be turned on and off. Continuous illumination does not work even with food present. (4) The key light should signal a high probability of food; that is, it should come on just before the food, and it should be on for a brief time relative to the time it is off (the inter-trial intervals). As the key light loses its power to signal reinforcement (by being left on too long, for instance) it also loses its power to autoshape pecking.

Autoshaping works with water reward as well as food. The peck at the key with water reward has a different topography from that with food reward: the pigeon seems to be sipping at the key instead of pecking at the key as it does with food reward. Autoshaping also works with electric-shock reduction. Pigeons will peck at a key when the key light is turned on just before electric shock is reduced. This may be because the shock, turned on gradually, elicits attack at the lit key. Responses of animals other than pigeons can also be autoshaped. Monkeys, for instance, have been trained by autoshaping to press a lit panel. Rats have been conditioned by autoshaping to press a lever with a light directly over it.

Autoshaping is a phenomenon that is being studied intensively now in several laboratories. New information may change the picture,

---

*A "releaser" is meant by ethologists to imply that the whole pattern of the response is ready to be performed but is normally inhibited. A releaser removes inhibition.

but it seems now as if the autoshaped peck emerges from a combination of innate patterns of behavior, innate releasing stimuli, and classical conditioning.

Why is autoshaping important? It may seem as if we have spent too much time on this phenomenon. Why worry about the responses of a seemingly insignificant organism in an artificial environment? But autoshaping is important for several reasons. On one hand it has shown psychologists that the supposedly simple case of a pigeon pecking a key in a Skinner box is actually much more complicated than it at first appears. The activity of pigeons studied in the Skinner box is not purely instrumental but is superimposed on the innate behavior patterns of the pigeon and "contaminated" by classical-conditioning effects. On the other hand, autoshaping offers a unique opportunity to study how these various types of conditioning interact with each other and with the organism's behavior patterns under conditions in which behavior is more easily observed and measured than in most other experimental environments and certainly more than in the natural environment. The Skinner box offers the possibility that the various components of behavior can be studied in interaction and the contribution of each evaluated. Finally, autoshaping is worth studying because it involves the basic components of all learning—human and otherwise—innate patterns shaped to a greater or lesser extent by environmental contingencies. Autoshaping, as an instance of such an interaction, takes its place among the other activities we have considered in this chapter on the limits of learning.

DIFFERENCES IN ASSOCIABILITY

In classical conditioning the CS-US relationship gives rise to an altered response. In instrumental conditioning the response-reinforcement relationship gives rise to an altered response. The limitations we have so far been discussing refer to the influence of the situation in which learning takes place on the alteration of the response. Motor reactions to the situation either facilitate or hinder the response. Now we turn to a more fundamental type of limitation—a limitation of the associability inherent in the CS-US and response-reinforcement *associations* themselves. It turns out that associations, like motor reactions, are by no means arbitrary. That this is so can perhaps best be illustrated by describing an experiment by John Garcia and Robert A. Koelling published in 1966. In previous experiments it had been found extremely easy to train rats to form an association between sickness (usually caused by X-radiation) and taste (that is, rats would avoid the food they had eaten before becoming sick), but it had been difficult to train rats to form an association between sickness and visual or auditory stimuli. These experimental results fitted in with what was known about rats' natural avoidance of poisons. For centuries man has been trying to get rid of rats by poisoning them, but without much success. For instance, if the basement of a butcher shop containing barrels of salted meats were infested with rats, the owner might poison a small dish of sugar and leave it out for the rats. But the rats would each eat only a drop of the sugar (even though it tasted good), would become sick, and would thereafter avoid sugar. They would keep eating the meat, they would not die, and they would not leave the cellar. This phenomenon, of tasting a bit of new food and then, if becoming sick, avoiding it thereafter, is known as bait-shyness. It is an annoying habit of rats, which on their part is quite adaptive since it makes them difficult to poison. What Garcia and Koelling wanted to investigate was the relative ease with which rats associated sickness with taste, but not with sights or sounds.

Garcia and Koelling tested four groups of rats in classical conditioning experiments, diagrammed in Figure 4.4. All the rats were given the same CS, what the experimenters called "bright-noisy-tasty water." By means of a drinkometer each lick at a tube was counted and followed by a brief flash of light and a click. The water in the tube was flavored with saccharin (or salt for some of the rats), so each lick was followed by a gustatory, a visual, and an auditory stimulus. This combined CS was then paired with different aversive stimuli (US's) for the four groups of rats. Two groups were given aversive stimuli that made them sick; one sickness group was given X rays while they were drinking and the other was given the poison lithium chloride in the drinking water (not shown in Figure 4.4). The other two groups were shocked—one immediately after each lick and the other with the shock delayed slightly (only the immediate-shock group is shown in Figure 4.4). Interspersed with the conditioning trials (each conditioning trial consisted of a 20-minute daily period of drinking paired with the aversive stimulus) were trials on which plain water was presented, without the aversive stimulus. In addition, prior and subsequent to the pairing of CS and US, each group was tested with the tasty water and bright-noisy water separately. Figure 4.4 shows the results for one sickness group and one shock group (the other groups followed suit). During the pre-test, the rats in both groups drank large quantities of both the bright-noisy water and the tasty water, in about equal proportions. During the experiment proper, both groups of rats gradually

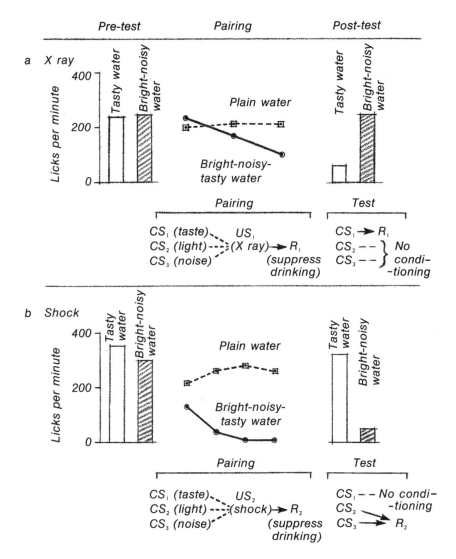

Figure 4.4 *Garcia and Koelling's association experiment, with X-ray and shock used as the aversive stimuli.*

came to stop drinking the bright-noisy-tasty water (although on alternate days they drank plenty of plain water). Evidently both sickness and shock caused the rats to stop drinking. But on the post-tests, the rats that had been made sick did not drink the tasty water and did drink the bright-noisy water, and the rats that had been shocked did not drink the bright-noisy water but did drink the tasty water. Although both sickness and shock suppressed drinking, each became associated with only some of the stimuli accompanying drinking. Sickness became associated with taste (and not with lights and sounds), whereas shock became associated with lights and sounds (and not with taste).

These results clearly show that one cannot simply pair CS's and US's arbitrarily and expect conditioning to occur. Whether conditioning occurs will depend on which CS's are paired with which US's. For the rat, tastes and sickness "belong together."

Other experiments have shown that for other animals the belongingness of taste and sickness is not so strict as for rats. For instance, the quail quite readily associates visual stimuli with sickness. This makes sense from a biological point of view since the rat has poor vision and eats many different kinds of food with many different tastes, but the quail has excellent vision and eats very few kinds of food, mostly consisting of hard grain, which it swallows whole and therefore hardly tastes. If the quail had to depend on taste to avoid poisoned food it would have a great deal of difficulty surviving.

If animals show an avoidance of tastes associated with sickness, they might also be expected to show a preference for tastes associated with recovery from sickness. Although this complementary effect is not so strong or all-pervasive as the taste-sickness effect, some studies have found preferences in rats for foods associated with recovery from sickness.

A peculiarity of taste-sickness associations is that they are best formed with novel tastes. Rats can learn to associate familiar tastes with sickness, but only after many trials and with a difficulty commensurate with that of associating sights and sounds with sickness.

Perhaps the most remarkable difference between taste-sickness association and the other types of learning that have been studied is the long delay possible between CS and US with the taste-sickness effect. To give an idea of the difference, Figure 4.5 shows, in parts (a) and (b), two standard delay functions, the first for classical and the second for instrumental conditioning, and in part (c) a delay function for taste-sickness learning. The various functions found in various laboratories differ in detail but there has been general agreement that the optimum delay between CS and US in classical conditioning is about 0.5 second, and that in instrumental conditioning, immediate reinforcement is necessary. (When reinforcement has operated with a delay, it has generally been assumed that the delay is bridged by secondary reinforcers—stimuli associated with primary reinforcement—which themselves follow immediately after the response). The delay function in Figure 4.5c, published by Garcia, Ervin, and

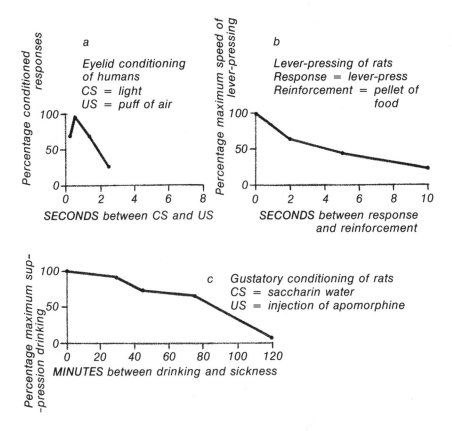

Figure 4.5 How delay affects conditioning with classical, instrumental, and gustatory procedures. (Data for (a) from B. Reynolds, "The acquisition of a trace conditioned response as a function of the magnitude of the stimulus trace." J. Exp. Psych., 1945, 35, 15–30. Data for (b) from C. T. Perin, "A quantitative investigation of the delay of reinforcement gradient." J. Exp. Psych., 1943, 32, 37–51. Data for (c) from J. Garcia, F. R. Ervin, and R. A. Koelling, "Learning with prolonged delay of reinforcement." Psychonomic Sci., 1966, 5, 121–122.)

Koelling, is of quite a different order, with conditioning at a high level even after a 1-hour delay. In this study each group of rats was given a sweet solution and then made sick later after a period indicated on the abscissa. There were five pairings of taste and sickness for each rat. Then the rats were tested for how much sugar solution they would drink. Even the group with 3-hours delay drank less than the controls. Subsequent studies have found taste-sickness conditioning with delays between CS and US of up to 6 or 8 hours.

The question why such delays are possible with taste-sickness conditioning and seemingly not possible with other combinations of

CS and US has not been finally settled. One theory is that tastes are not interfered with by other stimuli during the delay period, whereas stimuli such as sights and sounds are. Another theory is that tastes linger in the mouth during the delay period so that they are still there when sickness comes on. But control experiments show that despite intervening tastes, even novel ones, rats still associate sickness with tastes experienced several hours earlier. Furthermore, taste-sickness associations are formed when sufficient plain water is drunk during the intervening interval to wash away the taste. More significantly, rats learned to discriminate between high and low concentrations of a sour solution when one concentration was followed by sickness and the other was not, by avoiding the particular concentration paired with sickness. Since the two concentrations have similar aftertastes it would be hard to explain taste aversions as aversions formed for after-tastes. Thus, the theory that tastes linger in the mouth is also not confirmed. Again, a mechanism useful for survival has been found. Long delays between CS and US help the rat to survive. Otherwise the rat would not learn to associate slow-acting poisons with their tastes and poisoning rats would be an easy job.

Psychologists studying the taste-sickness association speculate that a separate physiological system governs this important type of association. It is as if when a rat becomes sick, this mechanism looks back over the past several hours and if any novel foods have been eaten, provides the rat with an aversion for those foods. This physiological mechanism, whatever it might be, is a primitive structure. Taste aversions have been taught to deeply anesthetized rats. In an anesthetized rat the higher nervous centers are presumably not functioning.

Pre-established associative tendencies play a part also in instrumental conditioning. The Polish psychologist Jerzy Konorski and his students have found, in experiments testing various discriminative stimuli with instrumental responses of dogs, that certain stimuli, responses, and reinforcers seem to work together better than others. For instance, "go-no go" response alternatives, in which the reinforcer follows the response but is withheld if the response is withheld (for example, food reinforces lifting of the paw in the presence of the stimulus) work best with discriminative stimuli that vary in intensity or quality (for example, a metronome signals reinforcement availability; a buzzer signals that reinforcement is unavailable, even if a response is made). Under these conditions dogs will learn to respond (lift a paw) or withhold response under appropriate stimulus conditions. If, instead of buzzer versus metronome, the "go-no go" response is taught with a single stimulus, say the buzzer, coming from in front of the dog to signal reinforcement availability and from behind the dog to signal unavailability, the dog learns slowly, if at all, to respond and withhold its response appropriately.

Conversely, when the response is itself directional (for example, lifting the left paw followed by food in the presence of one stimulus, lifting the right paw followed by food in the presence of another stimulus), then directional stimuli (buzzer from the front or from the rear) are quite appropriate (the dog learns fast) but stimuli differing in intensity or quality are inappropriate (the dog learns slowly or not at all). Konorsky believes that the ease or difficulty of discrimination with various arrangements of stimuli, responses, and reinforcers is due to the properties of the nervous system. The behavior of his dogs cannot be explained simply in terms of their orientation to various stimuli or to other responses elicited by the discriminative stimuli or the reinforcer, since the dogs can be trained fairly easily to respond in a direction opposite to the direction of the stimulus (for example, raising the right paw when the buzzer comes from the left), which should be difficult if orientation toward the stimulus were the critical determinant of ease of learning in his experiments.

The fact that in both classical and instrumental conditioning certain types of stimuli and responses are seemingly easier to associate than others probably has something to do with the structures of the nervous system, particularly the brain (with classical conditioning, primitive brain structures; with instrumental conditioning, perhaps more complicated structures). If learning is mediated by the brain it stands to reason that, whatever mechanisms the brain uses, it will be more disposed to some sorts of learning than others because they are more suited to those mechanisms. The mechanisms themselves are almost completely unknown at the present time. To what extent they are innate structures and to what extent they are formed by experience is undetermined as well. It may be, for instance, that some early common experience with tastes and sickness by rats, conceivably during nursing and weaning or possibly even during the fetal stage, lays down the pattern of the mechanism; or it may be that the mechanism is inherited by the rat, just as its two eyes, four legs, and tail are inherited. But most likely, the adult rat's tendency to associate taste and sickness derives from a combination of biological evolution and experience. The same would hold for other sorts of associative tendencies, such as those discovered by Konorski.

PREPAREDNESS

The evidence of differences in associability has led Martin E. P. Seligman to define a dimension he calls *preparedness*. An organism may be prepared, unprepared, or contraprepared to form a given association—preparedness presumably reflecting the survival value of the association for the species as a whole. In this view, Garcia's rats are prepared to associate tastes with sickness but unprepared or even contraprepared to associate tastes with electric shock. Similarly, Konorski's dogs are prepared to associate directional stimuli with directional responses but unprepared or contraprepared to associate directional stimuli with "go-no go" responses. A contraprepared association is one the organism shows extreme resistance to learning. A canary, for instance, might be contraprepared to associate the image of a cat with anything but danger, although even such learning is not impossible. Preparedness does not refer to a hard-and-fast category but to a dimension along which associations may vary. In the previous chapter we have seen that a cockroach, normally unprepared to associate a bright light with an approach response may nevertheless be taught to do so.

Preparedness is measured by ease of learning—for instance, number of trials to reach a certain probability of responding—but stands, according to Seligman, for something more than just ease of learning. Seligman speculates that the way in which an organism learns a prepared association differs from the way in which it learns an unprepared association. Some evidence indicates that there may be different rules of learning for prepared and unprepared associations. For instance, prepared associations may be learned with long delays, may extinguish more slowly once learned, may be less subject to interference from other stimuli, may be learned even under anesthesia, and may be learned by humans despite "knowledge" to the contrary (as when people are afraid of heights, snakes, and certain other natural phenomena even while admitting that their fears are irrational).

To be really useful, the concept of preparedness would have to summarize some group of characteristics that prepared associations show and unprepared associations do not. As it stands now, there is little evidence that properties such as long-delay learning are common to all easily learned associations. Until a set of rules is found consistent from one easily learned association to another, or until a common underlying physiological mechanism is found for easily learned associations, the concept of preparedness will be limited in usefulness except as a synonym for ease of learning.

Another difficulty with the concept of preparedness is that it focuses wholly on the organism doing the learning and not at all on its environment. When a child fails to learn the multiplication tables, is it because he was unprepared to learn them or because his teacher was unprepared to teach them to him? Certainly both are responsible. Even with simpler learning situations it is not always clear where the problem lies. To take an example from the beginning of this chapter, it was once thought that pigeons could not learn to escape electric shocks by pecking a key. The association in question is that between key-pecking and shock reduction. Is this association unprepared? One might suspect so, but when electric shock is increased gradually pigeons easily learn to peck to escape and even to avoid shock. *Now* the pigeon is seen to have been prepared to learn to peck a key to escape shock. What counts, obviously, is the way the stimuli are presented as well as the way the organism is constructed.

Many of the methods we use to teach animals and humans various associations are traditional, the results of historical accident. It is tempting to define preparedness in terms of these traditional techniques, and then when learning does not occur, to blame the failure on the organism rather than the technique. But a new technique, if it works, soon becomes standard and what seemed unusual at first soon becomes simple. A child may seem unprepared to learn a given subject unless unusual methods are used. But once the unusual methods become usual the child is seen to have been prepared all along. The prominent developmental psychologist Jerome Bruner has claimed that no subject is too difficult to be taught at some level to any child, no matter how young. This would seem a more constructive attitude to have, in general, than the attitude that some organisms simply can't be taught certain things. And it is an attitude that, despite the material in this chapter, is not out of line with the facts.

Bibliography

This was an easy chapter to write, mostly because a single book was available that contains much of the material covered. The book, edited by Martin E. P. Seligman, is *Biological Boundaries of Learning* (New York: Appleton-Century-Crofts, 1972). Most of the articles listed below are reprinted in Seligman's book where, in addition, several other articles on the subject are reprinted. Another book on the same subject has recently been published that contains original articles by workers in this field. Edited by R. A. Hinde and J. Stevenson-Hinde, it is titled *Constraints on Learning: Limitations and Predispositions* (London: Academic Press, 1973).

The following is a list of articles referred to in this chapter:

Bolles, R. Species-specific defense reactions and avoidance learning. *Psychological Review*, 1970, *77*, 32–48.

Breland, K., and Breland, M. The misbehavior of organisms. *American Psychologist*, 1961, *16*, 681–684.

Brown, P., and Jenkins, H. Auto-shaping of the pigeon's key peck. *Journal of The Experimental Analysis of Behavior*, 1968, *11*, 1–8.

Dobrezecka, C., Szwejkowska, G., and Konorski, J. Qualitative versus directional cues in two forms of differentiation. *Science*, 1966, *153*, 87–89.

Garcia, J., Ervin, F., and Koelling, R. A. Learning with prolonged delay of reinforcement. *Psychonomic Science*, 1966, *5*, 121–122.

Garcia, J., and Koelling, R. A. Relation of cue to consequence in avoidance learning. *Psychonomic Science*, 1966, *4*, 123–124.

Thorndike, E. L. *Animal Intelligence.* New York: Macmillan, 1911.

Williams, D., and Williams, H. Auto-maintenance in the pigeon: Sustained pecking despite contingent non-reinforcement. *Journal of the Experimental Analysis of Behavior*, 1969, *12*, 511–520.

5

Relations Between Stimuli, Responses, and Reinforcement

CONNECTIONS AND CORRELATIONS

Association by Contiguity

In this chapter we will focus on the relations between major variables (stimuli, responses, and reinforcement) in classical and instrumental conditioning. In classical conditioning the experimenter controls the relation between the CS and the US. In instrumental conditioning the experimenter controls the relation between response and reinforcement. What property of these relationships is most critical in determining behavior?

The first, most obvious, and most popular answer to this question is "temporal contiguity." In classical conditioning the CS and the US are presented together. When a dog is exposed to a bell and then food powder, it is the conjunction in time, the 1:1 correspondence between the bell and the food powder, that is said to increase the probability of salivation the next time, when the bell is presented alone. In instrumental conditioning, when a rat is given a pellet of food immediately after pressing a lever, it is the conjunction in time, the 1:1 correspondence between the bar-press and the pellet, that is said to increase the rate of bar pressing. This is nothing more or less than the principle of *association by contiguity*, which we discussed in the first chapter, a principle that has served psychologists long and well.

By and large, "association by contiguity" is still the way most psychologists describe what subjects learn when they are instrumentally or classically conditioned. The dog learns the connection between the bell and the food powder. The rat learns the connection between the bar-press and the food pellet. It is hard to talk about learning at all without implying some form of association by contiguity. Recently, however, behaviorists have become somewhat suspicious of temporal contiguity as a universal description of all relations between stimuli, responses, and reinforcement. What is wrong with assuming a 1:1 relationship between stimulus and response or between response and reinforcement? What is wrong with describing these relations solely as connections?

The Relation Between Stimuli and Responses

To say there is a 1:1 correspondence between stimuli and responses, for example, is to say that each occurrence of a conditioned response must be caused by a specific stimulus. But consider the instrumental act of a fireman shoveling coal into the boiler of a locomotive. We may reasonably ask: Where is the 1:1 stimulus for this behavior? The stimulus can be considered to consist of those elements of the environment, the gauges and dials on the boiler, that tell the man the pressure is low. These dial or gauge readings are measurable. An observer may notice a correlation between the dial reading and the rate of shoveling. At this level we usually find the most consistent relationships between stimuli and responses.

At a more molecular level, are we able to account for each shovelful of coal in terms of its own special stimulus? In order to do this, we would be forced to hypothesize about the *proprioceptive* feedback from muscular movements and attempt to relate that feedback to internal stimuli provided by the fireman's central nervous system or his thoughts, wishes, ideas, and intentions. However, none of these hypothetical internal stimuli are at present easily measurable, and if the behaviorist relies on anything, it is the desirability of measuring the effects he studies. Therefore, until more precise techniques are developed to provide meaningful 1:1 relationships between each response and its stimulus, we should be satisfied to describe the stimulus-response relation in these complex cases in terms of a correlation between events such as (1) the reading on the fireman's pressure gauge and (2) his rate of shoveling.

It is often the case that order is found on a molar level but not on a more molecular level. The physicist finds order in the relations between the pressure, volume, and temperature of a gas although the individual molecules of gas move in random and unpredictable ways; the economist can estimate reasonably well the total amount of money in savings banks in the United States next year without being able to tell whether or not a given individual will deposit or withdraw money. Similarly, the behaviorist does not need to refer to unmeasured stimuli within the organism or to refer to unmeasured thoughts, hopes or dreams within the organism in order to justify his molar descriptions of behavior.

Some classically conditioned responses may have a specific stimulus by which they are elicited, much like the unconditioned knee jerk, which is elicited by striking the knee with a rubber hammer. However, some responses are elicited by more molar environmental events. As we noted, the rate at which a dog breathes is correlated with temperature; a high temperature existing over a relatively long span of time can be a US, with rate of breathing (only measurable over a relatively long time span) as the response with which it is correlated.

In instrumental conditioning (and in the case of the fireman stoking coal), the stimulus signals the existence of a certain relationship between behavior and reinforcement; the gauges tell the fireman whether shoveling will be reinforced.

The Relation Between Responses and Reinforcement

Virtually the same argument applies to the relation between response and reinforcement as to that between stimulus and response. According to the principle of association by contiguity, we ought to find a 1:1 correspondence between response and reinforcement; if it appears that a response is acquired, then it must be reinforced somehow; each instrumental act must have its own reinforcement. The trouble with this notion is the same as the trouble with the supposed 1:1 correspondence between stimulus and response: in everyday life it is hard to find such correspondence.

Consider again the man stoking coal. What is the reinforcement for this response? Possibly the increase in speed of the locomotive. Taking a broader view, the reinforcement could be the fireman's salary or the things he buys with his salary. In any case, we would be hard put to find a specific reinforcer for each shovelful of coal. What we do find is a general correlation between coal shoveling and speed of the locomotive. The faster the coal is shoveled the faster the locomotive goes. As long as the locomotive goes fast enough, the fireman will be paid every week and he will be able to feed himself and his family. As soon as we try to go beyond these correlations—as soon as we try to discover reinforcers for each response—we find ourselves making unverifiable hypotheses about unmeasurable events within the organism. It is indeed a stimulating exercise to speculate about what sort of events could be reinforcing each response. One theory has it that the fireman's sense of his own muscular effort in lifting the shovel becomes associated with the increased speed of the locomotive (the reinforcing event), and, hence, is reinforcing in itself. Thus the reinforcer for each response becomes the feeling of having made that response. Another theory about the reinforcer for each response is that the fireman is rewarded by the satisfaction of accomplishment after each shovelful of coal. These theories, however, contain dangerous pitfalls for the behaviorist, since they involve unmeasured entities within the organism.

Do Organisms Learn Correlations?

If we reject the notion of 1:1 correspondence, we can offer in its place the possibility that the organism learns a set of correlations. (Again, we use the term "learning" with the proviso that it corresponds to overt behavioral effects. We need not posit anything within the organism's mind or even within its nervous system.)

Figure 5.1 shows the correlation between stimulus and reinforcement in simple classical conditioning. A bell is paired with food powder as it is presented to a dog. One unalterable feature of this pairing is that whatever the frequency of the bell, the frequency of the food powder goes along with it. Short intervals between successive bells are accompanied by short intervals between successive presentations of food powder, and *vice versa*.

Figure 5.1 also shows the correlation between response and reinforcement in simple instrumental conditioning in which a rat is reinforced for each bar-press by a pellet of food. With the 1:1 correspondence specifically provided in the experiment (and shown on the left side of Figure 5.1) goes the correlation of frequencies shown on the right. Let us consider the rat that is in a chamber with the bar. Sometimes the rat presses the bar at a slow rate and sometimes at a rapid rate. When the bar is pressed at a slow rate, food comes at a slow rate. When the bar is pressed at a rapid rate, food comes at a rapid rate.

a

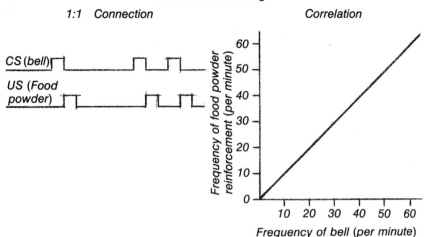

Classical conditioning

1:1 Connection

CS (bell)

US (Food powder)

Correlation

Frequency of food powder reinforcement (per minute)

Frequency of bell (per minute)

b

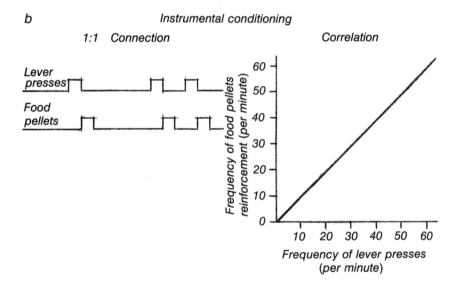

Instrumental conditioning

1:1 Connection

Lever presses

Food pellets

Correlation

Frequency of food pellets reinforcement (per minute)

Frequency of lever presses (per minute)

Figure 5.1 *Repeated 1:1 connections are expressed graphically as perfect correlations. The top half of the figure illustrates a perfect correlation in classical conditioning; the bottom half illustrates a perfect correlation in instrumental conditioning.*

We notice that in situations of this kind, rats tend to press the bar rapidly. It is possible that the critical feature of the relationship between response and reinforcement is their correlation in rate.

The particular kind of correlation in Figure 5.1b (where a response is followed immediately by a reinforcement) represents the most common experimental learning situation, but other correlations can also be learned. For instance, when the correlation between responding and reinforcement is zero, when the reinforcements are programmed at a given rate no matter what the rate of responding, this fact too is learned. Figure 5.2a shows such a zero correlation. This would apply, for instance, to any control mechanism that has broken down. If an elevator button does not work, the frequency of elevators arriving at a floor, while not necessarily decreasing to zero, would nevertheless be out of the control of the operator. In other words, the correlation between the act of pressing the button and the elevator arriving at a floor would be zero. Likewise, if a water faucet breaks, the flow of water may increase drastically and be out of control. In this case, the correlation between turning the handle and the flow of water would be zero.

A zero correlation is represented by the horizontal line in the correlation plot of Figure 5.2a. Evidence that a zero correlation has been learned would be the cessation of a response. When good control (exemplified by a water faucet) breaks down, the correlation changes abruptly from a high value to zero, and organisms react appropriately. In the case of the water faucet, people would soon stop turning an ineffective faucet.

When poor control (exemplified by an elevator) breaks down, the change is less likely to have an immediate effect on behavior. When we are exposed to a positive correlation like the one in Figure 5.2b, and then switched to a zero correlation such as that of Figure 5.2a, we find it extremely difficult to realize that the correlation has changed. When the elevator button was working, even with no presses at all, there were some occasions on which the elevator stopped at that floor (when someone inside the elevator wanted to get out there). The more the button was pressed, the more times the elevator stopped at the floor. This would produce a positive correlation. The correlation shown in Figure 5.2b is a rather simplified version of such a positive correlation. When the correlation is changed to that of Figure 5.2a, when the button is out of order, it will be a long time before people stop pressing it. Very likely, people will press the button even more frequently, responding according to the old correlation which, unfortunately for them, no longer applies.

In general, the greater the change (from the old correlation function between rate of reinforcement and rate of response to the new function), the easier it is to learn; in our terms, the more likely it is to affect behavior.

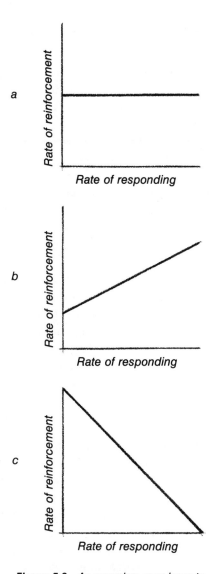

Figure 5.2 An organism may learn to respond to these kinds of correlations between rate of responding and rate of reinforcement. (a) Zero correlation between response and reinforcement. (b) Slight positive correlation between response and reinforcement. Some reinforcement occurs without responding; reinforcement is increased slightly by responding. (c) Negative correlation between response and reinforcement. The more responding, the less reinforcement.

Correlation Versus Schedules

There are two possible areas of confusion with respect to the distinction between connections and correlations. First, correlation between responses and reinforcement must not be confused with the presentation of reinforcement on a pre-arranged schedule, such as a fixed-interval or variable-ratio schedule. Traditionally, when a schedule of reinforcement, such as those described previously, is programmed, a specific response always produces reinforcement immediately. For instance, in a fixed-ratio of ten responses, every tenth response produces reinforcement immediately and reliably. In a situation where responses are only correlated with reinforcement but not in 1:1 correspondence with reinforcement, reinforcements may come between responses or just preceding responses as well as immediately after responses.

The only relation required for a positive correlation in rate is that increased responding somehow produce increased reinforcement. While reinforcement delivered on a schedule will always determine some correlation function between responding and reinforcement, reinforcement correlated with responding does not imply that some schedule of reinforcement (as a schedule is traditionally understood) is in effect.

Correlations and Contingencies

A second area of confusion applies to the contingency tables shown in Figure 2.14. A contingency table represents a set of conditional probabilities. As long as the probabilities are 1.0 and 0, there is no difference between saying that an organism learns a set of probabilities (as in Figure 2.14a or 2.14b) and saying that an organism learns the connections shown on the left-hand side of Figure 5.1.

When the conditional probabilities of the contingency table are less than unity but when reinforcement (when it comes) comes immediately after each response, the situation is like the schedules of reinforcement described above.

When the conditional probabilities of the contingency tables are less than unity *and* when reinforcement need not follow immediately upon the response, as in Figure 2.14c, the situation is like that we have been describing as based on correlations between the variables.

In general, correlation functions such as those of Figure 5.1 provide a better description of contingencies than tables such as Figure 2.14c. Conditional probabilities are usually measured in terms of relative frequencies. The correlation functions of Figure 5.1 provide a better picture of relative frequencies. However, in some experiments, conditional probabilities are deliberately set on a trial-by-trial basis. In such cases contingency tables such as that of Figure 2.14c would better represent the conditions imposed. Which of the two representations is a better picture of what is learned by the organism is an empirical question not yet fully settled.

Negative Correlations

Negative correlations between rate of responding and rate of reinforcement like that illustrated in Figure 5.2c affect behavior usually by reducing its frequency. If a rat is given food when it *doesn't* press a bar and bar-presses reduce the frequency of food, the rat will soon stop bar pressing and, in fact, avoid the vicinity of the bar, even though bar-presses were previously used to obtain food.

Studies of Correlations

In the case of a positive correlation between an act (bar pressing) and reinforcement (food), when each bar-press produces its own reinforcement, we may ask which is more important, the fact that each bar-press produces food or the fact that rapid bar pressing produces frequent reinforcement? In the simple situations of Figure 5.1, where each bar-press is specifically reinforced, it is hard to decide between 1:1 connections and correlations. It may be that *only* 1:1 connections can be learned. If so, we would have to invent connections in more complex situations, where none are provided by the environment, as in the example of the fireman stoking coal. Such invention would, in effect, be an abandonment of our strategy as behaviorists: to deal only with that which can be measured, observed, and confirmed. Fortunately, there is some evidence that correlations can be learned, in fact, that they are learned in situations in which they are not specifically arranged by an experimenter.

One experiment that tests whether correlations can be learned when they are not accompanied by direct connections between responses and their consequences is the one by Herrnstein and Hineline described previously. They found that rats would learn to press a bar when presses were not followed by any consequence other than a reduced frequency of shock. In their experiment there was no 1:1 connection between responses and shocks or even between responses and shock-free periods. Instead, when the rats pressed at a rapid rate, shocks came at a slow rate and when rats pressed at a slow rate shocks came at a rapid rate. Under these conditions rats learned to press rapidly.

Another interesting experiment in this area was done by three researchers at the University of Pennsylvania, Martin Seligman, Steven Maier, and Richard Solomon. In our example of the broken elevator button, we talked about changing from one correlation to another; before the button broke, there was a positive correlation between button pressing and elevator arrivals (Figure 5.2b). We speculated that the change from this positive correlation to zero correlation would be hard to detect. Subjects would respond according to the correlation that they had originally learned, even after that correlation was changed (that is, people would press the elevator button frequently even after it had been disconnected). Seligman, Maier, and Solomon varied a set of correlations in the opposite direction. Whereas, in the example of the elevator, the correlation between button pressing and elevator arrivals was first positive and then zero, the correlation in this experiment was first zero and then positive.

On the first day of the experiment, dogs were exposed to electric shocks programmed independently of their behavior. Nothing the dogs could do prevented the shock or enabled them to escape it (each shock lasted five seconds). Any responses the dogs made were completely uncorrelated with electric shock. On the next day, the dogs were put into a shuttle box and again shocked. This time, however, the shocks were preceded by a signal and the dogs could jump over a barrier to escape the shock (or, if they were fast enough, to avoid it). Most of the dogs in this experiment did not learn to escape. The dogs seemed to "give up" and passively "accept" the shock. Some of the dogs learned to escape after they were dragged by the experimenters across the barrier. Even then, some of them did not learn. In this respect their behavior contrasted vividly with dogs who had not been previously exposed to the inescapable shock. These dogs quickly learned to escape, and then to avoid the shock in the shuttle box. Obviously the prior exposure to inescapable shock had a strong effect on the dogs' subsequent behavior in the shuttle box. It severely retarded their learning to avoid the shocks.

Once again, it is tempting to draw analogies to human behavior. Often, when people are put in situations where they cannot avoid pain no matter what they do, and then the situation is changed so that they can avoid pain, they have a difficult time learning the proper avoidance responses. A child who is beaten regularly no matter what he does may not learn to "behave well" when conditions are changed so that beatings only follow "bad" behavior. What is it, then, about the initial conditions where responses and shocks are uncorrelated that affects behavior later when they are correlated? Seligman, Maier, and Solomon have a vivid name for the effect of the uncorrelated initial condition. They call it *learned helplessness*. The dogs learned in the initial condition that nothing they did could affect the shock. Then, when they were exposed to a situation when they could avoid shock, they had to "unlearn" the helplessness that they had previously acquired. In our terms, the dogs first learned the zero correlation between shock and responding; then, when exposed to the positive correlation they failed to react to the change in correlation. They had to "unlearn" the zero correlation.

By analogy, a zero correlation between *positive* reinforcement and behavior would also retard the acquisition of a response correlated with reward. In the human case, rewarding a child no matter what he does would be as bad as punishing a child no matter what he does because both would retard the child's acquisition of behavior that leads to reward or avoids punishment. Just as learned helplessness results from uncorrelated punishment, *learned omnipotence* could result from uncorrelated reward.

The evidence provided by the Seligman, Maier, and Solomon experiment is that correlations, even when they are zero correlations, are learned (in the sense that they have a potent effect on behavior). It would be difficult to explain this experiment in terms of connections, because the important feature of the first stage of the experiment, when shocks and responses were uncorrelated, was that there were no connections established. If there were no connections, what could have been learned? In terms of correlations, however, the experiment is easy to explain, because zero correlations exist on the same continuum as positive correlations. There is no reason why they cannot be learned just as easily as positive correlations. Then, the zero correlation, already learned, interferes with the effect of the positive correlation imposed later.

One might ask, why substitute one highly speculative notion, that organisms learn correlations, for another, that organisms learn connections. If "connections" send us off on a hunt for unobserved stimuli and reinforcers, doesn't this new "correlation" theory send us off on a hunt for unobserved correlations? The answer is, that it does, but the critical difference is not whether we must look for previously unobserved events, but *where* we must look for them. The unobserved stimuli and reinforcers postulated by connectionists have usually been postulated within the organism, where we cannot observe them, while the correlations we are speculating about must be found between the organism's responses and its environment, an area in which we are able to look.

As behaviorists, we observe the organism as it interacts with its environment. Whatever rules or laws we have uncovered are rules and laws regarding this observable interaction. It is this aspect of modern behaviorism that most distinguishes it from other approaches to psychology. When a rat presses a bar to obtain food, for instance, we focus our attention on the relation between the food and the bar-presses rather than on the relation between the food and the hopes, expectations, fears, wishes, and dreams of the rat. If the rat learns a complex series of movements, we focus on the environmental manipulations necessary for the complex series of movements to occur rather than on the way they are encoded in the rat's mind or even in its brain.

STIMULUS CONTROL

Stimulus control is another term for stimulus discrimination. If an organism comes to respond one way in the presence of a stimulus and another way in its absence, then that stimulus is said to "control" the organism's behavior much as a red light controls traffic.

Stimulus Control in Classical Conditioning

We have already discussed stimulus control (discrimination) in classical conditioning. Recall the experiment of Shenger-Krestovnikova with circles and ellipses as stimuli for dogs (Figure 2.6). The circle (CS) was followed by food powder while the ellipse was not. At first dogs salivated when circles or ellipses were presented; they later came to salivate only when circles were presented (except when the circles and ellipses were almost identical). From one point of view, the dogs learned to discriminate between the circles and ellipses. From another point of view the circles gained control of the dog's salivation.

The most common form of discrimination conditioning consists of alternating two stimuli (like the circles and ellipses), with one followed by the unconditioned stimulus and the other not followed by the unconditioned stimulus. Because this form of discrimination conditioning is so common, there are special terms for the stimuli; the stimulus followed by the unconditioned stimulus (the circle) is called the CS+; the stimulus not followed by the unconditioned stimulus (the ellipse) is called the CS−.

There are, however, other ways to obtain stimulus control in classical conditioning. For example, instead of circles followed by food (and ellipses followed by no food), Shenger-Krestovnikova's experiment might have had circles followed by more food and ellipses by less food. The dogs then might have come to respond during exposure to both circles and ellipses, but to respond more during circles. Alternatively, Shenger-Krestovnikova might have adjusted the amount of food proportionally to the roundness of the ellipse. [In Figure 2.6, (b) would be followed by the least food, (c) by more food, (d) by still more food and (a) by the most food.] The dogs might then have come to salivate in proportion to the roundness of the stimulus. Still another alternative would have been to follow circles by food, and ellipses by electric shock to the paw. Then circles might have come to elicit salivation and ellipses, withdrawal.

Stimulus Control in Instrumental Conditioning

In instrumental conditioning the relation between behavior and reinforcement (or punishment) is very important, however, *signaling stimuli* (which are neither reinforcing nor punishing in themselves) can also play an important role. In classical conditioning the CS is correlated with reinforcement. In that sense the stimulus plays a primary role in classical conditioning. In instrumental conditioning, however, nonreinforcing stimuli play only a secondary role: They indicate changes in the correlation between behavior and reinforcement (or punishment). A good example of a stimulus serving such a secondary function in human behavior is an out-of-order sign on a Coke machine. This sign tells us about the relationship between dimes and Cokes but is not itself directly associated with either. Signs that signal a relation between responses and reinforcement are called *discriminative stimuli.*

As in classical conditioning, the most common discrimination procedures involve alternate presentation of two stimuli; in the presence of one stimulus, reinforcement is obtained; in the presence of the other, reinforcement is not obtained. As with classical conditioning, the stimuli for this special discrimination procedure also have special names. A discriminative stimulus that signals a positive correlation between responding and reinforcement is called an S^D ("ess dee"). A discriminative stimulus that signals the absence of reinforcement regardless of responding is called an S^Δ ("ess delta"). Figure 5.3 shows this common discrimination procedure with the two types of conditioning.

Classical discrimination procedure

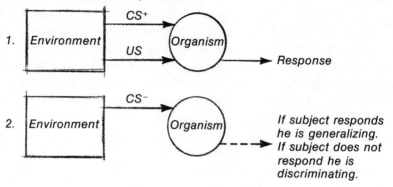

Instrumental discrimination procedure

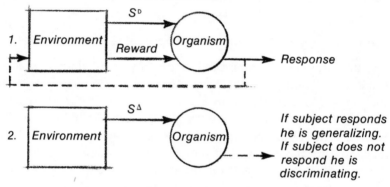

Figure 5.3 *Discrimination procedures for classical and instrumental conditioning.*

It is important to note, however, that alternation of stimuli signaling reinforcement and no reinforcement (as in Figure 5.3) is only one of many discrimination procedures—only one form of stimulus control. A discriminative stimulus may signal any relation between responding and reinforcement. The color of the sky in the morning, for example, gives an indication of whether a trip to the beach that afternoon will be reinforced by the opportunity to swim. But blue skies in the morning do not guarantee fair weather, nor do grey skies guarantee rain. Blue skies signal one relation between response and reinforcement, grey skies, another. Thus, while we may refrain from going to the beach on a grey day, such a signal is not, properly, an S^Δ because it is *possible* that our response (going to the beach) would be reinforced (nice weather at the beach) even when skies are grey in the morning.

Successive Discrimination and Simultaneous Discrimination

Within the confines of instrumental conditioning, discrimination has been studied in two ways. One way, called *successive discrimination*, is alternately presenting two different discriminative stimuli. The other way, called *simultaneous discrimination*, presents two discriminative stimuli together.

The alternating green and red of a traffic light, telling us to go (respond) in the presence of the green and stop (not respond) in the presence of the red is an example of successive discrimination. The adjacent green and red lights marking open and closed toll booths on a highway or bridge are an example of simultaneous discrimination. They tell us not whether to go or stop, but whether to go one way or another. In general, simultaneous-discrimination situations can produce finer distinctions in responses to stimuli than successive-discrimination situations. There are two reasons for this greater sensitivity of simultaneous discrimination. First of all, the stimuli themselves are easier to tell apart when presented simultaneously. It is easier, for instance, to tell a darker from a lighter shade of grey when the two greys are adjacent than when they are seen at different times. Secondly, even when the stimuli are clearly distinguishable, the properties of simultaneous procedures tend to create greater differences in performance than the properties of successive procedures. In successive discriminations, responding appropriate to one stimulus when it appears does not preclude responding appropriate to the other when it appears.

In simultaneous discriminations, on the other hand, when the organism is responding appropriately for one stimulus, it is losing time during which it might be responding appropriately for the other.

It is easy to see how simultaneous discrimination is more sensitive than successive discrimination in everyday life. At home, where dinner is put before someone, he often has the choice only of eating it or not. Observing a person's eating habits at home may tell you little about his preferences for food, since many people will eat whatever is put in front of them. In a restaurant, however, a choice is available, and eating one food often precludes eating another. Here, the same person is liable to be more "discriminating."

Connections

In classical conditioning the stimulus (the CS) is said to cause the response; in instrumental conditioning the stimulus is said to set the occasion for the response.

The CS in classical conditioning is like an airraid siren signaling an event to come and generating a direct response. The discriminative stimulus of instrumental conditioning is like the "Open" sign in a store window signaling that *if* we were to turn the knob of the door, the door would open.

This distinction rests on the distinction we previously made between elicited and emitted responses. During classical conditioning, responses are preceded by the US and are said to be elicited, or caused, by the US. After conditioning has taken place (when responses begin to occur after the CS), the responses are, by extension, said to be elicited or caused by the CS. During instrumental conditioning, on the other hand, responses are not preceded in any strict way by any stimulus. They are said to be emitted by the organism. The discriminative stimulus never invariably indicates reinforcement. It may indicate that reinforcement is available *provided* some response is made. Thus, when responding increases in frequency during the discriminative stimulus, we do not say that the stimulus elicits or causes the responses, but that the stimulus *sets the occasion* for the responses to occur.

Accordingly, when pecking of pigeons at a key is reinforced when the key is green and unreinforced when the key is dark, and the pigeon pecks more frequently at the green key, we say that the green key sets the occasion for the response as opposed to the notion that the green key *causes* the response. Similarly, when a man is paid for working on weekdays and not paid for working on weekends we say that the stimuli that tell him what day of the week it is (for example, checking a calendar) set the occasion for his work. It would be awkward to say that checking a calendar *causes* the man to work. We also realize that these stimuli, while controlling whether the man works or not, do not exert exclusive control. It is rare to find a 1:1 correspondence of weekdays and working.

Testing for Control by S^D and S^Δ

Let us return to the procedure illustrated in the lower part of Figure 5.3. Two discriminative stimuli are alternated. One (the S^D) signals a positive correlation between responding and reinforcement. The other (the S^Δ) signals a zero correlation, with no reinforcement programmed, regardless of responding. The behavior usually observed under these conditions is straightforward: responding during the S^D, no responding during the S^Δ.

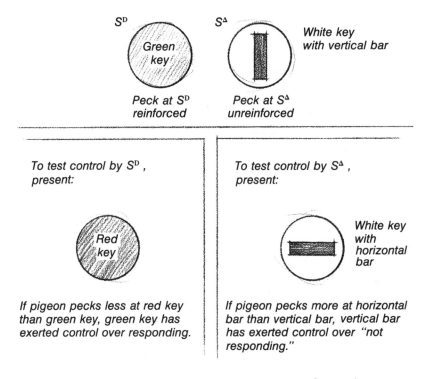

Figure 5.4 *Procedures for testing control by S^D and S^{Δ}.*

A particular instance of such a discrimination, involving a pigeon and a key, is illustrated at the top of Figure 5.4. The pigeon's pecks are reinforced when the key is green (S^D) and not reinforced when the key is white with a vertical bar (S^{Δ}). After alternate exposure to the two discriminative stimuli, the pigeon comes to peck at the key when it is green and not to peck at the key when it is white with a vertical bar.

What has the pigeon learned about the two discriminative stimuli? Consider these three alternatives:

a. The pigeon learns to peck when the key is green (S^D).
b. The pigeon learns not to peck when the key is white with a vertical bar (S^{Δ}).
c. The pigeon learns to peck when the key is green *and* not to peck when the key is white with a vertical bar.

A parallel set of questions can be raised about virtually any discrimination. A little boy may be rewarded for kissing his mother and not rewarded for kissing his father. Does he learn (1) to kiss his mother, (2) not to kiss his father, or (3) both?

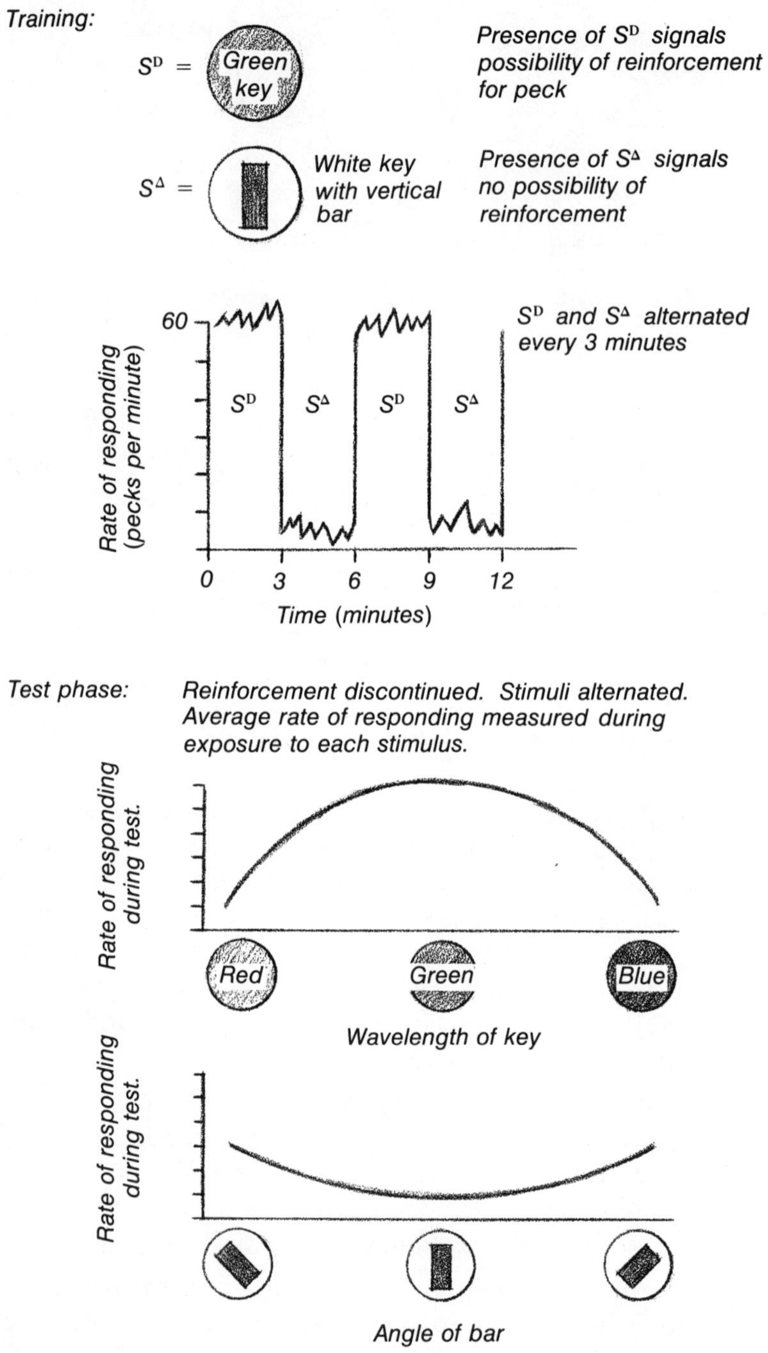

Figure 5.5 Hypothetical experiment to test discrimination.

Which alternative the boy learns depends on what he ordinarily does. If he ordinarily kisses nobody, he must learn to kiss his mother, and he need learn nothing specific about his father. If he ordinarily kisses everybody, he must learn not to kiss his father, but nothing specific about his mother. If he ordinarily kisses some people he must learn to kiss his mother *and* not to kiss his father.

The same sort of reasoning applies to the pigeon. If it ordinarily does not peck, it must learn to peck the green key. If it ordinarily pecks, it must learn not to peck the white key with the vertical bar. If it sometimes pecks, it must learn both.

Whether alternative (a), (b), or (c) applies in any given case depends on the organism (both its species and its previous experience), the stimuli, the reinforcement, the response, and the relation between the reinforcement and the response. The question that concerns us here is how to test the alternatives.

Alternatives (a) and (b) imply that one of the stimuli has no effect. Alternative (a) implies that the S^Δ has no effect, and alternative (b) implies that the S^D has no effect. One way to test either of these alternatives is the hypothetical experiment shown in Figure 5.5. The rationale for the tests follows a somewhat complicated argument. The stimulus that is supposed to have no effect is varied. If it is argued, as it is in alternatives (a) and (b), that one of the stimuli has no effect, then its variation also ought to have no effect.

If, on the other hand, varying either stimulus has the effect of producing variation in behavior, then alternative (c) must have been correct.

An important practical point of the tests is that the S^D and S^Δ must be capable of separate variation along different continua. In the illustration in Figure 5.5, the continuum is color for the S^D and angle of the bar for the S^Δ. Suppose otherwise, that the S^D and S^Δ varied along the same continuum—that the S^D was a simple white key, the S^Δ was a grey key (and the continuum is brightness). Then in the test phase, any new stimulus (a new shade of grey) would be a variation of both the S^D and the S^Δ. If the pigeon pecked less during the new stimulus, there would be no way of knowing whether it was because the stimulus was less like the S^D or more like the S^Δ. In the example in Figure 5.5, on the other hand, where the S^D and S^Δ are on two continua, we can be fairly certain that while the red key is not like the S^D, it is no more like the S^Δ than the green key was.

Another practical problem with the procedure in Figure 5.5, is what to do about reinforcement while the test stimuli are presented. For tests of the efficacy of S^D, for instance, the usual solution is to stop reinforcement altogether during the test and alternate the original S^D and a group of test stimuli varying along the same dimension (color, in the case of the example in Figure 5.5). This would be a simple generalization experiment where responding would be expected to fall off as the stimuli became more different from the original S^D, provided the S^D had an effect, i.e., provided either alternative (a) or (c) was true. Otherwise (if alternative (b) were true), responding would not drop off, but would remain at a high value as the color of the stimulus was varied.

For tests of the efficacy of S^Δ, a corresponding procedure is followed. Reinforcements are discontinued, and the original S^Δ is alternated with test stimuli varying along the same dimension (tilt of the bar across the white key in Figure 5.5). This experiment shown in Figure 5.5 (bottom curve) would test generalization of the S^Δ. Responding would be expected to increase as the stimuli became more different from the original S^Δ provided the S^Δ had an effect (provided either alternative (b) or (c) were true). Otherwise (if alternative (a) were true), responding would not increase but would remain at the same low value as the angle of the bar was changed.

While the specific hypothetical experiment of Figure 5.5 has not been performed exactly as described here, enough similar experiments have been performed for us to be certain that in the case described (pigeons pecking a key), alternative (c) is correct. Both S^D and S^Δ gradients have been found. Figure 5.5 shows a hypothetical S^D and an S^Δ test-phase gradient. Usually S^Δ gradients are somewhat shallower than S^D gradients. Some experimenters have speculated that this is because the S^D is the only stimulus signaling reinforcement, while the S^Δ shares the property of signaling nonreinforcement with the myriad other stimuli in the pigeon's environment. Since the S^D is unique and the S^Δ somewhat more general, the pigeon is likely to respond in the presence of a new stimulus as if it were another of the general, more common "S^Δ"s. In the generalization test, therefore, the particular S^Δ of training does not produce as much discrimination in responding as the S^D of training. This is another way of saying that while alternative (c) is correct, alternatives (a) and (b) are not equally incorrect. There is some truth to alternative (a) in the case of Figure 5.5.

Some psychologists interpret the test-phase gradients shown in Figure 5.5 as reflections of processes inside the organism. The S^D gradient is said to mirror an excitatory process inside the organism. The excitation is a continuous state said to underlie emissions of discrete responses. The S^Δ gradient is said to mirror an inhibitory process inside the organism. The inhibition is said to underlie the nonemission of the response.* It is arguable whether the concepts of excitation and inhibition are necessary to mediate between environment and behavior. As behaviorists, we would prefer to relate stimuli such as the green and white keys directly to the organism's behavior.

Complex Discriminations

Most experiments in the laboratory use discriminative stimuli of a simple kind—they use tones, lights, bars, and so forth. Yet, we know that humans and animals are capable of much more complex discriminations. We recognize the faces of our relatives, the handwriting of our friends, and their voices. Animals also are capable of making complex discriminations of this kind. Dogs recognize their masters' faces, and the famous RCA trademark reminds us that a dog can recognize his master's voice as well.

As an illustration of the complex discriminations that are possible, consider the following experiment with pigeons. Thousands of photographs were taken of vehicles of various kinds. The pictures were then sorted into two groups, those that contained trucks or parts of trucks, and those that contained only cars. The pictures were shown in random order to the pigeons, but the same picture was never shown twice to the same pigeon. While the pictures were being shown, the pigeons could peck a key. Occasionally, a peck would produce some food, but most of the time pecks had no effect. The critical point of the experiment was that for some pigeons pecks were reinforced only if the picture contained a truck or part of a truck. For other pigeons, pecks were reinforced only when the picture contained cars or parts of cars. In other words, for the first group of pigeons, trucks were "S^D"s and cars were "S^Δ"s; for the other group, conditions were reversed. As far as the experimenters could tell, there was no difference between the two groups of photographs other than the cars-versus-trucks distinction. The two groups of photographs were equally light, equally colorful, and equally complex. Yet, within a few weeks of daily exposure to the photographs, the pigeons came to peck rapidly when exposed to a picture containing a truck (if that was the S^D) or a car (if that was the S^D) and slowly or not at all when the picture contained the S^Δ vehicle. How was this discrimination made? Possibly each pigeon had its own strategy. Perhaps some counted the axles on the vehicles. Perhaps some recognized the distinctive hoods or fenders of trucks or

---

*The notion that inhibition is associated with nonreinforcement comes from Pavlov's conception of extinction as a positive inhibitory process (see Figure 2.4).

simply discriminated the size of the vehicle. (Although, since some vehicles were close and some far away, this could not be a simple size discrimination. It would have to be based on the relative size of the vehicle compared to its surroundings.) The complexity of the discrimination can be appreciated when we realize that with all our modern technology, we are now only on the threshold of our ability to build machines to make equivalent discriminations.

The important point here is that whatever the detailed strategy of the individual pigeons, there was an invariance in the molar properties of their behavior (pecking did occur in the presence of the S^D). Furthermore, whatever the strategy of the individual pigeons, their behavior is subject to manipulation in the same way by reinforcing pecks in the presence of the S^D. When differential reinforcement was discontinued, the discrimination deteriorated, and the pigeons responded equally during the two kinds of pictures. For the behaviorist, this covariance between properties of behavior (responding) and properties of the environment (cars or trucks) is the important part of the experiment. The strategy of a particular pigeon is a matter for speculation only insofar as it leads to future experiments. (For instance, if the pigeons counted axles, they would do badly in discriminating cars from two-axled trucks.) When the particular strategy hypothesized does not lead to specific behavioral consequences, the behaviorist loses interest in it.

Bibliography

There is very little published specifically on connections and correlations. The previously cited theoretical accounts by Guthrie, Hull, Tolman, and Skinner, all have a point of view on the subject. Tolman was first to call himself a molar behaviorist, and *molar behaviorism* (the view that stimuli and responses need not be discrete sensory or muscular events) is probably the best way to describe the present approach. However, the most direct influence on the material in this chapter is the work of B. F. Skinner. He showed that behavior could be accounted for quantitatively without the notion of a 1:1 correspondence between stimulus and response. The present account extends his ideas to account quantitatively for behavior without a 1:1 relation between responses and reinforcement. See R. J. Herrnstein's "Method and theory in the study of avoidance" (*Psychological Review*, 76, 1969, 49–70) for a formal application of these notions to avoidance learning.

A recent theoretical article that argues strongly for a law of effect based on correlations rather than connections is, W. M. Baum's "The correlation based law of effect" (*Journal of the Experimental Analysis of Behavior*, 20, 1973,

137–153). Another theoretical article on the same topic is T. J. Testa's "Causal relationships and the acquisition of avoidance responses" (*Psychological Review, 81*, 1974, 491–506.

The experiment by Seligman, Maier, and Solomon is described in their paper, "Pavlovian fear conditioning and learned helplessness," in *Aversive Conditioning and Learning,* edited by R. Church and B. Campbell (New York: Appleton-Century-Crofts, 1969).

In the specific area of stimulus control, there are many published works. See the article by H. S. Terrace in Honig's *Operant Behavior* (cited in the bibliography at the end of Chapter 3) for a clearly written account. See also the sections on stimulus control in the Mackintosh and Nevin-Reynolds books (also previously cited). For descriptions of experiments on inhibition see H. M. Jenkins's "Generalization gradients and the concept of inhibition," in *Stimulus Generalization,* edited by D. I. Mostofsky (Stanford: Stanford University Press, 1965, pp. 55–62). A thorough discussion of the concept of inhibition can also be found in E. Hearst, S. Besley, and W. G. Farthing's "Inhibition and the stimulus control of operant behavior" (*Journal of the Experimental Analysis of Behavior, 14*, 1970, 373–409). For experiments in complex discriminations in animals see "The complex discriminated operant: Studies of matching-to-sample and related problems" by W. W. Cumming and R. Berryman (in the Mostofsky book). Also see R. J. Herrnstein and D. Loveland's "Complex visual concept in the pigeon" (*Science, 146,* 1964, 549–551).

6

Some New Directions

The previous chapters have briefly sketched the history and the recent progress of the science of the behavior of organisms. In this chapter we take up the question: In what directions is this emerging science moving? The following sections cover only four of the many areas in which behaviorism is being extended and applied: (1) the treatment of dysfunctional human behavior, (2) the quantification of behavioral variables, (3) self-control, (4) language and the talking chimpanzees.

WARNING

In the physical sciences, trained engineers, familiar with both the physical sciences themselves and with machines and their operation, develop practical uses for the laws that scientists discover. In behavioral sciences we are all engineers in a sense. We are, ourselves, behaving organisms and we sometimes feel a pressing need for rules that will tell us how to behave. There is thus a strong temptation to draw analogies from pigeons to people—to attempt to apply laboratory data directly to our everyday lives. However, the behavior of an organism in response to the simple contingencies of an isolated laboratory environment may be quite different from the behavior of an organism exposed to the complex contingencies of a nonlaboratory environment. We hope to eventually apply what we have learned in the laboratory to the problems of everyday life. But such application must be undertaken with the utmost care.

Perhaps the greatest danger of premature application of the findings of behavioral science to the complex world outside the laboratory is that it gives us the illusion that we are acting scientifically when, in reality, our behavior is no more effective than it would be if it were guided simply by tradition. Since we know little of the complex effects of spanking on children, it is no more scientific to tell ourselves we are spanking a child "to reduce his maladaptive behavior" than to spank him "because we are mad at him." (It is for this reason that the examples that are drawn here from everyday life should not be regarded as direct guides to action.)

DYSFUNCTIONAL BEHAVIOR

In the laboratory we are concerned with complex contingencies of reinforcement and with quantifying the variables that control behavior. We tend to take for granted the basic principles by which such control is obtained, the principles outlined in this book. At several institutions, however, researchers have been resolutely applying these principles to the treatment of dysfunctional human behavior. These applications have been successful as measured against results with more traditional methods of treating behavioral disorders.

One way to look at dysfunctional behavior is to regard it as behavior that has evolved "out of synchrony" with changes in the environment. According to this view, when the environment changes too suddenly or drastically, an organism may not be able to "keep up"—to compensate adequately, to behave so as to maximize reward under the changed contingencies.

Someone who is unhappy about his behavior may seek help from a therapist. It is up to the therapist to provide the appropriate environmental gradations that will reward the patient for approximations to the desired behavior.

Sometimes it is society, rather than the individual himself, that desires a change in his behavior. Murder is an obvious example of a dysfunctional behavior that harms human society. Then there are those individuals who cannot function in the particular society in which they live. Some cannot hold a job; some cannot interact with other people; some cannot communicate rationally; others cannot even eat or attend to their own bodily needs without constant assistance. In the United States alone, more than a quarter of a million people are held in federal and state prisons, and more than half a million people are held in mental institutions. The basic question regarding an institutionalized person is: Do we want to use the most effective means we know to change his or her behavior for the better (that is, to bring it into conformity with the environmental contingencies)? If we refuse to try, we will continue to expose the inmate to the contingencies of reinforcement in our present institutions. This course of action often does provide a crude but effective means of modifying behavior—for the worse.

The techniques used in behavior modification are varied. At present, behavior modification outside the laboratory is more of an art than a science; each therapist evolves his own techniques for application of behavioral principles. Let us consider two examples:

(1) In a mental hospital (as in any hospital or institution where boredom is a strong factor) the attention of the staff is a potent reinforcer. Almost every mental hospital is "short staffed," and there is a tendency for staff members to pay most attention to those patients who give the most trouble. Thus, a behaviorist would contend that there is a built-in mechanism in most mental hospitals to reinforce trouble-making and disturbances of various kinds. An easy way for a patient to get personal attention under these circumstances is to refuse to eat. In fact, in many mental hospitals there is a large number of patients who must be coaxed to enter the dining room and once there, who must be fed like infants. A vicious circle develops. Patients refuse to eat, becoming the center of attention. This, in turn, reinforces their refusal to eat and gets them more attention. Clearly, positive feedback is at work in the situation.

In a report published in 1962, Teodore Ayllon and Erick Haughton, on the staff of a hospital in Saskatchewan, Canada described a technique they devised to break the vicious circle. They selected a group of thirty schizophrenic women with a history of refusal to eat. Several attendants usually took thirty minutes to get the women into the dining room. Ayllon and Haughton then changed the contingencies. The attendants were instructed to ignore the patients. A bell sounded to announce that the dining room was open. Thirty minutes later the doors of the dining room were closed and patients were no longer allowed in. Whoever did not enter within 30 minutes did not eat that meal. Although, at first, few patients entered the dining room within the allotted time, eventually almost all of them did. Then the time was decreased from 30 minutes to 20 minutes to 15 minutes and to 5 minutes. Finally, almost all of the patients entered the dining room within five minutes of the bell without the assistance of the attendants. Next, Haughton and Ayllon made entrance to the dining room contingent on dropping a penny (which the patients received from a nurse) into a slot. Then, in order to receive the coin, each patient had to press a button simultaneously with another patient at another button. At the end of the experiment, all the patients, selected originally for their refusal to eat, were engaging in cooperative behavior in order to obtain admission to the dining hall. Here is an example of making one reinforcer (attention from staff) independent of a behavior (refusal to eat) and making another reinforcer (food) dependent on a behavior (sharing a task with another person). The first reinforcer lost its effect on the patient's behavior and the second reinforcer gained effectiveness.

(2) A second example also involves the gradual shaping of a response, this time a verbal response of a *catatonic schizophrenic* patient who had been completely mute for nineteen years prior to the incidents reported here. To say the least, the patient, referred to as S (for Subject), was withdrawn and exhibited little psychomotor activity. The case history that follows is not unique. It is from a report published in 1960 by Wayne Isaacs, James Thomas, and Israel Goldiamond of Anna State Hospital in Illinois.*

> The S was brought to a group therapy session with other chronic schizophrenics (who were verbal), but he sat in the position in which he was placed and continued the withdrawal behaviors which characterized him. He remained impassive and stared ahead even when cigarettes, which other members accepted, were offered to him and were waved before his face. At one session, when E removed cigarettes from his pocket, a package of chewing gum accidentally fell out. The S's eyes moved toward the gum and then returned to their usual position. This response was chosen by E as one with which he would start to work, using the method of successive approximation. (This method finds use where E desires to produce responses which are not present in the current repertoire of the organism and which are considerably removed from those which are available. The E then attempts to "shape" the available behaviors into the desired form, capitalizing upon both the variability and regularity of successive behaviors. The shaping process involves the reinforcement of those parts of a selected response which are successively in the desired direction and the nonreinforcement of those which are not. For example, a pigeon may be initially reinforced when it moves its head. When this movement occurs regularly, only an upward movement may be reinforced, with downward movements not reinforced. The pigeon may now stretch its neck, with this movement reinforced. Eventually the pigeon may be trained to peck at a disc which was initially high above its head and at which it would normally never peck. In the case of the psychotic under discussion, the succession was eye movement, which brought into play occasional facial movements including those of the mouth, lip movements, vocalizations, word utterance, and finally verbal behavior.)

*In case histories, the subject is often referred to as S, the experimenter as E.

The S met individually with E three times a week. Group sessions also continued. The following sequence of procedures was introduced in the private sessions. Although the weeks are numbered consecutively, they did not follow at regular intervals since other duties kept E from seeing S every week.

Weeks, 1, 2. A stick of gum was held before S's face, and E waited until S's eyes moved toward it. When this response occurred, E as a consequence gave him the gum. By the end of the second week, response probability in the presence of the gum was increased to such an extent that S's eyes moved toward the gum as soon as it was held up.

Weeks 3, 4. The E now held the gum before S, waiting until he noticed movement in S's lips before giving it to him. Toward the end of the first session of the third week, a lip movement spontaneously occurred, which E promptly reinforced. By the end of this week both lip movement and eye movement occurred when the gum was held up. The E then withheld giving S the gum until S spontaneously made a vocalization, at which time E gave S the gum. By the end of this week, holding up the gum readily occasioned eye movement toward it, lip movement, and a vocalization resembling a croak.

Weeks, 5, 6. The E held up the gum, and said, "Say gum, gum," repeating these words each time S vocalized. Giving S the gum was made contingent upon vocalizations increasingly approximating gum. At the sixth session (at the end of Week 6), when E said, "Say gum, gum," S suddenly said, "Gum, please." This response was accompanied by reinstatement of other responses of this class, that is, S answered questions regarding his name and age.

Thereafter he responded to questions by E both in individual sessions and in group sessions, but answered no one else. Responses to the discriminative stimuli of the room generalized to E on the ward; he greeted E on two occasions in the group room. He read from signs in E's office upon request by E.

Since the response now seemed to be under the strong stimulus control of E, the person, attempt was made to generalize the stimulus to other people. Accordingly, a nurse was brought into the private room; S smiled at her. After a month, he began answering her questions. Later, when he brought his coat to a volunteer worker on the ward, she interpreted the gesture as a desire to go outdoors and conducted him there. Upon informing E of the incident, she was instructed to obey S only as a consequence of explicit verbal requests by him. The S thereafter vocalized requests. These instructions have now been given to other hospital personnel, and S regularly initiates verbal requests when nonverbal requests have no reinforcing consequences. Upon being taken to the commissary, he said, "Ping pong," to the volunteer worker and played a game with her. Other patients, visitors, and members of hospital-society-at-large continue, however, to interpret non-verbal requests and to reinforce them by obeying S.

Some nonbehaviorists object to this kind of direct treatment of dysfunctional behavior on the grounds that it treats "only the behavioral symptoms of the disorder" rather than "the underlying disorder," which is said to exist in "the mind" of the patient. These critics contend that as long as the basic psychological problem is not found by subtle and sophisticated techniques and revealed to the patient, elimination of one symptom will tend to be replaced by the substitution of another. In actual instances of behavioral treatment, however, dysfunctional behaviors have been eliminated, and such a hypothetical substitution of symptoms is virtually never found. *

But will a successful treatment in a mental hospital (or therapist's office), where the environment is largely under control, persist when a person returns to the normal complex environment outside of the institution? Behavioral modifications wrought in an institution could easily be extinguished in other environments. Clearly, it is important that appropriate behavior continue to be rewarded in the "outside world."

Often dysfunctional behavior seems to be subject to the effect of positive feedback. For some reason a man has a mild behavioral disturbance; his relatives and friends overreact to the mild disturbance and upset him; this increases the disturbance, which, in turn, provokes stronger reactions. A behavioral therapist's treatment of such behavior would be designed to break this pattern in a direct fashion. Relatives who have refused to have a patient home for visits because they are upset by the patient's strange appearance or behavior may change their attitude when the patient's appearance and behavior are less strange. Their changed attitude may well reinforce normal behavior outside the institution.

QUANTIFICATION OF BEHAVIORAL VARIABLES

While some applications of behavioral techniques can be made at present, true behavioral engineering awaits better quantification of behavioral variables. There is a forbidding stretch of terra incognita between the laws of conditioning and the practical manipulation of behavior. Pavlov's and Thorndike's qualitative laws say little to a mother confronted with an unruly child, a teacher struggling with a balky class, or a legislator concerned with the public good. The

---

*Even if the critics were correct, and behavioral therapy treated only symptoms, surely it would be better to get rid of the symptoms and not the underlying disease than to "cure" the disease and leave all the symptoms intact. (A man would not worry about a cold without its symptoms to tell him that he has it. Similarly, he would worry a great deal if the symptoms of runny nose, headaches, sneezing and high temperature persisted even though his "basic cold" had been cured.)

"controlling agency" is often without a clearly defined response to control, let along access to potent stimuli, reinforcers or punishers. But even with the essentials for conditioning (stimuli, responses, and consequences), the quantitative ingredients for a practical course of action are still lacking. It is, for example, insufficient to assert that good driving would be encouraged by an incentive program. In order to be useful, the information must be quantitative. Will an incentive program stimulate enough good driving to justify its cost?

Where response and consequence can be measured as monetary quantities or their equivalents, classical economics has been able to deal quantitatively with behavior; the modern science of game theory is an extension of an analysis of behavior from an economist's point of view. However, the limitation of a quantification of behavior in purely economic terms is not only that it assumes men will always act rationally (to maximize money gained) but also that it focuses only on situations that permit monetary analysis. Organisms are often found in situations that do not easily lend themselves to such a characterization—for example, a mother with her child. Yet in both monetary and nonmonetary situations, presumably in accordance with a single set of psychological laws, the behavior of organisms is governed by its consequences.

Laws relating the parameters of reward and punishment to behavior can be regarded as a sort of behavioral economics. An application of quantitative techniques in the area of choice was made in 1970 by Richard Herrnstein at Harvard University. Herrnstein wanted to relate the behavior of an organism in a choice situation to behavior in a single response situation (see Figure 2.24 for characteristics of the two situations). In a sense, he reasoned, all behavior is choice behavior. Imagine a pie chart representing ways the behavior of a single organism can be classified; we can think of the organism as constantly engaged in choosing between various alternatives represented by pie-shaped sections of the chart. The more one alternative is chosen, the bigger the section of the circle in the representation. A pigeon's pecks on a key can be represented in this way (as shown on the left in Figure 6.1). If we assume that each peck takes an equal amount of time, the rate of pecking is a measure of the time spent pecking; the faster the rate of pecking, the larger the section of the pie. We can therefore think of the pigeon as constantly choosing between pecking and not pecking, with choice represented by the relative sizes of the sections. However, we cannot draw an accurate pie chart because we have no way of knowing how long a peck takes. We measure the moment that the key is depressed—but the pigeon starts to peck before our moment of meas-

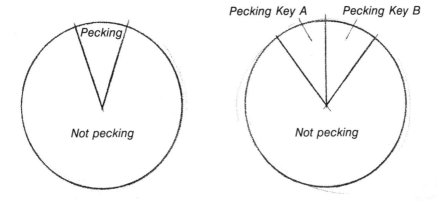

Figure 6.1 *Division of a pigeon's time into "pecking" and "not pecking" with (left) a single key and (right) with two keys.*

urement and continues afterward. Our measure gives us the rate of pecking, but it cannot give us the duration of each peck. We *assume* that all pecks have equal duration. Thus, if our measurements doubled we should double the size of the slice of the pie in Figure 6.1 that represents pecking. But we do not know the size of the original slice that we are to double.

Now consider two keys in the chamber. (The situation changes to that shown on the right in Figure 6.1.) With two keys we consider the pigeon to be faced with a three-way choice. The pigeon may peck on Key A or Key B, or may choose not to peck. Similarly, three keys in the chamber would mean a four-way choice: pecking on any of the three keys or not pecking.

It is easy to measure the rate of pecking on one key and compare that rate to the rate of pecking on another key. In this comparison a remarkably simple relationship is usually found. If the pigeons are made hungry and pecks on the keys occasionally produce food, the rate of pecking on each key is a constant fraction of the rate at which food reinforcement is obtained by pecking the key. In other words, if

P_A stands for the rate of pecking Key A,
P_B stands for the rate of pecking Key B, and
R_A stands for the rate of reinforcement obtained by pecking Key A,
R_B stands for the rate of reinforcement obtained by pecking Key B,

then

$$\frac{P_A}{P_B} = \frac{R_A}{R_B} \tag{1}$$

No matter how many keys there are in the chamber, the equation above holds between any pair of the keys. Since we are assuming that each peck has the same duration (without knowing what the duration is), relative rate of pecking equals relative time spent pecking. Thus, equation (1) says that the pigeon distributes its time pecking a key in proportion to the rate at which reinforcement is produced by pecking that key. The total reinforcement may come from many small individual presentations of food or a few large food presentations. What counts is the overall rate of delivery.

Generalizing this result, we say that an organism distributes its time among several activities in proportion to the rewards to be derived from engaging in those activities. If this generalization holds, we may turn back to the case of Figure 6.1a, where the activities of the pigeon with which we were concerned were pecking a single key or not pecking that key. If we use the symbol N to represent time not pecking the key, and R_N to represent any reward involved in not pecking the key (from resting, preening, pecking the floor, and so forth), we have:

$$\frac{P_A}{N} = \frac{R_A}{R_N} \tag{2}$$

Logically, another way of saying the same thing is:

$$\frac{P_A}{P_A + N} = \frac{R_A}{R_A + R_N} \tag{3}$$

Again, as opposed to the two-key situation of Equation 1, we have no way of measuring N and R_N, but we can assume that R_N is constant for a given situation and a given pigeon, and, because $P_A + N$ exhaust whatever the organism can do with a single key, this sum equals a constant. Thus:

$$P_A = \frac{(P_A + N)R_A}{R_A + (R_N)} \tag{4}$$

where the items in brackets are constants. Equation 4 makes a prediction that can be tested. It predicts a certain relationship between the rate of an activity and the reinforcement of that activity, holding all other reinforcements constant.

Herrnstein has found that, by and large, this prediction is confirmed in experiments with animals. Figure 6.2 shows the rate at which a pigeon pecks a single available key as a function of the reinforcements delivered to that pigeon for pecking. The reinforcements were programmed on a variable-interval schedule (see Chapter 3

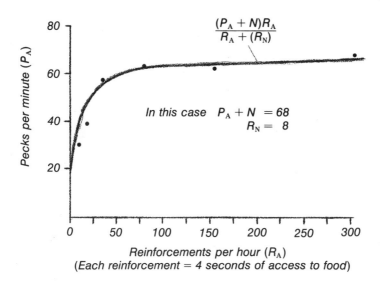

In this case $P_A + N = 68$
$R_N = 8$

Figure 6.2 *The rate of pecking of a pigeon as a function of the rate of reinforcement on a variable-interval schedule of reinforcement. The points are fitted by Equation 4. The constant $(P_A + N)$ is the rate at which this pigeon would peck if it spent all its time pecking. The constant (R_N) is the equivalent rate of reinforcement for nonpecking. [Data from A. C. Catania and G. S. Reynolds, "A quantitative analysis of the responding maintained by interval schedules of reinforcement," Journal of the Experimental Analysis of Behavior, 1968, 11, 327–383.]*

for a discussion of schedules). The points on the graph show the data for one particular pigeon. The solid line is Equation 4. The constant $(P_A + N)$ can be interpreted as the rate of pecking if the pigeon spent all its time pecking. The constant R_N can be interpreted as the rate of reinforcement from other sources than that specifically arranged by the experimenter.

Whether Equation 1 and Equation 4 (which is another form of Equation 1) will prove valid over the long run and whether N and R_N are meaningful in the sense that they can predict an individual's behavior in other situations are open questions and we await practical applications of this quantitative work. However, we can see from Equation 4 the direction they might take. Two ways of changing a given behavior (P_A) are by manipulating reward for that behavior (R_A) and by manipulating reward for other behavior (R_N). When faced with these alternatives in practical situations, how can we decide which to take? For instance, if a traffic engineer wants people to take an alternate route, is it better to make the first route harder to travel on or make the alternate route easier to travel on? Should a mother reduce crying in her child by reducing the reinforcement for crying (by ignoring it) or by increasing attention to the child during periods without crying?

Equation 4 tells us the surprising fact that manipulating reward for *other* behavior will occasionally have a stronger effect on a given response than manipulating reward for that response itself. Which is more effective depends on the relative size of the two rewards in the first place. In general the change in reward that will have most effect on a response is that which involves a larger percentage change in reward. In other words, a given change in a big reward (adding $5 to $100) will have less effect than the same change made in a small reward (adding $5 to $5). Thus, a good rule to remember is to change the reward that is initially smaller in order to have the greatest effect.

SELF-CONTROL

Frequently, people want to change and better control their own behavior. Some people want to study more, some less. Some want to work harder, some to learn to relax. Some people want to be more assertive with their employers or employees or with their relatives; some want to be less combative. Such behavior changes can often be brought about by behavioral techniques. A person can be rewarded for approaches to the desired behavior in a manner that parallels the way a pigeon is rewarded for desired approximations to a peck on a key. In a previous section we have seen that this relatively small-scale process (called *shaping*) bears certain similarities to the general process of the evolutionary development of species.

Self-control is actually a misnomer for self-induced change, for although some patterns of behavior may come from within ourselves in the sense that they were acquired before birth or soon thereafter, whatever causes a behavior to appear at a given time must come from interaction with the environment. Thus *self*-control really refers to the use of certain aspects of environment to control behavior.

The kinds of behavior that we shall place under the rubric of self-control are most easily defined by listing some examples. A person can exert self-control by biting his tongue, clapping his hand over his mouth to keep from laughing, putting a box of candy out of sight to keep from eating, or putting an alarm clock out of easy reach of his bed. All these are overt performances of one sort of behavior in order to

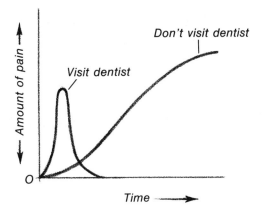

Figure 6.3 *Hypothetical diagram of the way pain would vary on visiting the dentist and without visiting the dentist.*

change the probability of later engaging in another sort of behavior. Less overt strategies of self-control are observed when an overweight person refrains from dessert or when someone refuses a cocktail at a party because he is driving home later. A close look at the contingencies in each of these examples reveals a common issue: *immediacy* versus *delay* of reinforcement or punishment.

Take the temporal issue away and the issue of self-control goes away as well. If it were suddenly discovered that cottage cheese was just as fattening (and therefore had the same ultimate consequences for me) as a roast beef sandwich, and if I still ate the cottage cheese, I would have to admit that I simply liked the cottage cheese better. The decision would become, like one between blue and brown suits, simply one of taste.

Psychologists have long noticed the now-versus-later character of self-control. Self-control comes into play not only when subjects prefer larger rewards in the future to smaller rewards in the present but also when they avoid greater pain in the future in return for lesser pain in the present. In the latter context, visiting the dentist shows self-control and not visiting him shows a lack of self-control. The reason for indecision between two alternatives—one clearly better than the other—is that the better alternative is only better in the long run (Figure 6.3). The worse alternative offers immediate benefit. The difference between someone who is controlling himself and someone who is not controlling himself is thus not in where the control is located (inside his skin or outside his skin); the difference is in whether or not his present behavior is taking future contingencies into account.

Does self-control explain why someone works at an unpleasant job? Yes—but only if there are rewards that extend further in time than the job itself. If the unpleasantness and the rewards occur only during the work, self-control is not a factor.

If we want to know how self-control is learned, the question to ask is, how do we shift the temporal locus of control from immediate to distant consequences?

We have argued in previous chapters that the cause of a behavior can be the relationship between that behavior and events in the environment. To take one example, Herrnstein and Hineline (Figure 3.20) arranged this set of contingencies for a rat: the rate of irregularly delivered brief electric shocks varied inversely with the rate of bar pressing. If the rats pressed faster, the shocks came slower; if they pressed slower, the shocks came faster. The rats learned to press the bar even though no single bar press avoided any single shock. In effect, they learned that the rate of bar presses and the rate of shocks were the critical variables.

Suppose in the Herrnstein-Hineline experiment that each bar press had cost the rat something. We could imagine that the effort of pressing was increased or that a low-intensity shock followed upon each press. In such a situation, the immediate consequences of pressing the bar would be painful (or effortful) but the long-term consequences of not pressing the bar would be still more painful. The picture would be something like that shown in Figure 6.3. Replace "Visit dentist" by "Press bar" and "Don't visit dentist" by "Don't press bar" and you have a fair picture of the rat's situation. Will rats press bars under these conditions? In a recent experiment, J. V. Lambert, P. J. Bersh, P. M. Hineline, and G. D. Smith found that rats consistently pressed the bar when a press produced a single shock immediately but avoided several shocks of equal intensity later on.

Can we say that the rats in the Lambert *et al.* experiment were exhibiting self-control? If the criterion for exhibiting self-control is choosing a larger future good over a smaller present good, then these rats were exhibiting self-control; they avoided a more painful experience in the distant future in favor of a less painful experience in the immediate future. If, on the other hand, we insist that exertions of "ego-strength," "internalization," "expectancy," or other cognitive or motivational events must also go on somewhere within the rat, we shall have the difficult task of trying to verify their occurrence. But such explanatory efforts are unnecessary. The behavior itself is all the evidence we need that self-control is going on. In short, it is the rat's behavior in relation to the contingencies imposed that constitutes self-control.

Similar arguments apply as well to human self-control. Human behavior is more complicated than rat behavior. But this is not because human behavior is controlled from the inside and rat behavior from the outside but because the environmental events controlling human behavior generally occur over a much longer interval than those that control the behavior of the rat. According to this view, when we refuse the third martini at a party (if we do refuse it), it is not because an internal force directs our behavior but because we are responding to a set of contingencies spread out widely in time before and after we are offered the drink. The wider contingencies include potential events on the way home and the next morning; the narrower contingencies include only events at the party itself. Why humans should act in accordance with the wider contingencies rather than with the narrower ones is a good question, which we shall discuss later. For now, let us say that the question is answered no better by referring to internal forces or states than it is without them.

The kind of self-control we have just described—turning down a drink—might be called "brute-force" self-control. When the temptation is offered, it is simply refused. The martini is turned down at the party, the bakery is passed without a purchase, the dessert is pushed away, and so on. The direct cause of such behavior is the long-term correlation between the behavior and its consequences.

An objection might be raised that the view espoused here applies well enough to brute-force self-control but not to more sophisticated techniques of self-control, such as those developed by Weight Watchers or Alcoholics Anonymous or those we are constantly inventing in everyday life to manipulate our own behavior. For example, consider the following ways in which a student might get himself to study:

1. He simply studies despite the temptation to go to the movies instead.
2. He rewards himself for studying by going to the movies after he studies.
3. He has previously deposited a fairly large sum of money with a friend. He has instructed the friend to check every half-hour during the evening to see that he is studying. If the friend does not find him studying, the friend is further instructed to send the money to a political party whose views are exactly contrary to those of the student.

We have already briefly discussed alternative 1 ("brute force"). What about alternatives 2 and 3? They are both forms of self-control because their object is to increase the likelihood that behavior will be in accordance with its long-term consequences. They are fairly representative of types of self-control often recommended by behavior therapists and might be called, respectively, "self-reinforcement" and "commitment."

Let us consider self-reinforcement first. A little analysis reveals that the reinforcements given to oneself do not support the behavior upon which they are contingent. Suppose, for a moment, that the student in our example increased his studying by going to the movies afterward. Now suppose that this self-reinforcement continued but that external reinforcers—the good grades, the knowledge, the social approval to be gained from studying—were withdrawn. How long would studying continue without them? What would the point of studying be? Would going to the movies continue to "work" as a self-imposed reinforcer for studying? One does not have to do an experiment to answer these questions negatively. In what sense, then, was the movie a reinforcer? This is a critical question because the test for a reinforcer must be whether it can support behavior. If we take away external reinforcers leaving only a form of self-reinforcement that supports no behavior other than that involved in its consumption, then self-reinforcement loses its effectiveness.

It seems likely that self-reinforcement is a form of secondary reinforcement. Going to the movies might have increased studying not because of its reinforcing properties (that is, the student's enjoyment of the film) but because of its stimulus properties (that is, what it meant to the student: "I am improving my study habits and will get better grades"). This hypothesis could be tested by substituting neutral events for rewards. For instance, a student who treats himself to a peanut after each 10 minutes of studying ought to study as well if, instead of eating it, he simply transfers the peanut from one dish to another as a way of counting 10-minute periods of studying. The question is clearly empirical, but the research on self-reinforcement, whether with humans or animals, has rarely addressed it directly.

A behavior therapist might ask the student to institute a program of self-reinforcement for studying as sort of a cast or mold for forming a new pattern of behavior, but the therapist might not be satisfied until the cast was removed. The program might start with going to the movies as a self-reinforcer, switch to a more convenient and less time-consuming activity like eating a peanut after each 10 minutes of studying, then switch to a program of record-keeping, then switch to nothing. Presumably, by this time, the contingency between studying and grades would be directly controlling studying. Relapses might be treated by returning to prior supports. The sequence from movies to peanuts to record-keeping to nothing may not constitute a gradual reduction of primary reinforcement but rather the association of a series of less and less vivid secondary reinforcements with future rewards.

Self-reinforcement may simply be like emphatically saying to oneself *"Yes. I did just do that."* following a behavior. Because of the extra emphasis put on a desired behavior in this manner, the feedback in self-reinforcement may well be more intense than the proprioceptive and kinesthetic feedback of most behaviors. Other things being equal, correlations between intense stimuli should affect behavior more than correlations between weak stimuli do. Were this not the case, self-reinforcement should not work.

Now let us turn to the sort of complicated strategies exemplified by alternative 3, in which the student has made an agreement with his friend to send his money to an opposing political party if he does not study. This self-control requires a commitment. It is rather like the signing of a contract specifying various kinds of performance in the future and setting forth penalties for failure to comply. George Ainslie and Leonard Green and I have shown that commitment of this kind is predicted by the simple descriptions of choice advanced by Herrnstein (described in the previous section). Ainslie's argument (and his experiment) differ in detail from Green's and mine, but the main arguments are the same and will be summarized here.

Figure 6.4 is a diagram of the commitment decision process in alternative 3. There are two decisions in question. Decision X, between studying and not studying, takes place in the evening when the student is supposed to study. At the time decision X is made the short-term consequences of not studying are very likely to determine the student's choice. Thus, not studying is the probable result. Decision Y takes place the morning before. Decision Y is between making the commitment and not making it. Assuming the commitment is effective (that the student absolutely will not tolerate the sending of his money to an opposing political party), making the commitment is equivalent to choosing the lower branch of Figure 6.4, to studying, and to experiencing the consequences of studying. At the time decision Y is made, the value of studying is likely to be higher than that of not studying and the student will probably agree to the commitment.

Once decision Y is available, and if we assume that the contingencies are effective, commitment behavior should follow *automatically*.

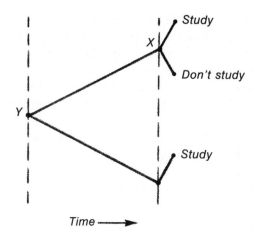

Figure 6.4 *Flow diagram of commitment to study. Choice at X is between studying immediately and not studying. It is assumed that a student would not study at X. Choice at Y is between having a choice later (top arm) and being forced to study later (bottom arm). A student who would not study at X might nevertheless commit himself to study by choosing the lower arm at Y.*

To make the point that this exercise of commitment is not dependent on ego strength, internalization, resistance to frustration, or other sophisticated cognitive or motivational phenomena, Ainslie showed with rats (and Green and I with pigeons), that relatively naive animals would exhibit commitment. The experiment Green and I did closely follows the schema of Figure 6.4. The pigeons were placed in a Skinner box with two translucent plastic disks side by side on one wall. Below the disks and equidistant from each was a hopper where food could be presented.

Choice X for the pigeons was indicated by illuminating one of the two disks with red light and the other with green light (as illustrated in Figure 6.5). If the pigeon pecked the red disk, the hopper opened immediately and gave the pigeon access to food for 2 seconds. If the pigeon pecked the green disk, the lights in the chamber went out for 4 seconds and then the hopper opened for 4 seconds. Thus, a peck at the green disk produced a reward twice as large, but delayed 4 seconds.

Choice Y for the pigeons was indicated by illuminating both disks with white light. If the pigeon pecked the left-hand disk 15 times, the

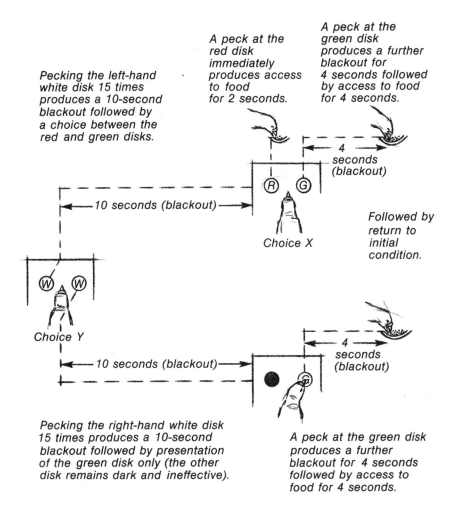

Pecking the left-hand white disk 15 times produces a 10-second blackout followed by a choice between the red and green disks.

A peck at the red disk immediately produces access to food for 2 seconds.

A peck at the green disk produces a further blackout for 4 seconds followed by access to food for 4 seconds.

← 4 → seconds (blackout)

←—10 seconds (blackout)—→

Choice X

Followed by return to initial condition.

Choice Y

←—10 seconds (blackout)—→

← 4 → seconds (blackout)

Pecking the right-hand white disk 15 times produces a 10-second blackout followed by presentation of the green disk only (the other disk remains dark and ineffective).

A peck at the green disk produces a further blackout for 4 seconds followed by access to food for 4 seconds.

Figure 6.5 *The commitment experiment.*

lights turned off for a 10-second blackout followed by Choice X (illumination of the disks with red and green light). If the pigeon pecked the right-hand disk 15 times, the lights turned off for a 10-second blackout followed by illumination of one of the keys only with green light. A peck at the green key then produced the delayed large reward. The other key was dark and there was no way (once the right-hand disk had been pecked 15 times) to obtain the small immediate reward. Thus, pecking the right-hand disk (when it was white) *committed* the pigeon to accepting the larger, delayed reward. Pecking the left-hand disk (when it was white) allowed a choice later between the large delayed reward and the small immediate reward. *

In order to draw a parallel between the behavior of pigeons in this experiment and the kind of commitment exhibited by the student we have to show (1) that the pigeons were indeed tempted by the immediate small reward—that when offered the green and red disks together (Choice X), they would peck the red disk and obtain an immediate reward, and (2) that the pigeons would commit themselves at Choice Y to obtaining the larger delayed reward by pecking the right-hand disk more than the left-hand disk.

The results on the first point were unequivocal. After two weeks of daily sessions in the apparatus, of about an hour each, when the red and green disks were presented together to any of the five pigeons in this experiment, the red disk was pecked more than 95 percent of the time. This was not due to a preference for one side of the chamber to the other, because the red and green lights were randomly switched from side to side. It was not a color preference, because the pigeons switched within a session to pecking the green disk when the consequences of pecking the two colors were reversed. Thus preference for the red disk can be ascribed only to a preference for the small immediate reward over the large delayed reward.

The results on the second point were less striking. When both disks were white (Choice Y) 3 of the 5 pigeons pecked the right-hand disk, committing themselves to the large reward, more than they pecked the left-hand disk. But, because 2 of the birds pecked the left-hand disk more, it was possible that the preference we measured was simply the result of chance, that the pigeons were randomly pecking on the two white disks and ignoring the contingencies of the experiment. To test this we varied the time of the blackout after the 15 pecks of Choice Y. Blackout time was 10 seconds in the original experiment. We now varied it up and down between 1 and 16 seconds. If the pigeon's distribution of pecks on the 2 white keys was random in the first experiment, it might be expected to remain so as the blackout was varied. On the other hand, if the pigeons were exhibiting commitment, they might change their behavior systematically as the time between the commitment response (Choice Y) and the temptation (Choice X) was varied. Reasoning by analogy to human behavior, the closer the temptation, the more difficult it should be to make the

---

*After the 4-second delayed reward, the disks turned white again and a new trial began. However, after the 2-second immediate reward, a further blackout of 6 seconds preceded the next trial. This equalized total trial duration for the two alternatives of Choice X.

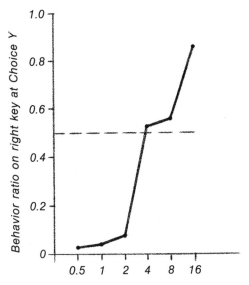

Figure 6.6 *Average behavior ratio on the right-hand white disk for the experiment illustrated in Figure 6.5. The abscissa represents variation of the blackout time between 0.5 and 16 seconds (instead of the 10 seconds indicated in Figure 6.5).*

commitment. In fact this is exactly what we found. When we reduced the blackout interval to 1 second, 4 of the 5 pigeons pecked more on the left-hand disk (no commitment). When we increased the interval to 16 seconds, 4 of the 5 pigeons pecked more on the right-hand disk (commitment). All of the pigeons shifted their preference in the expected direction as the duration of the blackout was varied. Figure 6.6 shows the average percentage of commitment responses at various values of blackout duration. We took this as evidence that animals other than humans could exhibit self-control, or at least the kind of self-control required for commitment. Since other current theories of self-control require a degree of sophistication on the part of the subject that a pigeon is not supposed to possess, they cannot account for the pigeons' behavior in our experiments. This behavior can be accounted for, however, by viewing commitment in terms of contingencies. Suppose, instead of assuming conflicting forces within the pigeon, we assume that the pigeon actually prefers what it chooses—the immediate small reward in Choice X and the large delayed reward in

Choice Y. As it happens, virtually all quantitative models of choice behavior do predict this reversal of preference. Perhaps the simplest of these models is a modification of Herrnstein's equations that we just discussed: an animal's preference between two alternatives varies directly as the ratio of the magnitudes of the alternatives and inversely as the ratio of their delays. This can be written in abbreviated form as

$$\frac{P_A}{P_B} = \frac{M_A}{M_B} \times \frac{D_B}{D_A},$$

where P reflects value of an alternative to the subject, M = magnitude of reward, D = delay of reward, and the subscripts stand for alternatives A and B. Let us say that in regard to our experiment the subscript A stands for the small immediate reward and the subscript B stands for the delayed large reward. The latter was always twice the former (4 seconds exposure to food versus 2 seconds) so $M_A/M_B = 0.5$. At choice X, $D_A = 0$ (or close to 0) and $D_B = 4$ seconds (the delay between pecking the green disk and delivery of food). Under these conditions P_A/P_B is much greater than unity, which would account for the strong tendency to choose the immediate small reward over the delayed large reward at Choice X. At Choice Y, 10 seconds must be added to each delay so that

$$\frac{P_A}{P_B} = 0.5 \times \frac{4 + 10}{0 + 10} = 0.7,$$

representing preference for alternative B, the delayed large reward, but not by nearly as much as preference for the small immediate reward in Choice X.

This is a model that does not account for the time between presentation and pecking of the red and green disks; furthermore, it oversimplifies reality by treating the time of hopper presentation as if it were a simple measure of magnitude of reward. As simple as it is, however, the model does begin to account for commitment behavior without postulating unobserved conflicts within the organism. Furthermore, it leads to testable predictions. For instance, it predicts that the pigeons in the present experiment would be indifferent to Choice Y when the blackout time is 4 seconds:

$$\frac{P_A}{P_B} = 0.5 \times \frac{4 + 4}{0 + 4} = 1$$

On the ordinate of Figure 6.6, a behavior ratio of 0.5 represents indifference between the alternatives (that is, equal rates of pecking on the two disks); points above the horizontal line show a preference for the right-hand disk (commitment); points below the horizontal line

Some New Directions

show a preference for the left-hand disk (no commitment). Although individual pigeons varied considerably as to the point at which their functions crossed the horizontal line, the average function crosses the horizontal line near the abscissa value where the blackout equalled 4 seconds, as the choice equation predicts.

In the past, most of the research on human self-control has focused on the personality of people who are good at controlling themselves. The old, it seems, do it better than the young, the sane better than the schizophrenic, the intelligent better than the unintelligent, the rich better than the poor. Obviously, self-control is a good thing to have. But environmental events that can generate self-control (that is, that can shift the cause of behavior from short-term to long-term events) have not been systematically examined.

The preceding analysis tends to suggest that future investigation of human self-control should be directed to the following areas:

1. Practice with long-term contingencies controlling one activity may increase the likelihood that they will control other activities. The notion that there are "addictive personalities" implies that some people cannot or do not respond to long-term contingencies in several behavioral areas. Can they be taught to behave generally in accord with such contingencies? Perhaps a person who has learned not to overeat will have an easier time learning not to smoke. This implies that the way to begin in the cure of harmful habits may be through control of other habits. For instance, alcoholics might first be trained to keep their weight under control or to stop smoking. Control of eating an ice cream sundae by the next day's consequences might transfer to control of getting drunk by the next day's consequences.

2. The long-term antecedents and consequences of certain events might be isolated from those of other events by techniques to make them more vivid or salient. The subject is in pretty much the same state with respect to observation of events controlling his behavior as the observer is. The way that we know better than anyone else what causes our behavior is not that we have access to internal sources of control but simply that we have more behavioral data.

The salience of the relationship between a behavior and its consequences may be increased by (a) counting and timing events with mechanical or written aids, and (b) the techniques of self-reinforcement (and self-punishment). Simply counting calories has been found to be as effective in short-term weight reduction as self-reward, external monetary reward, aversive imagery in connection with food, and relaxation training. The reason for this may be that the reward for eating less is losing weight regardless of the subsidiary rewards inserted between the two events. These subsidiary rewards do no more than emphasize the relation between eating and losing weight, a function performed just as well by counting calories.

3. Finally, commitment strategies should be studied. An application of commitment in a practical setting is a device invented by Nathan H. Azrin and J. Powell. It is a cigarette box that can be locked for two hours after a cigarette is removed. When a person starts to smoke one cigarette he is most willing to postpone his next cigarette. At that point he cheerfully locks his cigarette case for two hours. Thirty minutes later, when he might ordinarily be ready for another cigarette, and, presumably, when the immediate reward of smoking outweighs the long term reward of not smoking, he is prevented from succumbing to temptation by his prior decision to lock the case. Azrin and Powell report sharp reductions in the rate of smoking of chain smokers with this device. Like self-reinforcement, commitment may be kept in force permanently. Behavior according to long-term contingencies is guaranteed as long as the commitment is in force. If I habitually keep my alarm clock across the room from my bed, I will have to get out of bed every morning to turn it off. This technique of getting myself up in the morning is one that can conveniently be used every day. But often commitment strategies involve awkward or expensive apparatus, and because they are commitments they limit choice. Ironically, in the long term, it may be better to occasionally behave according to short-term contingencies (in other words, to act impulsively). Rigid commitment does not allow such behavior and may be undesirable for that reason. Commitment strategies thus might be instituted only as a temporary measure to bring behavior into conformity with long-term consequences. Once these consequences are experienced, they may serve to maintain behavior by themselves. For instance, consider the following studies being done by G. T. Wilson at Rutgers University's Behavior Research Laboratory. The aim of these studies is to extend control outside of the laboratory and into the everyday life of the alcoholic by a series of graded commitments. It has been found easy to control drinking in a laboratory setting—where four alcoholics live together for several weeks at a time. This is accomplished by the administration of a severe electric shock immediately following each drink; however, this procedure alone does not transfer to the everyday life of the alcoholic. Immediate punishment is a form of contingency notoriously absent from everyday life.

In future studies alcoholics will be asked to commit themselves in the morning (when they are feeling the ill-effects of their drinking) to a contract that specifies that they be shocked after each drink they take that night. Eventually, if the commitment is made each morning, drinking may cease in the laboratory setting. If so, the control of drinking would have been transferred from the immediate shock to a longer-term relationship between shock, hangovers, and drinking. It seems likely that nondrinking established in this way can carry over to everyday life, where temporally extended rewards for nondrinking are present in other forms.

It may be naive to expect that harmful habits with complex and varied etiologies should be curable by such a straightforward technique, but, straightforward as the technique may be, it has not yet been tried, perhaps because of a tendency to look for inner forces when faced with problems of self-control. If this technique or a similar one does work, it will be the best kind of evidence that such a focus is misplaced.

LANGUAGE

Consider again the beaver laying one stick upon another. Whether the beaver can be said to be playing with the sticks or building a dam depends *not* on what it is doing at this very moment (a still photograph or a 2-second film clip would not settle the issue) but on what it has done previously and what it is going to do. Similarly, a pianist plays a note in an arpeggio as one single act, but, if he is skilled, the act not only occupies the fraction of a second of its technical boundaries but bears an intimate relation to the pianist's actions during the rest of the arpeggio and the rest of the piece. He leads up to it and down from it. The coherent nature of the act can be appreciated if we consider the feelings of the pianist and his audience if he were to be suddenly interrupted.

As psychologists we are concerned with discovering (or devising) rules that govern such behavior. These rules may be logical rules or grammatical rules or formal rules, like those of chess or baseball. All are rules governing behavior, and all take on meaning only when they are considered in a broad (molar) context. As the philosopher Ludwig Wittgenstein says, ''It is not possible that there should have been only one occasion on which someone obeyed a rule. It is not possible that there should have been only one occasion on which a report was made, an order given or understood; and so on—To obey a rule, to make a report, to give an order, to play a game of chess, are *customs* (uses, institutions). . . . To understand a sentence means to understand a language. To understand a language means to be master of a technique."

Wittgenstein is saying that language is on a continuum with other kinds of behavior (with that of the beaver and the pianist). We cannot tell whether a person is speaking a language (in the sense that he is guided by the rules of the language) or merely parroting it until we see how effective his use of language is.

There are many ways in which language may be used effectively. Consider the following list (from Wittgenstein):

Giving orders and obeying them.
Describing the appearance of an object, or giving its measurements.
Constructing an object from a description (making a drawing).
Reporting an event.
Speculating about an event.
Forming and testing a hypothesis.
Presenting the results of an experiment in tables or diagrams.
Making up a story; and reading it.
Play-acting.
Singing round songs.
Guessing riddles.
Making a joke; telling it.
Solving a problem in practical arithmetic.
Translating from one language to another.
Asking, thanking, cursing, greeting, praying.

All these are ways of using language. Each way has something in common with some of the others, but they *all* do not have any one thing in common.

The psycholinguist Roman Jakobson has listed five ways language is used.

1. *Emotive.* Used primarily to express emotion, as during arguments or during lovemaking.
2. *Phatic.* Used merely as a means of contact between two organisms, as between a mother and baby, where the sounds of each (especially those of the mother) serve mainly to establish their presence.
3. *Metalinguistic.* Used about language itself. For instance, when speech is being taught, or a child's pronounciation is corrected. The child will say a sentence incorrectly ("I gone to school"), and the mother will repeat the sentence correctly ("I went to school"). Such a correction is a metalinguistic use of language.

4. *Poetic.* Used when the structure of language is emphasized for its own sake—as in a poem. ("red red rose," "luscious lady," etc.).
5. *Conative.* Used with behavior of some kind as its object ("Get out of here", "Pass the salt", etc.).

Jakobson's five classes are interesting, but they are inadequate. For example, when we try to put Wittgenstein's list of the uses of language into Jakobson's categories, we see that not all of them fit. Language has long been described by psychologists in this piecemeal way, no doubt because it is such an elusive concept.

Meaning as Association

The associationistic philosophers speculated that every environmental stimulus calls up images to the mind that are (a) a faint copy of the stimulus itself and (b) a faint copy of other stimuli that have previously accompanied (been associated with) the stimulus in question. If the stimulus is a word, the meaning of the word would be the images that are associated with its sound (see Figure 1.4). For instance, if every time a mother hands her child a cookie she says "cookie," the child will associate the sound of the word with the image of the cookie itself. Then, when the mother says "cookie" without handing the child anything, the image of a cookie will rise spontaneously in the child's mind. According to the associationists, the meaning of a word consists of the images it evokes.

Psychologists have not been able to get inside a person's head to study meaning by examining the images evoked by words, but they have asked people to give them indirect reports. In an experiment by Clyde Noble, subjects were given a word, say "kitchen," and then asked to write down all the other words that the original word reminded them of. For instance, they might write "knife," "fork," "apron," etc. Noble reasoned that the words the subject wrote down might stand for ideas generated by the original stimulus word. The more of these words suggested by the original word, the "more meaning" that stimulus word was said to have. Noble determined for each stimulus word an "m-score." This was the average number of response words that his subjects could write down in one minute. "Kitchen" turned out to have a high m-score. More abstract concepts such as "justice" had a lower m-score. By itself, the m-score of a word is a rather useless piece of information, but Noble found that m-score was a reliable predictor of how well words were remembered and how quickly associations between them and other words could be taught.

A more refined approach to the study of responses to words was made by James Deese. He examined not the *number* of associations to a word, but the *kind* of associations. He reasoned that two words were alike in meaning when the responses to those two words overlapped. For instance, "kitchen" might produce "knife," "fork," "table," "window," and "porch" might produce "swing," "air," "front," "table." The word "table," common to both response groups, makes the words somewhat similar in meaning according to Deese. The more such common responses are found, the more similar the words are in meaning.

A further analysis of associations reveals two general types, called *syntigmatic* and *paradigmatic*. Syntigmatic associations are those that refer to sequence. For instance "table"–"cloth," "yankee"–"doodle," "red"–"rider," "cool"–"cat," "play"–"ground" would be syntigmatic because they normally occur in sequence. Another thing to note about such associations is that they are not usually reversible. Many people will respond "cloth" to the stimulus "table," few people will respond "table" to the stimulus "cloth".

Paradigmatic associations, on the other hand, represent associations, not of sequence, but of kind. For instance, "table"–"chair," "Yankee"–"Southerner," "red"–"green", "cool"–"cold," "play"–"movie" would be paradigmatic. Unlike syntigmatic associations these are generally reversible.

It has been found that children tend to give more syntigmatic associations, changing to paradigmatic associations as they get older.

This general approach, treating language as association between individual words, has illuminated only a small corner of the immense area of linguistic behavior. It fails to consider at least two important complexities of linguistic behavior:

1. It does not consider linguistic behavior as extended in time. Instead, it considers immediate responses to immediate stimulation and thus misses those aspects of language (such as following grammatical rules) that can only be understood over a period of time.

2. It does not consider the functional properties of language. It ignores the question of the *uses* of language. From the above studies, the mind of the person associating words appears as a passive receptacle of stimuli. But we know that a person plays an active role in what he learns.

The following sections tackle some of this complexity in a more direct fashion. In these sections we will lose a little of the elegant simplicity of associationism and its quantitative precision. We hope, in return for these sacrifices, to gain a better approximation to the world as it actually is.

Language and Thought

One line of speculation about the relation between language and thought stems from the early behaviorists, whose concern was to explain behavior—including thought—on simple mechanistic principles. Thought has been considered, through the ages, to be part of the spiritual nature of man. The early behaviorists denied man any spiritual nature, hoping to explain all behavior in terms of stimulus–response connections. Yet, they could not deny that man thinks (this seemed to them as fundamental a fact to them as it did to Descartes—"I think, therefore, I am."). They resolved their quandry by regarding thought as a kind of action—but action of so small a magnitude that it could not be seen. For instance, when a man was asked to think of hitting a nail with a hammer, he was said to actually move the muscles in his hand slightly. This movement, no more and no less, was supposed to comprise his thought. When sensitive measurements were taken it was found that such movements often occurred without the awareness of the man making them. That is, the man said he thought of hitting the nail with the hammer, but he didn't realize he was making any movements. Although concrete actions such as hitting a nail with a hammer could be represented by small movements of the arms, most thoughts, especially of the more abstract kind (thoughts of justice, for instance) would be represented by unspoken language—that is, unnoticed movements of the tongue and larynx. Sensitive instruments indeed do pick up such movements occasionally.

The problem with notions such as these is that they are inherently untestable. When movements are not found corresponding to certain thoughts, one can always imagine that they still occur but at a level too minute for the instruments used to detect.

A more subtle relationship between language and thought was postulated by the Russian psychologist L. S. Vigotsky. According to Vigotsky, thought and speech are two separate processes that develop for a while independently and then come together. Thought without speech would be exemplified by the kind of intelligent behavior exhibited by Köhler's chimpanzee Sultan when he moved a box underneath a banana hanging out of reach and then jumped up from the box to get the banana (see p. 45, Chapter 1). This kind of behavior seems complex enough to us (the observers of it) that we are tempted to say it was thoughtful.* Vigotsky would agree with our judgment, but he would say that it lacks a component of most adult human thought, namely combination with inner speech. Vigotsky claims that most "intelligent" acts of children below about three years of age are of this kind—perhaps the acts have a complex nature, but they are not accompanied by either overt or covert language. This, according to Vigotsky, is thought without speech.

Similarly, he contends, there can be speech without thought. Jakobson's categories of emotive and phatic uses of language are examples, as well as affective expression and the babbling of infants in their cribs.

According to Vigotsky thought and speech join in humans when they are about three years old. At first a word is treated as a property of an object rather than a symbol of that object. For instance, the sound "chair" is something that a chair *has*, like color and shape. A child treats each object as if there were something (like a record) inside the object constantly saying the object's name. Thus a cookie is not only round and small and good-tasting, but it also has the sound "cookie" built into it. Later, the sound of the word is separated from things like shape, size, and color and comes to be a symbol for the object.

While this is going on, the child develops a kind of speech that has been often noticed but seldom studied. Vigotsky calls it egocentric speech. It goes on practically all the time with little children but can be noticed particularly when they are put to bed at night and are alone in their crib. They start talking, repeating words they heard that day—stringing phrases together. To an outsider what the child says makes little sense. Sometimes the child's egocentric speech is social—referred to other things and designed, however poorly, to tell somebody else something. But often the speech is directed to himself. A two year old, Tommy, will say, "Tommy bad boy" or "Tommy go home," etc. This speech serves as a sort of feedback tending to organize behavior better. Tommy can perform intelligent acts (as Köhler's chimpanzees can) without speech, but he can do them better when he gives himself an order first. Tommy may go into the kitchen when he is hungry but he will go faster if he first tells himself to go into the kitchen. Thus, much of the actual vocalization of young children is

---

*A behaviorist would claim that the "thoughtfulness" lies wholly in the behavior itself. A cognitive psychologist would claim that other events in the monkey's head determine the thoughtfulness of the behavior. Since these other events are never observed, we ignore the distinction.

self-directed. Anyone who has observed a three-year-old child has noticed it. After a child's fourth or fifth birthday, however, egocentric speech becomes less noticed in childrens' vocalization and finally drops out altogether. From then on, audible speech becomes a social act. Vigotsky's theory is that egocentric speech becomes *more* egocentric as time goes on, finally becoming inner speech. The child, in other words, keeps on with egocentric speech, in fact more than ever, but now no one hears it because the child says it to himself. Egocentric speech loses all communication function and becomes a complex stimulus for one's own behavior. Some evidence for this is that just before egocentric speech disappears it becomes even more frequent and less intelligible to others. In other words, it becomes more egocentric. By this time it has lost all function as a communication device and becomes purely a mechanism for self-direction. What remains in the external vocalization is social speech. Thus, adults have essentially two languages, a private one that guides their actions and structures their thoughts, and a public one that serves for communication.

An interesting study in this area was done in Russia with a pair of twins who were raised together and who were both retarded in speech. It seemed to the experimenters that the twins had been so close to one another that they could understand each other's egocentric speech and had never had to develop social speech with others. In effect, their egocentric speech had never become internalized. The experimenters reasoned that if the twins were separated they would have to develop social speech. Indeed, within three months of their separation the children spoke and understood normally. One twin was given systematic training in social speech. While both twins improved, the one with systematic training improved more rapidly.

Russian psychologists have been very interested in the way in which speech serves to organize behavior. Following Pavlov as well as Vigotsky, they call language the "second-signal system." What do they mean by this? In Pavlov's early experiments with dogs, the sound of the bell is a signal for food. But the word "bell" would be a signal for the sound of the bell; it would be a second signal whose function is to direct attention to the bell. Environmental signals themselves direct *action.* Language is said to direct *attention.* The function of language would be to put the organism in a position, prior to the signal itself, so that it could act promptly when the primary signal came; hence, the name "second-signal system." Linguistic second signals can come from the outside or may, like Vigotsky's inner speech, be generated by a person to himself. How the second-signal system guides behavior is shown in an experiment by the Russian, S. A. Luria. He had children squeeze a rubber bulb when a light came on. Then he introduced a discrimination: when the light was green the child was to squeeze, when the light was red the child was not to squeeze. Prior to three years of age, children find this task very difficult. They just keep squeezing constantly. However, Luria trained the child to say "squeeze" when he saw the green light and "don't squeeze" when he saw the red light. Then Luria trained the child to actually squeeze the bulb when the child, himself, said squeeze but not to squeeze when he said "don't squeeze." Thus Luria succeeded in teaching children to perform a task correctly with the mediation of language which they could not perform without the mediation of language.

Like the early behaviorists in America, the Russians believe that inner speech is accompanied by small muscular movements. They differ from the early behaviorists in that they do not identify such movements with thought. Rather, they see these movements as an aid or guide to thought. When thought runs smoothly it is likely to be unaccompanied by inner speech. But, when difficulties arise, thought needs guidance from inner speech and hence, with difficult problems, such small movements are more likely to arise.

An experiment by the Russian psychologist, Sokolov, illustrates the point. He asked his subjects to read a passage silently while he measured small movements at various points on their bodies —including the neck and face, where visually undetectable speech movements would be likely to occur. Later, to insure that they had understood the passage, he asked them to write a summary. The subjects had three kinds of passage to read: (a) Standard Russian (their native language), (b) Easy English, (c) Difficult English. Sokolov found, in general, that the subjects made many minute movements at the start and few at the end of all passages and that there was a sudden increase of such movements at paragraph breaks. In particular, he found that the number of minute movements was higher when the material to be read was more difficult. In other words, the more difficult it was to think, the more the aid of inner speech was necessary.

Another experiment on the second-signal system was done by Luria. To appreciate this experiment, we must recall that the second-signal system regulates, not responding itself, but attention to signals that, in turn, regulate responding. The response to language is not action per se but attention or orientation. Thus the response for which language is a stimulus is called "an orienting response" and the linguistic stimulus plus the response are together called "an orienting reflex." Now, it seems that when people are attending to something, the blood volume in their extremities (such as a finger) decreases while the blood volume in the head increases. Thus a sudden increase in the difference between the head and finger blood volumes, measured by a plethysmograph, could be labeled as an orienting response. Luria and his colleagues found that when they presented a new stimulus to a subject, the orienting response increased; the response then decreased with repeated presentations. In other words the orienting response decreased with familiarity, as one would expect attention to decrease.

Luria and his colleagues read a list of words to their subjects, and kept repeating the list. After the initial orienting responses died down, they told the subjects to watch for a particular word (word X) from the original list and press a button after that word was presented. They noticed then a resurgence of the orienting response after word X—but not generally after the other words. When they presented the subjects with other words from the list similar in sound to word X, they found that the subjects did not make orienting responses. However, when they presented the subjects with other words from the list similar in *meaning* to word X, they did sometimes get orienting responses. This indicates that subjects translate the sound of the word into its meaning at a very early level of processing in the nervous system—even before the nervous system decides whether or not to pay attention to the word.

Although thought and speech certainly bear an intimate relation to each other we should be careful before we identify the two. Subjectively, we can all remember having thoughts with no apparent visual or verbal content. Further reasons for caution come from pathology. An aphasic (someone with a severe language impairment) may be able to act intelligently in all other respects.

An even stronger line of evidence against the thought-equals-language argument is the presence of ambiguous sentences in the language. Consider the sentence "It is drinking water," which could have at least two meanings depending on context. In one context these words would accompany one thought; in another context, another thought.

So, although the proposition that thought and language are one has not been fruitful in explaining either thought or language, it is nevertheless clear that language and thought are closely interwoven processes. Recently, American psychologists have taken a fresh look at language and have investigated some of its structural characteristics. We will turn to these studies next.

Grammar (Words in a Sentence)

Grammar comprises a system of rules regarding the use of language. To get these grammatical rules into proper perspective, let us consider two other systems of rules. First, consider the rules of chess. Virtually everyone who learns to play chess learns the rules and can discuss them. You can ask the chess player about the rules that limit the movements of his pieces and he will tell you what they are. Then if you watch him play you will notice that the actual movement of the pieces generally conforms to the rules he has articulated. On the other hand, consider Newton's laws of motion. Almost everything in the universe obeys this set of rules: a stone, a human body, an apple, a molecule, a mountain. Yet, despite the fact that Newton's laws of motion are obeyed by a stone, only a visitor from another universe could conceivably expect the stone to articulate the rules. The rules of grammar lie somewhere between the rules of chess and Newton's laws of motion. The rules of grammar are like the rules of chess in the sense that they are social, and that their use is acquired over time (that is, their use must be learned), and that they are frequently disobeyed. On the other hand, the rules of grammar are like Newton's laws in the sense that most of us cannot articulate them and even those of us who can articulate them are not conscious of obeying them while speaking. Although no one could play chess until the rules had been established, it is certain that people were speaking grammatically before anyone thought to codify the rules of grammar. Some psychologists have tended to think of the rules of grammar as things existing in the heads of people who speak grammatically. Others see grammar as a convenient description of how people organize and comprehend sentences.

The group of psychologists who believe that the rules of grammar are in people's heads distinguish between competence and performance. Competence is "having the rule." Performance is using it. Another group of psychologists, among whom most behaviorists would place themselves, would see grammatical rules as molar descriptions of behavior from which there may be molecular deviations in the form of "ungrammatical expressions." According to this view, "competence" would be a molar description of behavior (over periods of time long enough to include several instances of comprehension and production to be sure that the person said to be competent is not just accidentally stringing words together grammatically), and "performance" would be a molecular description of immediate behavior.

The problems posed by the facts of grammatical speech were spotlighted by Carl Lashley in a paper written in 1951 called "The problem of serial order in behavior." Lashley argued that much behavior, of which grammatical speech is merely one example, exhibits properties that cannot be attributed to a chain of reflexes in which each behavioral link is determined only by a preceding link; rather, the entire sequence must be planned in advance. To support this view, Lashley argued that languages are translated by thoughts, not by individual words. For instance, when translating from German to English, Lashley found that he read the German text and then translated an entire thought to English (which has a different word order) without remembering a single word of the German text. The ease and speed with which translators (at the U.N., for instance) transpose the word order of two languages shows that word-for-word translation is not what they do. According to Lashley serial order in behavior results from an interaction of spatial and temporal systems. The order of a sentence, for instance, is predetermined according to grammatical rules and somehow represented completely in the nervous system even before the sentence is begun. Then, when the sentence is about to be uttered, this representation is scanned and the elements flow sequentially to the vocal cords.

Consider the following sentence, cited by Lashley: "Rapid righting with his uninjured hand saved from loss the contents of the canoe." When you hear someone read the sentence you understand "righting" not "writing," but only when you hear the word "canoe." Thus, there must be an integrating mechanism for the sentence as a whole. The sentence must be planned in advance before it is uttered because its meaning is ambiguous until the entire sentence is out. One cannot imagine a speaker starting the sentence without already having determined how it is to end. The planning of a sentence in a language is done according to grammatical rules. But the problem of serial order is more general than just sentences. There are hierarchies of order: the order of vocal movements in pronouncing a word, the order of words in a sentence, sentences in a paragraph, and paragraphs in a discourse. Within each, three sets of events need to be accounted for: The activation of the elements (words), without regard to order, the events to which the elements refer (meaning), and the order itself (grammar).

It has been suggested that a sentence is stored in memory as a kernel with variations. That is, the sentence "John was not hit by Mary" would be stored as "Mary hits John" plus the fact that the sentence is passive, negative, and in the past tense. Many psychologists feel that the principles of this sort of grammar are the same principles by which people understand and produce sentences. But this is likely to seem true for any grammar that concisely describes the sentences people actually do produce.

Remember, we said that grammar may be thought of as a molar description of the use of language, and that ungrammatical expressions may be thought of as molecular deviations from that molar description. Another kind of variation in grammar was studied by Jaques Mehler. He gave subjects lists of sentences and asked them to recall the sentences later. He was interested in the errors made in recall. He found two major kinds of errors: (a) omissions of words and (b) changes of grammatical structure (syntactic errors). As the time between initial learning and testing increased, the omission errors went down but the syntactic errors went up. Subjects tended to remember sentences in a simpler form than that in which they were presented. In other words, subjects would say they heard "Mary hit John" when they really heard "John was hit by Mary."

An experiment to separate the effect of grammar from the effect of other properties of sentences was done by William Epstein. He found that a grammatically structured series of nonsense words was easier to learn than unstructured nonsense. There were four categories of things to learn:

1. Structured nonsense (like jabberwocky or doubletalk), for example:
   The frumous grably frabled a plinky trucket in his glimp.
2. Unstructured nonsense, for example:
   Frabled glimp trucket grably plinky frumous.
3. Structured but meaningless sentences, for example:
   Colorless green ideas sleep furiously.
4. Unstructured meaningless sentences, for example:
   Ideas furiously green sleep colorless.

Epstein first showed subjects each complete string of words on a card. He found that structured meaningless sentences were learned best and unstructured nonsense was learned least well. The structured nonsense was learned better than the unstructured nonsense. Why? The material was equally familiar (or unfamiliar), equally meaningful, and, since none of the nonsense had presumably occurred before in the subjects' experience, the sequential probabilities of one word following another were the same. The only explanation for the ease in learning the structured nonsense is that the structure (or syntax) itself was responsible for the ease of learning even though there were more words ("the," "and," "of" included) in the structured material.

After showing some subjects the entire sentences on cards, Epstein took other subjects and showed them the sentences word by word (one word at a time). This kind of presentation de-emphasized the structure, so that the sentences were not perceived as units, and all four categories were learned equally slowly. Epstein reasoned that the ability of subjects to learn sentences depended on their ability to organize those sentences into a small number of units. The unstructured material was difficult to organize. But the structured material already came in with an organization (that of grammar) and thus was easy to organize—there was less to remember.

So, what have we learned about grammar? First, that it is a set of rules, to some extent arbitrary (like the rules of chess) and to some extent natural (like Newton's laws). Our speech generally obeys these rules but sometimes does not obey them. When we make mistakes, they are often in the direction of simpler grammatical forms. In order to speak a sentence we have to plan it in advance because the grammatical rules we follow sometimes force us to make adjustments in the beginning of sentences to prepare for what we are going to say at the end. The fact that we can do this shows that we do indeed have some sort of outline (or molar appreciation) of what we are about to say—similarly, the outfielder does not run to where the ball *is* but to where the ball is going to be. In understanding sentences the rules of grammar help us organize the input and thus remember them better. Even nonsense, when it is syntactically consistent (like "Jabberwocky"), can be organized in this way.

Little work has been done by psychologists on how sentences are put together in discourse, but recently two young psychologists, John Bransford and Jeffrey Franks have broken into the area. They concentrated on how listeners understand groups of sentences.

They presented subjects with groups of sentences like the following:

(a) The rock rolled down the mountain.
(b) The rock crushed the hut.
(c) The hut was tiny.
(d) The hut was at the edge of the woods.

Note that the ideas in these four sentences could be expressed in a single sentence:

(e) *The rock, which rolled down the mountain, crushed the tiny hut at the edge of the woods.*

Now, the subjects in this experiment were *never* presented with sentence (e). They only saw (a), (b), (c), and (d), mixed with several other groups of sentences like (a), (b), (c), and (d), expressing other ideas. Some were long sentences and some were short. Later the subjects were given long lists of sentences and asked, first, whether the new sentences were on the old list, and second, how confident they were that they recognized the sentences. Bransford and Franks found that most of their subjects thought they had seen the composite sentence (e), and were, in fact, more confident that they had seen (e) than that they had seen the original sentences (a), (b), (c), and (d). This study shows that incoming material does not directly affect behavior. Behavior differs from input by

1. being more efficiently organized (having fewer units of information than the input) and
2. being more consistent with other (previously emitted) patterns of behavior.

Reinforcement and Language

It is clear that reinforcement plays a role in the use of language. There are several lines of evidence, but our own common sense tells us the answer. We say "Please pass the salt" as long as the salt is passed. When it is not passed, we will stop saying "Please pass the salt" and start saying something else. An experiment by the psychologist Greenspoon indicates that linguistic behavior can be modified sometimes without the awareness of the subject. Greenspoon in an interview, the real purpose of which was disguised from the subject, would occasionally nod his head and say "mmm-hmm" in a tone indicating he understood what the subject was saying. He said this each time the subject uttered a plural noun, and recorded the frequency of plural nouns. He found that "rewarding" subjects with "mmm-hmm" increased the frequency of their plural nouns and withdrawal of "mmm-hmm" decreased the frequency again. Afterwards the subjects said that they were not aware that their utterance of plural nouns had changed during the experiment. There is some dispute about whether all subjects were *really* unaware of what was going on—but this is irrelevant to our purposes. The point is that their behavior changed according to the contingencies.

A more difficult question is: Can language be taught in the same way that a rat's pressing a lever can be taught, by reinforcing correct behavior and punishing or extinguishing incorrect behavior? First of all, it is necessary to define the area of the problem. Many of Wittgenstein's categories undoubtedly can be taught. The critical ability we seek to find out about is the ability to form sentences that one has never heard or used before (with familiar elements that have been used before). Can this be acquired by traditional reinforcement techniques or is it an inborn property of the human brain? That is, is grammar learned by reinforcement or is it an inherited structural property of the nervous system?

There is little question but that reinforcement plays a part in the learning of words. Each child learns his parents' language. The child babbles and certain sounds are reinforced. There is evidence that as babies get older their babbling takes on more of the character of the speech of their parents. When a child duplicates the sounds of his parents he gets rewarded by his parents; also, the very sounds he makes remind him of his parents (from whom primary reward comes) and take on a secondarily reinforcing quality.

According to Jakobson, understanding of speech proceeds by successive discriminations. First consonants are distinguished from vowels, then aspirated consonants (for example, p, t, h) from nonaspirated consonants (for example, f, m, r).

The problem, though, is not with understanding sounds, it is with using grammar. How does one acquire grammatical rules? Some linguists (Noam Chomsky is the best known) have found certain grammatical universals that seem to characterize languages. (WARNING: here comes the nature–nurture controversy again.) Are these universals inborn—part of our evolutionary heritage—or are they the way various cultures react to similar environmental forces (for instance, one could discover farming techniques—sowing, reaping, etc., that cross cultural lines—but is this because these farming actions are innate or because one must do the same sorts of things everywhere to produce crops)?

One way in which this question has been approached is to try to teach animals (particularly chimpanzees) to talk. The reasoning goes like this: As far as we know, only humans have a grammatical language. Perhaps this is because only humans are born with the special mechanism necessary for grammatical language. If animals can be taught to speak grammatically, we could speculate that the language behavior of humans is merely a highly developed form of other behavior and not a special characteristic of humans alone. Complete evidence in this area is still to come, but it is instructive to look at some of what has been done so far.

First, there is the case of Vicky, a chimpanzee that was raised from infancy by a husband–wife team of psychologists along with their own child. At first, Vicky outperformed the human baby in nearly every respect, but slowly and surely the human baby caught up. Vicky could (finally) understand some human speech but she never learned to speak beyond uttering a few rudimentary words like "milk," "Ma ma," and so forth. As soon as the human baby learned to speak, she quickly outdistanced the chimp.

In a more successful experiment, the chimp Washoe was raised by two psychologists and "spoken to" in only deaf-mute language—with the fingers. The reasoning behind this was that Vicky's problem might not have been with grammar as such but with the mechanics of speaking. Although chimps seem to have a reasonable approximation of the human vocal apparatus, they may not have enough of the subtle nerve-muscle connections to coordinate lips, tongue, diaphragm, and jaw in the way that humans do. However, chimps do have remarkable coordination in their fingers. When Washoe was addressed in deaf-mute language and rewarded by approval for appropriate gestures of its own, the chimp soon learned to form words, and even sentences. In fact, Washoe could construct original sentences out of familiar words, a common criterion for the use of grammar. Washoe's vocabulary is limited and her grammar is simple, but the rudiments of human speech are there.

Another attempt to teach chimps to use language is the more formal approach of David Premack. Premack constructed a special language for chimps. Premack reasoned that a simple language might contain a few nouns, like "honey," "bread," "Sarah" (the name of the chimp): a few verbs like "take," "give," "insert"; and a few functional words and signs like "yes," "no" and a question mark. Each word in Premack's language was represented by a plastic marker. These differed in color and shape.

Premack first taught Sarah to identify the colored markers by having the chimp put available markers on a board when it wanted something like a banana. Then it learned the difference between "give banana" and "take banana." Then Premack reinforced the correct answering of questions with "yes" or "no" markers and by gradual stages he got the chimp to use markers to form sentences such as "Sarah, insert banana (in) pail" or "Sarah insert apple (in) dish." Premack found that Sarah could not only correctly use the specific sentences she was taught but she could also use the sentence structure correctly with new words. That is, she could identify and use the sentence, "Sarah insert milk (in) pail" even though she had only learned the sentence with apples and bananas.

Premack found, furthermore, an even more sophisticated operation could be taught to Sarah. She could actually discuss the words (plastic markers) themselves. She could correctly understand and produce the marker for "apple" then another marker standing for "is the name of," then an apple itself. This is one of the most rigid criteria for having a language, being able to discuss the language itself.

Vicky, Washoe, and Sarah teach us that although humans certainly possess something that makes it easier for them to learn languages, it is by no means impossible to teach animals to exhibit the essential elements of language use. We can conclude that language is only quantitatively different from the other forms of behavior that are subject to the principles of learning.

Bibliography

Two books dealing directly with the application of behavioral techniques to human problems are J. Dollard and N. E. Miller's *Personality and Psychotherapy* (New York: McGraw-Hill, 1950) and B. F. Skinner's *Science and Human Behavior* (New York: The Macmillan Co., 1953). Many other behaviorists have speculated about applications to human problems. A classic (but now out-of-date) attempt at such application is J. B. Watson's *Behaviorism*, originally published in 1924 and now available as a paperback (New York: Norton, 1970).

A collection of articles specifically dealing with behavior modification in clinical settings is L. Krasner and L. P. Ullman's *Research in Behavior Modification* (New York: Holt, Rinehart & Winston, 1965). Another book by these authors is *A Psychological Approach to Abnormal Behavior, I. Concepts* (New York: Prentice-Hall, 1969). Pioneering work on clinical application of behavioral principles has been done by Joseph Wolpe. An inspiring account of successes with various techniques that Wolpe has developed can be found in a paperback by J. Wolpe and A. A. Lazarus, *Behavior Therapy Technique: A Guide to the Treatment of Neuroses* (Long Island City, New York: Pergamon Press, 1966). A recent textbook on abnormal psychology that takes a behavioristic approach is G. Davison and J. M. Neale's *Abnormal Psychology: An Experimental Clinical Approach* (New York: Wiley, 1974). There are several collections of studies dealing with the application of behavioral studies to human problems. A good one is *Human Learning* (New York: Holt, Rinehart & Winston, 1964), edited by A. W. Staats. In this book, an interesting experiment is reported by C. D. Ferster, J. I. Nurnberger, and E. B. Levitt on the control of eating. The Ayllon and Haughton report on "Control of the behavior of schizophrenic patients by food" appears in the *Journal of the Experimental Analysis of Behavior* (1962, 5, 343–352). The study in which the schizophrenic child is reinforced for uttering sounds is reported in *Journal of Speech and Hearing Disorders* (1960, 25, 8–12).

A book I have recently written (H. Rachlin, *Behavior and Learning*, San Francisco, W. H. Freeman, 1976) contains some further explanation of recent quantitative studies of choice as well as a more extensive exposition of other topics in this book. Perusal of recent issues of the *Journal of the Experimental*

Analysis of Behavior, Journal of Comparative and Physiological Psychology, Journal of Experimental Psychology, and Psychological Review, is the best way to keep abreast of developments. An early attempt to quantify reinforcements in the manner discussed here was that of C. J. Warden. Using his "obstruction box," which contained an electrified grid, he ranked various species with respect to the number of times they would cross the grid to reach a reward on the other side. (His works on this subject are no longer in print, but may be found in libraries.)

Quantitative accounts of the interaction of reward and punishment are often subsumed under theories of conflict. A review of studies of conflict can be found in a paperback by A. J. Yates, Frustration and Conflict (New York: Wiley, 1962). Logan's experiments with rats in a straight alley may be found in his book Incentive: How the Conditions of Reinforcement Affect the Performance of Rats (New Haven: Yale University Press, 1960). Logan's studies of choice and the equations derived therefrom, were used by Ainslie to predict crossover points in his experiment. Logan's equations are from his article "Decision-making by rats: delay versus amount of reward" (Journal of Comparative and Physiological Psychology, 1965, 59, 1–12).

The equations on pages 203 and 204 are from R. H. Herrnstein, "On the law of effect" (Journal of the Experimental Analysis of Behavior, 1970, 13, 243–266).

Self-control is discussed in the above-mentioned book by Skinner (Chapter XV), and several experiments in the area have been performed by W. Mischel and reported in Progress in Experimental Personality Research, Vol. 3 (New York: Academic Press, 1966), edited by B. A. Maher. Ainslie's experiments were performed prior to those Green and I did but were published later. Ainslie described his experiments in the Journal of the Experimental Analysis of Behavior (1974, 21, 485–489). The reference for my experiment with Green is "Commitment, choice, and self-control" (by H. Rachlin and L. Green, in the Journal of the Experimental Analysis of Behavior, 1972, 17, 15–22). Azrin and Powell describe their locking cigarette box in the Journal of Applied Behavioral Analysis (1969, 2, 39–42). The Lambert, et al. experiment in which rats faced a problem similar to visiting the dentist appears in the Journal of the Experimental Analysis of Behavior (1973, 19, 361–367). An interesting theoretical analysis of self-control from an economist's point of view can be found in R. H. Strotz's "Myopia and inconsistency in dynamic utility maximization" (Review of Economic Studies, 1956, 23, 165–180).

The psychology of language is an area in which there are literally hundreds of books. We can do no more than give the reader a start. Two well-written books on the subject are, Roger Brown's Words and Things (Glencoe, Ill.: The Free Press, 1958) and George Miller's Language and Communication (New York: McGraw Hill, 1951).

A collection of readings edited by S. Saporta contains articles by Chomsky, Jakobson, Lashley, Skinner, Vigotsky, and others mentioned in this chapter.

More recent work is presented in a report of a conference held in 1969, edited by G. B. Flores d'Arcais and W. J. M. Levelt, called Advances in Psycholinguistics (Amsterdam: North Holland Publishing Company, 1970). Ludwig Wittgenstein's Philosophical Investigations, translated by G. E. M. Anscombe (New York: The Macmillan Co., 1958), is notoriously difficult but is nevertheless enjoyable to read and repays the effort spent in trying to understand it.

The Bransford and Franks experiment appeared in *Cognitive Psychology* (1971, *2*, 331–350).

Descriptions of the work with talking chimps have been published in many places but is summarized nicely in an introductory book by Roger Brown and Richard Herrnstein, *Psychology* (Boston: Little Brown and Co., 1975).

Glossary

ASSOCIATION. The connection of two or more sensations, ideas, images, or other mental phenomena. Laws of association are laws formulated to account for the establishment of such connections.

BEHAVIOR. (1) Any action of an organism. (2) The actions of an organism. (3) Actions of organisms.

BEHAVIORAL THERAPIST. A psychologist who is concerned with helping people change their behavior so as to better adapt it to their environment.

BEHAVIORISM. A branch of experimental psychology, the object of which is to discover laws describing the behavior of organisms.

BEHAVIOR RATIO. When an organism is free to make any of two or more responses in "choice" experiments, the behavior ratio is the measure of choice. It is the number of responses to one alternative divided by the total responses to all alternatives.

BELONGINGNESS. A term coined by E. L. Thorndike to indicate that certain associations are more easily formed than others because in some sense the components belong together. See also *Preparedness*.

CHOICE. The possibility of more than one response. Essentially every situation in which behavior may vary is a choice situation. Even with one alley or one manipulandum (a lever, a disk, or the like), an organism may choose to run or not to run, to press a lever or not to press it. Choice can be measured most easily, however, when two similar alternatives are available as in a T-maze or multi-lever Skinner box. One frequently used measure of choice is the *Behavior Ratio*.

CLASSICAL CONDITIONING.   As an operation, classical conditioning refers to the pairing in fixed temporal relation of (a) a neutral stimulus with (b) a stimulus correlated with a response—a reflex. (For example, a bell—a neutral stimulus—may be paired with food powder, which is originally correlated with salivation—a reflex. An organism exposed to such repeated pairings often comes to respond to the originally neutral stimulus as it did to the other stimulus. In this example, the organism would come to salivate upon presentation of the bell.)

CONDITIONED REINFORCEMENT.   Another name for *Secondary Reinforcement.*

CONDITIONED RESPONSE.   The response elicited by the conditioned stimulus alone (after the process of classical conditioning has taken place). In some cases this is only quantitatively different from the response originally elicited by the unconditioned stimulus (the unconditioned response). In other cases there may be qualitative differences between the conditioned and unconditioned responses.

CONDITIONED STIMULUS (CS).   A stimulus that does not ordinarily elicit a certain response but that comes to elicit that response by virtue of its pairings in a classical conditioning procedure with another stimulus, an unconditioned stimulus, that does ordinarily elicit the response.

CONSCIOUSNESS.   That part of one's *Mind* that one knows. A conscious mental process would be a process that one knows about, like doing mental arithmetic; an unconscious mental process would be a process about which one has no knowledge. John Stuart Mill's *Mental Chemistry*, in which sensations get combined into ideas, would be described as an unconscious mental process, since we seem to have many ideas without being aware of component sensations.

CONTINGENCY.   A set of conditional probabilities relating the occurrence and nonoccurrence of events. In classical conditioning, the critical contingencies are between the conditioned and unconditioned stimuli. In instrumental conditioning the critical contingencies are between responding and reinforcement. The word "contingency" has also been used in a more general sense, as in *Contingencies of Reinforcement*, a recent book by B. F. Skinner. Here, contingency refers to the general relationships between behavior and the environment (without reference to any specific set of correlations or probabilities).

CORRELATION.   In general, any relation between two variables. If the knowledge of the value of one variable helps you predict the value of the other, then the variables are correlated. In a positive correlation, increases in one variable correspond to increases in the other, as in the correlation between rising atmospheric temperature and trips to the beach. In a negative correlation, increases in one variable correspond to decreases in the other, as in the correlation between rising atmospheric temperature and skiing.

CRITICAL PERIOD. A period during the early life of an organism when it can most easily acquire certain behaviors. The behaviors may be exhibited at a later time but their nature is determined by events during the critical period. For instance, the object that a duckling learns to follow during a critical period may become a focus for sexual behavior months later.

CUE. Another term for a discriminative stimulus (S^D or S^Δ).

DISCRIMINATION. Reliable differences in behavior in the presence of two or more stimuli.

DISCRIMINATIVE STIMULUS (S^D AND S^Δ). An S^D ("ess dee") is a stimulus during which there is a correlation between responding and reinforcement. An S^Δ ("ess delta") is a stimulus during which there is no correlation between responding and reinforcement. Somewhat confusingly, both S^D's and S^Δ's are called "discriminative stimuli."

DISINHIBITION. Removal of an inhibitory force, resulting in the action of the excitatory force formerly inhibited. (For instance, experimental extinction of classically conditioned salivation was thought by Pavlov to consist of the development of an inhibitory force opposing salivation. If, during extinction, a loud noise or other strong stimulus is presented, salivation suddenly increases. This is thought to be due to the disinhibitory effect of the noise.)

DUALISM. In the history of Western philosophy, the nature of man understood according to two principles—matter (the body) and spirit (the mind)—which are not derivable from each other.

ELICITED RESPONSE. When a stimulus is reliably followed by a certain response or set of responses, it is said to elicit that response or those responses. The notion of elicitation rests on an observed correlation between a stimulus and a subsequent response.

EMITTED RESPONSE. When a response is not found to be correlated with any prior stimulus it is said to be emitted. An emitted response may be brought into correlation with a subsequent stimulus by the environment, in which case the subsequent stimulus could reinforce or punish the response.

EMPIRICISM. (See *Nativism*.)

ESCAPE CONDITIONING. A form of instrumental conditioning in which responding is negatively correlated with aversive stimulation. Also called "negative reinforcement."

EVOLUTION. Gradual development. According to Darwin's theory of evolution of the structure of species, the mechanism of evolution works by survival (and reproduction) of those organisms most fitted to the environment. An analogous mechanism seems to govern functional changes of behavior in the repertoire of individual organisms. Behavior fitted to the environment is repeated while behavior not fitted to the environment is not repeated.

EXCITATION. Any increase in rate or amplitude of responding. Some psychologists refer to an "excitatory force," which is said to underlie the increases in responding actually measured.

EXPERIMENTAL PSYCHOLOGY. A branch of psychology in which behavioral observations are made in artificial and restricted environments, in which conditions can be controlled and behavior observed more easily than in natural settings.

EXTINCTION. In classical conditioning, the removal of a correlation between the unconditioned stimulus and conditioned stimulus. In instrumental conditioning, removal of a correlation between response and reward. In most cases, this is done simply by eliminating the unconditioned stimulus or the reward. However it may also be done by continued presentations of unconditioned stimulus or reward that are not correlated with conditioned stimuli or responses.

FEEDBACK. Any system in which a process is governed by its results. Most behavior involves feedback of some kind. (The act of picking up a pencil is governed to an extent by the position of the hand relative to the pencil. Thus the position of the hand is "fed back" by the visual system to govern further movements of the hand.)

FIXED-ACTION PATTERN. A complex unconditioned response.

FUNCTIONALISM. According to the Darwinian notion of evolution, the structure of species is determined by its function. Functional (that is, useful) traits remain after dysfunctional (nonuseful) traits disappear as organisms evolve from generation to generation. The original "functional psychologists" believed that the mind evolved along with the body. Because evolution "selects according to function," the mind is best understood through its uses, or functional qualities. According to Thorndike's Law of Effect, functional behavior is strengthened and repeated while nonfunctional behavior dies out within the lifetime of a single organism. Present-day functionalists attempt to understand behavior through its function as the organism interacts with the environment.

GENERALIZATION. In conditioning (whether classical or instrumental), an organism learns to behave in a certain way with the presentation of—or in the presence of—a certain stimulus or "stimulus situation." If this learned behavior also comes to be made in the presence of stimuli other than those used in conditioning, the organism is said to be generalizing from the training stimulus to the new stimulus. The closer the behavior in the presence of the new stimulus to the behavior in the presence of the training stimulus, the greater the generalization. The most generalization is to be found with stimuli similar to the training stimuli. Often generalization is ascribed to a failure to discriminate or pay attention to differences between stimuli.

GRADIENT. A function that relates a measure of responding to stimuli arranged along a continuum. See also *Generalization*.

GRAMMAR. A set of rules for speech and writing.

GSR (Galvanic Skin Response). A change in resistance on the palms of the hands caused, partially, by sweating. The GSR is part of the unconditioned response to electric shock and other painful stimuli. The GSR may, by classical conditioning procedures, come to be emitted after an originally neutral stimulus, such as a bell or light. The GSR is sometimes said to reflect a "central anxiety state" of the organism.

HABIT.   Any learned behavior.

IMPRINTING.   During a *Critical Period* in the life of an organism, certain responses may be elicited by a great variety of stimuli. Once a particular stimulus has served to elicit the response, however, it is imprinted: that is, it is better able to elicit the response than other potential stimuli. For instance, a duckling will follow any of a great variety of objects but once it follows a given object it continues to follow that object thereafter, ignoring or avoiding others.

INHIBITION.   Any decrease in rate or amplitude of responding. Some psychologists refer to an "inhibitory force" which is said to underlie the decreases in responding actually measured. According to Pavlov, all decreases in responding result from an active inhibitory force opposing the force of excitation. This implies that there is a distinction between decreases in responding due to loss of excitation and decreases in responding due to the active inhibitory force.

INNATE IDEAS.   "Mental contents" or "mental structures" that appear at birth or develop with maturation independently of experience.

INSTINCT.   Any innate behavior or any behavior acquired by all normal members of a species through the process of maturation.

INSTINCTIVE DRIFT.   The tendency of the form of learned behavior to change spontaneously to the form of instinctive behavior.

INSTRUMENTAL CONDITIONING.   Instrumental conditioning involves establishment of a correlation between some aspect of behavior and reinforcement or punishment. An organism is said to have been conditioned when its behavior changes so as to obtain (or retain) the reward or avoid (or escape from) the punishment.

INTROSPECTION.   A technique for observing mental events in which the mind is said to reflect on its own operations or contents.

ISOMORPHISM.   Having the same form. The Gestalt psychologists believe that consciousness has the same form as its representation in the nervous system. Thus, if a figure is seen as distorted, the distortion must take place somewhere in the nervous system.

LANGUAGE.   A pattern of behavior by which communication is ordinarily achieved.

LEARNING.   Any consistent change in behavior not brought about solely by maturation.

MEANING.   The context of a word or act. The more extensive and elaborate the context, the deeper the meaning.

MENTAL CHEMISTRY.   John Stuart Mill's term for the association of simple sensations to form an idea. The idea's properties may differ from those of its components just as the chemical properties of a compound (e.g., water) differ from those of its components (hydrogen and oxygen). (For example, the idea of visual depth may be composed of forms, textures, and shading, yet visual depth may have conscious properties other than those of form, texture, and shading.)

MIND. The repository of consciousness, sensation, thought, feeling, and so forth. According to Descartes, man could be divided into two parts: mind and body. The mind, unlike the body, is not machinelike and does not obey physical laws—but may obey laws of its own. Originally the task of psychology was to discover mental laws by the technique of *Introspection*. More recent attempts to discover mental laws have relied on observations of behavior. Currently, two kinds of psychologists are to be found observing behavior: those interested in behavior itself and those using behavioral observations to infer mental laws.

MOLARISM. A broad classification of environment or behavior. The belief that stimuli or responses broadly classified may be lawfully described without reference to smaller units. (See also *Stimulus, Response*.)

MOLECULARISM. A narrow classification of environment or behavior. The belief that complex processes, whether mental or behavioral, may be explained in terms of small units and rules for their combination.

NATIVISM. In the mental sphere, the belief that man's most basic or important ideas come to him without experience by virtue of his humanity. (Opposed to empiricism—the belief that man's most basic or important ideas come to him through experience.) In the behavioral sphere, the belief that basic behavior patterns are inborn and only modified slightly by experience or that the capacity to acquire certain behaviors is unique to certain species. (For example, while the particular language a person speaks is governed by his experience, a nativist would argue that humans are born with special mechanism that enables them to learn language and furthermore, that certain rules common to all languages are determined by the nature of this inborn mechanism. An empiricist would argue that the structure of language is determined by its function manifested only through experience.) The nativist-empiricist controversy is generally one of emphasis. There is general agreement that all behavior has innate and acquired components. The nativist stresses inborn patterns while the empiricist stresses the methods by which they may be modified.

NONSENSE SYLLABLE. A three-letter trigram (e.g., BAV, RUX, JIC, CIB) used by Ebbinghaus and others to study association. The principal advantage of nonsense syllables, according to Ebbinghaus, is that they have few previous associations; thus, any associations between them formed during an experiment can be studied independently of past experience.

OMISSION CONDITIONING. Omission is a form of instrumental conditioning in which the response is correlated with removal of a reward, otherwise continuously present.

OPERANT. All responses having a single common effect. Each instance of any response differs in some way, however small, from any other instance. Under what conditions can we say a response is repeated? One way to classify responses is by their common effect on the environment. All responses having a single common effect belong to the same operant class. For instance, all behavior that results in a bar-press could be considered a single operant. The definition of an operant is up to the observer of behavior (often the experimenter). He may base the delivery or removal of reinforcement or punishment upon the occurrence of the operant as he has defined it.

PARAMETER. A constant in an equation. A parametric experiment is one that tests a relationship with various parametric values. For instance, "days of deprivation" would affect the function relating "number of responses" in extinction to "number of prior reinforcements." An experiment that related responses in extinction to number of prior reinforcements at various deprivation levels would be a parametric experiment.

PERCEPTION. A process by which conclusions are reached as to the nature of the environment. Early mentalists believed that perceptions were sensations modified by associative experience. (For instance, when a melody is played a child and an adult might experience the same isolated sensations of individual notes but only the adult, because of his experience, will perceive the series of notes as a unit of melody.) The Gestalt psychologists, on the other hand, believed that perceptions as well as sensations could be independent of experience. (The notes of a melody might be seen as unitary by a child, not because of his experience with the notes but because the relation between the notes conformed to laws determined by the nervous system which tend to group certain of them together.)

PHENOMENOLOGY. A type of introspection which attempts to view immediate experience as a whole, naively, without analysis. According to the Gestalt psychologists, phenomenological observation is the preferred method of collecting psychological data.

PHYSIOLOGY. The study of the body, usually in terms of its parts (e.g., the nervous system) as opposed to study of behavior of the organism as a whole.

PREPAREDNESS. A term coined by M. E. P. Seligman to indicate that a given organism is better prepared to associate certain stimuli with each other (in the case of *Classical Conditioning*) and certain responses with certain reinforcers (in the case of *Instrumental Conditioning*). See also *Belongingness*.

PSEUDOCONDITIONING. Any conditioning obtained with a pairing that is shown to have been unnecessary for the establishment of the response is pseudoconditioning (not genuine conditioning). The essential element in *Classical Conditioning* is the pairing or correlation between the unconditioned and conditioned stimuli. The essential element in *Instrumental Conditioning* is the pairing or correlation of response and reinforcement. If a certain response can be made to appear without that pairing, then any experiment using pairing to establish that response is suspect; the pairing may not have been necessary.

PSYCHOLOGY. Originally a branch of philosophy devoted to the study of the mind. More recently, a science whose subject is the behavior of organisms. The observations of behavior (verbal behavior included) may or may not be used to infer mental processes.

PSYCHOPHYSICS. The study of sensation as a function of the physical properties of stimulation.

PUNISHMENT. A positive correlation between responding and aversive stimulation.

REFLEX. Originally, reflex referred to stimuli and responses related by specific nervous connections within the organism. Recently the concept of reflex has been broadened to include any relationship between a stimulus and a response. The stimulus may be any event in the environment and the response may be any behavior of the organism.

REINFORCEMENT. In *Classical Conditioning*, the presentation of the unconditioned stimulus. In *Instrumental Conditioning*, the presentation of a reward (positive reinforcement) or the removal of an aversive stimulus (negative reinforcement).

RESPONSE. Another word for a *Behavior*. Usually a response is defined as a rather discrete form of behavior such as a knee jerk, the pressing of a bar, or the pressing of a key. However, responses can also be broadly defined, e.g., "standing on one side of a chamber," or "not pressing a key."

SECONDARY REINFORCEMENT. A positive correlation of a response, not with reinforcement, but with a conditioned stimulus (CS) or a discriminative stimulus (S^D).

SENSATION. The conscious correlate of simple stimulation of the sense organs. Early mentalists believed that consciousness consisted only of simple sensations combined in various ways by association.

SOUL. The soul is said to be the spiritual and immortal part of man. Psychologists have tended to ignore the religious questions of the soul's immortality, its possible moral implications, and its role as the "essence of being." Stripped of religious implications, the concept of the soul approaches the concept of the *Mind*. The two concepts have generally been treated similarly by psychologists.

STIMULUS. Any environmental event. Stimuli may be classified broadly (for instance, any picture of a horse) or narrowly (e.g., a tone of a particular frequency and amplitude). With respect to behavior, stimuli may be relatively neutral, having no discernable effect on the organism, or they may elicit violent behavior. Stimuli may be positively reinforcing or punishing depending on whether they increase or decrease the strength of the behavior they follow. A neutral stimulus in one situation may be non-neutral in others.

STIMULUS CONTROL. Another word for the effects of *Discrimination* and *Generalization* in instrumental conditioning.

TEMPORAL CONTINGUITY. Happening at the same time.

THOUGHT. A process located inside the organism said to cause certain types of behavior, labeled "thoughtful." Behaviorists believe that behavior, however complex, is caused, not by thought, but directly by environmental events and contingencies. Cognitive psychologists believe that environmental events and contingencies act directly to cause only simple behavior. Otherwise, in their view, the environment acts indirectly, first causing thoughts which then, in turn, cause complex behavior.

VOLUNTARY BEHAVIOR. Behavior, the original cause of which is said to lie within the mind. Psychological theories that do not make use of mental concepts likewise ignore the concept of voluntary behavior.

Index